Backcountry Avalanche Safety

A Guide to Managing Avalanche Risk

TONY DAFFERN

RMB

Contents

RMB | Rocky Mountain Books Ltd.
rmbooks.com
@rmbooks
facebook.com/rmbooks

Cataloguing data available from Library and Archives Canada
ISBN 9781771602358 (paperback)
ISBN 9781771602365 (electronic)

Book design by Tony Daffern
All photos are by Tony Daffern unless noted otherwise.
Cover: Hard slab avalanche debris at Bow Summit in the Canadian Rockies. Photo Bob Uttl.

Printed and bound in China by 1010 Printing International Ltd.

Distributed in Canada by Heritage Group Distribution and in the U.S. by Publishers Group West

For information on purchasing bulk quantities of this book, or to obtain media excerpts or invite the author to speak at an event, please visit rmbooks.com and select the "Contact Us" tab.

We acknowledge the financial support of the Government of Canada through the Canada Book Fund and the Canada Council for the Arts, and of the province of British Columbia through the British Columbia Arts Council and the Book Publishing Tax Credit.

Disclaimer

The actions described in this book may be considered inherently dangerous activities. Individuals undertake these activities at their own risk. The information put forth in this guide has been collected from a variety of sources and is not guaranteed to be completely accurate or reliable. Many conditions and some information may change owing to weather and numerous other factors beyond the control of the authors and publishers. Individual climbers and/or hikers must determine the risks, use their own judgment, and take full responsibility for their actions. Do not depend on any information found in this book for your own personal safety. Your safety depends on your own good judgment based on your skills, education, and experience.

It is up to the users of this guidebook to acquire the necessary skills for safe experiences and to exercise caution in potentially hazardous areas. The authors and publishers of this guide accept no responsibility for your actions or the results that occur from another's actions, choices, or judgments. If you have any doubt as to your safety or your ability to attempt anything described in this guidebook, do not attempt it.

Cover: Hard slab avalanche debris at Bow Summit
in the Canadian Rockies. Photo Bob Uttl.

"We should condemn men for crossing snow slopes in a condition favourable to avalanches, as we should condemn them for indulging in a cruise in an unseaworthy ship."

Leslie Stephen, 1865

Foreword

In this book I stress the avoidance of avalanche hazard by good routefinding, by recognition and avoidance of hazardous slopes and by staying out of avalanche terrain during periods when avalanche hazard is high.

However, I recognize that days when the snow is stable usually outnumber days when it is unstable, and that there are skiers and snowboarders who want some guidance on riding safely in avalanche terrain. I therefore try to address the difficult problem of evaluating snow stability for backcountry powder seekers and make some recommendations on techniques to use when skiing or boarding steep backcountry slopes. But the book can only point the way; you must go out into the mountains and practise what you learn here. André Roch, in a 1979 address to some of the world's leaders in avalanche research, put it very succinctly when he said, "Remember this, my friends, the avalanche does not know that you are an expert!"

Acknowledgements

A work of this nature relies heavily on the knowledge, research and writing of others. This book is an attempt to organize and condense a vast amount of information normally available only to the snow science community or to professional mountain guides, and to interpret that information in light of my experience as a backcountry skier and climber. I have resisted the suggestion that every quote or source should be cited in referenced footnotes. There is a bibliography on page 205 for those of you who wish to read further on the subject.

However, I would like to thank several people who have made a major contribution to backcountry avalanche safety and whose work has had considerable influence on the presentation of material in this book.

Special thanks are due to Doug Fesler of Anchorage, Alaska, for permission to reproduce a major portion of his paper on choosing safe routes and making good decisions, which appears in the **Travel in Avalanche Terrain** chapter, and to the National Research Council of Canada, under the leadership of Peter Schaerer, who, in conjunction with the British Columbia Institute of Technology, developed the material on the Shovel Shear test and the rationale for hazard evaluation used in the chapter **Riding Steep Slopes**.

I would also like to acknowledge the contribution to backcountry avalanche safety made by Bruce Tremper and Brad Meiklejohn as a result of their addressing the issue of stability evaluation for the backcountry skier and for promoting safe skiing.

In the previous edition I neglected to mention Dale Atkins from RECCO and Bruce Edgerly from Backcountry Access, along with Manuel Genswein of Switzerland for their independent development of strategic shovelling, now considered a critical stage of backcountry avalanche rescue.

In particular I would like to recognize Grant Statham of Parks Canada for his work on the Avalanche Terrain Exposure Scale, and for his ongoing leadership in risk-based avalanche forecasting, which is the basis for Canadian avalanche forecasts.

Thanks also to Dale Gallagher for his help and encouragement, to Mrs. Martha Atwater for permission to reproduce the extract on page 158 from Monty Atwater's book *The Avalanche Hunters*, to Hodder & Stoughton for the quotation from Chris Bonington's *Everest: South West Face*, to Pete Martinelli for permission to use material from the *Avalanche Handbook*, and to Gord and Debbie Ritchie for their input on looking after an avalanche victim.

There were many people who assisted me in various ways. I hope the list is complete and apologize if I have missed anyone. Thanks to Dr. Eizi Akitaya, Tim Auger, Don Beers, Steve Couche, Greg Crawford, Kevin Cronin, Tom Davidson, Jim Davies, Roland Emetaz, Bruno Engler, George Field, Peter Fuhrmann, Dr. F. Furukawa, Lloyd Gallagher, Ethan Greene, Frank Grover, Kyle Hale, Clair Israelson, Bruce Jamieson, Seiiti Kinosita, Leon Kubbernus, Nick Logan, Rudolf Ludwig, Hamish MacInnes, Ian McCammon, Brad Meiklejohn, Kris Newman, Andy Nicol, Ron Perla, André Roche, Steve Rothfels, Tony Salway, Bob Sandford, Al Schaffer, Alf Skrastins, Peter Spear, Chris Stethem, Lars Suneby, Gery Unterasinger, Rod Ward and Knox Williams.

For this edition I co-opted guide and backcountry skier Kevin Hjertaas to cast a critical eye on the practical chapters, in particular **Travel in Avalanche Terrain** and **Riding Steep Slopes**. Thank you for your valuable input, Kevin.

Introduction

Snow avalanches are the greatest source of danger for mountain travellers in winter. They catch and very often kill the unwary who literally trigger their own destiny when they venture onto unsafe snow slopes in a moment of inattention or ignorance.

Historically, avalanche victims came from among those people who lived and worked in the shadow of the great mountains; whose houses, even whole villages, were destroyed every generation or two by catastrophic slides considered to be "acts of God" and so to be suffered with fortitude. Today, the most common victim is the climber, ski tourer, snowmobiler and the backcountry powder-hound.

Avalanches are complex natural phenomena, and in spite of modern technology and years of research no one can predict with certainty when or whether an avalanche will run. Avalanches may occur on any steep snow-covered slope. How steep and how much snow is required to initiate a slide are but two of the many factors to be considered when evaluating hazard. Another complication is that snow conditions vary in different geographical locations and at different times of the year. There is a vast difference between the fluffy powder snow of Colorado and the heavy, wet snow of Washington's Olympic Range.

Some winter seasons produce an inordinate number of avalanche accidents. British mountaineer and author Frank Smythe, writing in the 1929 *Alpine Journal*, theorized that years of low early snowfall and high winds in the Alps were accountable for the worst recreational avalanche casualties on record. Conversely, he noted that in seasons of heavy early snowfall and little wind there were few accidents. There is solid fact behind his theorizing: wind and a shallow snowpack have a great deal to do with avalanche accidents, as you will learn.

For instance, in the Christmas/New Year period of 2008, the snowpack all across Western Canada was thin and a period of unusually cold weather had substantially weakened the base. Then a series of winter storms accompanied by high winds swept across the area. Cornices formed and the slopes were loaded with fresh snow. Eight snowmobilers died in southern British Columbia and a skier and a snowboarder were killed out on the Coast. In the first two weeks of 2009 there were more storms—three more snowmobilers died—then a significant warming trend with spring-like conditions on a winter snowpack. Cornices weakened and fell and avalanches on wind-loaded slopes were easily triggered on a layer of weak facets formed during the earlier cold spell. Avalanche danger remained High in many areas for most of January. An unusual start to the winter season.

What are your chances of being caught in an avalanche and what might be the consequences? If you are a backcountry skier travelling on light touring skis along a marked trail, chances are that you'd never have a problem. Because of equipment limitations you'll rarely venture onto the steeper slopes and so would unconsciously avoid avalanche hazard by sticking to flatter terrain. It is ski tourers travelling off valley trails and over high alpine passes, skiers and boarders out to make turns, and ski mountaineers and climbers who are most at risk.

In a large number of avalanche accidents the recognition, evaluation and qualified acceptance of risk are absent; victims are often totally unaware of the danger. The majority of victims trigger the slide themselves. The chance of being caught by a naturally triggered slide is remote unless you are travelling during or immediately after a heavy snowfall or are climbing in the higher ranges of the world. Gerald Seligman, in his book *Snow Structure and Ski Fields*, published in 1936, quotes an old Swiss guide as saying, "I never fear that any avalanche will catch me unless I have myself brought it down." Statistically, the more time you spend high in the mountains, the more chance you have of being involved

Spring wet snow slides. Photo Alf Skrastins.

in an avalanche accident, either to your own party or to another group.

The answer to that second question — What might be the consequences? — is difficult to put numbers to. There are several sources of statistics compiled by various organizations in North America and Europe. Unfortunately they all depend on accident reports and don't count many unreported successful companion rescues.

It is estimated that in North America your chance of survival is about 85% if you get caught in an avalanche. Approximately 50% of those who survive either free themselves or are found because some part of their body or equipment was protruding above the surface of the snow. Of the people completely buried, only a dismal 35 to 40% live to tell of the ordeal, despite recent advances in transceiver technology and digging techniques.

Statistics compiled by the Colorado Avalanche Information Center on accidents in the USA from 1997 to 2007 indicate that if you are buried under 30 cm of snow you have a 75% chance of survival, which quickly drops to a 25–30% chance if you are buried a metre deep. All the statisticians seem to agree that if a person is buried under more than 2 metres of snow the chances of survival are almost nil. The weight of snow above the victim and the time it takes to dig down to them make survival unlikely in the majority of cases.

The most disturbing statistic, and the most important one for you to bear in mind, is the time factor. Again figures vary, but not by much. If your companions can dig you out within 15 minutes of the snow coming to rest, you have a 92% chance of survival. A few more minutes and your chance of survival is significantly reduced.

Obviously your first priority is to avoid being caught by an avalanche in the first place, but should the unthinkable happen, your greatest chance of survival lies in your companions locating you and digging you out in the fastest possible time.

The Colorado Avalanche Information Center data shows that since 1997 snowmobilers accounted for about 50% of backcountry avalanche fatalities, skiers and boarders 30%, snowshoers 8% and climbers and hikers 12%.

Some years ago Knox Williams, in his portrait of a typical avalanche victim, said: "The victim is a male, 27 years old, has had several years of skiing or mountaineering experience, and didn't know an avalanche from a snowball." Although the 20–30 age group still leads the way, the Colorado statistics show other age groups are catching up.

If you study published case histories of avalanche accidents you'll become aware of one important constant in backcountry accidents. **A large percentage of accidents occurred when avalanche danger was known to be high.** In some cases the victims chose to ignore warnings and proceeded with their trip; in others the victims were completely unaware of the possibility of avalanches. Many victims didn't know how to pick a safe route through avalanche terrain or, conversely, were unable to recognize potentially dangerous slopes. Few of those involved had any experience in evaluating avalanche hazard, even victims considered experienced leaders.

The biggest advance in avalanche safety in recent years has been in the art and science of Avalanche Forecasting. In the vast majority of avalanche accidents in the past 10 years, the forecaster was right on in predicting the Danger Level, and in most cases the written part of the forecast had warned about the hazard that resulted in the accident.

The bottom line is that your chance of getting caught in an avalanche is greatly reduced if you pay careful attention to the current Avalanche Forecast. Be patient, and wait until conditions are right!

The Anatomy of an Avalanche Accident

Three "experienced" skiers left the majority of their group skiing on the flats around the Lodge and headed out for a tour to a popular high mountain lake. Conditions were picture perfect, with cloudless skies and mild temperatures. *We won't need our transceivers, we're only going to the lake.*

Alf and his three friends *...wanted a carefree, easygoing kind of trip and a fairly short day of skiing.* After discussing potential avalanche hazard on the drive to the mountain they decided to head for the same high mountain lake. *Even so, we carried avalanche transceivers, snow shovels, avalanche probe poles, a first-aid kit and spare clothing with us as a matter of course.*

The local avalanche hazard forecast indicated: *Stability decreasing. Soft slab with buried surface hoar—difficult to detect.* It went on to add: *Safe routefinding imperative due to a weakening snowpack and warm temperatures. Slopes that have not recently avalanched should be considered as suspect.*

The ski in to the lake was fast and easy; wax was working and the trail was in good shape. There were tracks from other groups leading to a sunny, gladed plateau above the lake, a fine spot for lunch.

Beyond the plateau an attractive-looking snow-filled basin led up to a col between the main peak and its much lower outlier. The "experienced" group *...found some fresh ski tracks leading up the ridge between the lake and this basin* and followed them. After a short distance one of the party decided to turn back and wait for the other two at the lake.

They followed the tracks up through tightly packed trees and *decided to carry on to find a clear run out rather than ski down through the trees. We followed the existing ski tracks around the southwest ridge and came out at treeline halfway up from the valley below.*

Meanwhile, Alf's party lunched at the open gladed plateau above the lake, *...discussed the option of following the tracks into the basin and decided it might*

An overall view of the area described in "The Anatomy of an Avalanche Accident." The avalanche ran down the gully below the col in the centre of the picture. Alf's group were at the top of the treed ridge on the left of the gully. The slide started on the slope above the top of the trees to the right of the gully.
Photo Alf Skrastins.

be worth a look. Because it appeared that the other group would either be forced to lose the elevation they were gaining or would have to continue in a mid-slope traverse across steep terrain, Alf decided to choose an easier route through the forest to the bottom of the basin.

The lower section of the basin is divided by a treed ridge splitting the basin into two gullies. The entire ridgeline along the western and northern perimeter of the basin was crowned by very well-developed cornices, indicating heavy wind loading of the slopes in the basin, while the southwest-facing slopes on the east side of the basin showed evidence of cross-loading.

On emerging from the trees at the bottom of the most easterly gully Alf's group decided that this gully was a potential terrain trap. *We double-checked that all of our transceivers were transmitting and then probed the snow with our ski poles. We could feel approximately 25 cm of firm snow with a weak layer underneath.*

Proceeding a few metres farther to get a better view, one of the Alf's party, a qualified heli-ski guide, ...*did not like the "hollow, drum-like" sound of the snow as we crossed onto the southwest-facing aspect. Given this information we decided not to ski this half of the basin at all.*

Instead they followed the treed ground in the middle of the basin in order to get high enough for a good view of the area and to check out the other half of the basin. The heli-ski guide did a quick shovel shear test in the top 70 cm of the snowpack on the southeast aspect. The column of snow sheared very easily at about 40 cm below the surface while she was still in the process of isolating the column. *At that point we decided to avoid the open slopes altogether and to stick to the treed areas.*

The photograph mentioned in the text, taken a few minutes before the avalanche released. Photo Alf Skrastins.

11

A view of the avalanche path. The slope angle where the skiers triggered the slide is 35°. The average slope angle in the top portion of the gully is 36°. Photo George Field.

About 30 m above them, and across the gully on the southwest aspect, the two skiers had stopped to decide whether to go farther up or turn around. From here the existing tracks divided, one set going up the valley floor to the col, the other traversing the southwest-facing slope toward the mountain.

We briefly discussed avalanche hazards, noting that a large cornice was an apparent threat to both the valley floor and to the southeast aspect of the valley. We noted that the southwest aspect of the valley did not offer any apparent threat (there was no indication of avalanche activity and there were clusters of trees extending well above us).

One of them probed with his ski pole and felt that the snow was fairly consolidated. *We decided to continue to a group of trees 40 m above; we had no intention of carrying on to open slopes beyond.*

At the top of the trees, the slope ascended by Alf's party was wind-scoured and they were in a safe position. While stopped to take a photo Alf noticed two skiers following tracks made by an earlier party. *They had just made the switchback at the bottom of the convex roll in the upper portion of the gully. As they approached the switchback at the top of the roll I took a photograph of them and then put my camera away. I was about 200 m distant and 20 to 30 m higher than the skiers.*

One of the skiers fell while making the switchback at the top of the roll. When he got up they appeared to be having a discussion. As they continued toward a clump of trees a short distance away, a crack appeared in the snow between the skiers and the trees.

The initial size of the avalanche was small, a slab about 15 m square, and released with no warning. *I believe we were standing right on, or next to, the trigger point. We were immediately thrown on our sides and had no chance to ski off the slope.*

The skier on the right landed with his head slightly uphill and immediately pulled his skis underneath himself and used his arms to keep his upper body off the snow. The other skier fell with his head downhill and appeared to just hold his position on the snow and to look up at the slope behind him.

The slab broke up and the slab I was on missed the trees and carried me 50 m down the slope and began to slow down. At that point I thought the avalanche was over. However, this small slide triggered the rest of the slope.

Alf watched in horror. *The crack ran up the slope from the trees for about 60 m, then cut across the slope toward the ridgeline and then ran just below the ridge crest and below the cornice at the col. It widened very quickly as it ran. It was as if cloth were being ripped or a zipper were being opened. This was accompanied by a hissing sound, like air being let out of a big bag and a blanket being dragged across sand … all at the same time.*

I looked over my shoulder to see the entire wall of the valley above begin to move. The slab I was on picked up speed again and disintegrated. I was lying on my back and using my arms to try to "swim" upright.

The skiers were moving slowly downslope and the snow they were on was starting to break up as they moved. However, the snow on the steeper slope above them was moving faster than the snow they were on, and began to ride up over the top of the slab they were on.

The upright skier frantically pulled himself up on top of the slabs as they descended onto him. The other skier seemed unable to prevent the first of these faster slabs from covering him.

Successive waves of snow from the higher slopes overran the snow in the middle of the main slide, which ran down the main southwest-facing slope and into the gully. At the same time, a much thicker layer of snow from the slope directly below the col was also sliding in an easterly direction, running over the rest of the debris. This phase of the slide was accompanied by the low rumbling sound usually associated with avalanches.

After another 100 m the avalanche stopped.

My head remained above the snow during the entire slide. When the snow stopped my legs were buried to above my knees. I had lost one pole, my hat and glasses. My skis were still attached but were twisted around at an awkward angle. I was unhurt. When the slide stopped, Alf's group could no longer see the skiers. *I skied down the tree-protected ridge, looking down into the gully when possible. After a few turns I could see one skier on top of the snow at the very bottom of the slide.*

When he reached the bottom (*I descended within the trees a bit farther to avoid crossing a short, steep slope*), the skier on the surface was sitting on the debris, facing downhill, digging out his lower legs. There was no sign of the other skier. The guide was running back and forth down the debris looking for some sign of the missing skier.

After completing the initial search, and with only two hours of daylight left, Alf, whose skis were closest to the bottom, went for help while the others probed likely locations.

We suspected that since I had ridden the avalanche unhurt and on the surface all the way to the toe of the slide, something drastically different must have happened to my companion. Our initial probing was therefore directed at the trees below his entry point, and at a large, deep pile of debris lower down where the larger avalanche had intersected the initial slide.

He was found two hours later by a rescue team, face down under 70–100 cm of snow, still wearing his pack but missing both skis. He did not appear to have struggled at all.

I should note that my friend and I had over 30 years of combined backcountry skiing experience, but despite this we failed to recognize the danger of the slope we were on.

Because of our approach line through the trees on the southwest ridge, which obscured our overall view of the slope and potential avalanche patterns, the danger of the slope was far less obvious to us than to parties which approach the slope from the valley floor. Combined with the results of our pole probe, the fresh ski tracks already on the slope, and our decision to remain in the trees, these circumstances misled us to believe the slope had low risk of avalanche.

14 – Mountain Weather

Mountain Weather

Because changes in the snowpack leading to avalanche hazard are greatly influenced by weather, a knowledge of the effects of temperature change, sun, wind or rain on the snowpack is absolutely essential. It's possible for the backcountry traveller to decide whether avalanche hazard is likely to increase or decrease by making an intelligent interpretation of present meteorological conditions coupled with a knowledge of past weather.

Winter backcountry enthusiasts are primarily concerned with **changes** in weather conditions and with the effect of these changes on the old snowpack and on any new snowfall. It is important to remember that any **significant** change in the weather results in a change in the stability of the snowpack. The most important factors to consider are:

- **The amount of snow** and the intensity of the snowfall.

- **Wind speed** and direction of both prevailing and local winds.

- **Temperature changes**, particularly a sudden rise in temperature.

Opposite: An engraving from David Herrliberger's *Topographie der Eydgenossenschaft*, 1773, illustrating the common belief that avalanches were giant snowballs crashing down the mountain, gathering animals, trees and even buildings before annihilating the village below.

The Atmosphere

The earth's atmosphere consists of a mixture of gases, with oxygen and nitrogen making up about 90% of the volume. Other important constituents, as far as weather is concerned, are water vapour, ozone and carbon dioxide, all of which influence the radiation balance; and solid and liquid particles — dust, volcanic ash, tiny droplets of sulfuric or nitric acid, and salt from the sea — called aerosols. Aerosols, which may exist in the mountain atmosphere in concentrations as high as 150,000 particles per cubic centimetre, provide condensation nuclei for precipitation. The atmosphere is bound to the earth by the force of gravity; it has no upper surface, but blends gradually into interplanetary space. The pressure created by the atmosphere is greatest at the surface of the earth, and decreases with altitude. The usual measure of atmospheric pressure is the millibar (mb), which is approximately one 1000th of the atmospheric pressure at sea level. Sea level is usually considered to average 1013 mb, while pressure at approximately 5000 m (18,000 ft.) is about 500 mb. The lower atmosphere, in which most of our weather phenomena occur, and which contains most of the water vapour, is called the troposphere.

The transfer of heat from ground to air and the evaporation and condensation of water involving latent heat create an atmosphere that is constantly on the move, transporting heat and moisture and building momentum in the form of winds. The circulation pattern is further complicated by the earth's rotation on its axis, which gives an apparent deflection to air which would normally circulate directly between areas of high and low pressure.

Because atmospheric gases expand and contract as pressure changes, the density of the atmosphere varies with pressure. When air is heated, it expands, causing the density to decrease. In order to establish equilibrium, the warmer air, which is lighter than its surroundings, rises. Similarly, air that is cooled may become dense compared with

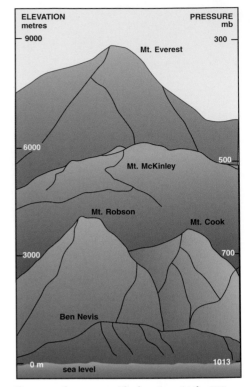

Decrease of pressure with elevation. At the 500 mb level airflow is free from friction with the earth's surface except where it passes over high mountain ranges.

its surroundings and tend to sink. Thus, low-level warm air will replace high-level cold air and vice versa.

Particularly applicable to precipitation is the fact that the temperature of a rising mass of air tends to fall as the air rises, because as atmospheric pressure decreases with altitude, the air expands, and like the air escaping from an inflated tire, it cools.

At this stage we must differentiate between air flows at different altitudes. At the 500 mb (5000 m) level the air flow is relatively free from friction with the earth's surface, except where it passes over high mountain ranges. These flows are called prevailing winds. At lower elevations, friction and terrain features have considerable effect on the air flow and give rise to secondary pressure systems below the main circulation which result in local wind systems.

Weather Patterns Producing Snow

Moisture, in the form of water vapour, must be present in the atmosphere for any appreciable amount of snow to fall. Most of the moisture providing snowfall on the western mountains of North America comes from the Pacific Ocean. As moist air is swept in over the Pacific Ocean as a result of the low pressure area which frequently develops over the Gulf of Alaska in winter, it produces heavy snowfalls in the Pacific Northwest and the Coast Ranges of British Columbia. Farther south, major storms tracking in across the Pacific from the west and southwest give rise to heavy precipitation in the Sierras. Warm, moist air from the Gulf of Mexico meeting cold Arctic air may result in heavy snowfalls on the eastern slopes of the Colorado Rockies. Inland, the amount of moisture available decreases rapidly, and only the higher, steeper ranges such as the Selkirks and the Rockies receive any large amounts of snow. The foothills of the Canadian Rockies tend to receive the most snow from northeasterly winds which blow when an Arctic high is over the Yukon and a low-pressure system is over Montana. The European mountains depend upon the Atlantic depressions for most of their snowfall. Ranges close to the ocean such as the Pyrenees suffer from unpredictable weather with heavy snowfalls and variable temperatures. Farther east, conditions are more predictable; snowfalls are lighter and drier. In the central and eastern Alps long periods of fine weather may be encountered in winter when a great high pressure area sits over northern Europe. The mountains of Scotland have the unpredictable weather and rapid changes of temperature associated with ranges close to the ocean, but because of their modest elevation are not subject to extreme snowfalls; they receive the majority of their precipitation as rain. The New Zealand Alps are a wall of high peaks rising from the ocean. Northwest winds bring warm, moist air from the Tasman Sea giving heavy snowfall and the most unpredictable weather of any popular mountain range

The Lifting of Moist Air

There are three important ways in which molecules of water vapour rise and produce snow. They are Orographic Lifting, Cyclonic Lifting and Frontal Lifting.

Orographic lifting is by far the most important lifting mechanism in the production of severe, avalanche-producing storms in the western mountains of Canada and the USA. As horizontally moving air masses are forced over mountain ranges, they rise and rapidly cool. The rate of lifting is ten times greater than that of Cyclonic or Frontal lifting. It was mentioned earlier that the amount of precipitation depends upon the moisture content of the air and the rate at which the air is lifted. In turn the rate of lifting depends upon the wind speed, the slope of the mountain barrier and how close to a right angle the wind hits the mountain range. Most of the snowfall in the Coast Ranges is caused by the orographic lifting of moist air from the Pacific Ocean. Farther inland there is less moisture in the air and the cloud layers tend to be thinner, so the amount of precipitation is reduced.

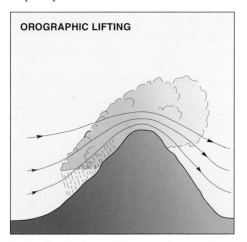

OROGRAPHIC LIFTING

Lifting of moist air over high mountain ranges. Because the air stops rising, the amount of condensation on lee slopes is greater.

Cyclonic lifting is the lifting of large air masses as the result of the general circulation pattern of the atmosphere. These air masses, or cyclones, are the areas of low pressure seen on the weather maps and may range in diameter from 100 km to 3000 km. In the northern hemisphere the air circulates in an anticlockwise direction around these low-pressure centres. In temperate latitudes cyclones produce much of the winter precipitation, though in mountainous areas they may be substantially modified by the terrain. In the absence of mountain barriers, the rate of lifting is rarely more than a few centimetres per second and the weather over areas dominated by cyclones is usually uniformly cloudy with moderate precipitation.

Frontal lifting The masses of air circulating around an area of low pressure have often come from different geographical regions, and as a result there may exist sharp transition zones separating cold, dry air such as the continental Arctic air mass from warmer, moister air of the prevailing westerlies. The boundary where two air masses meet is called a front. Be-

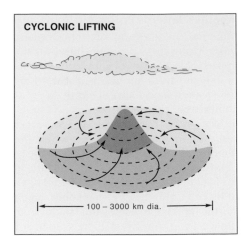

CYCLONIC LIFTING

|← —— 100 – 3000 km dia. —— →|

cause the cold air is denser, the warm air mass will always ride up over the cold air, and in the course of lifting often produces precipitation. The area where the warm air advances and pushes up over the cold air is known as a Warm Front, while the steeper Cold Front is formed when the cold air pushes its way beneath warm air. As the system decays, the cold front begins to overtake the warm front in a process called occlusion, which results in an Occluded Front. The principal frontal system in the atmosphere is the Arctic Front, where cold Arctic air and warmer tropical air meet.

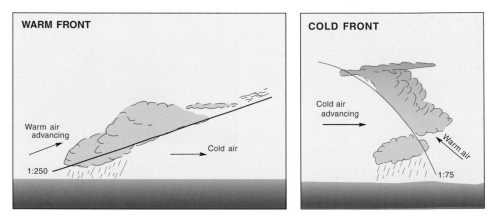

WARM FRONT

Warm air advancing

Cold air

1:250

COLD FRONT

Cold air advancing

Warm air

1:75

Snowfall

The depth of snowfall at any location is influenced by the amount of moisture present in the air and the speed at which the air rises. The warmer the air, the more moisture it can carry; the faster it rises, the greater the intensity of snowfall. The rate of lifting depends on the steepness of the mountain range together with wind speed and direction. Maximum snowfall occurs when a mountain range is at right angles to the moisture-laden winds.

It is important when considering the deposition of snow to differentiate between mountain ranges that confront major weather systems and smaller areas where deposition is dependent upon local wind patterns. Local winds may denude the windward side of a mountain where one would have expected the greater amount of snow to have fallen, and conversely, deposit snow on localized lee slopes.

The warmer the air, the more moisture it can hold. This results in a tendency for greater snowfalls from storms that originate in warmer areas such as the Pacific Ocean than from storms that originate in Continental Polar regions.

Snowfall Intensity

The rate at which snow falls, and the precipitation intensity, has a direct bearing on the development of avalanche hazard. High rates of snowfall—2 cm/hour or greater, especially when accompanied by wind—are usually responsible for major periods of direct-action avalanche activity. While

Direct-action avalanches

Loose-snow or storm-slab avalanches that fall during or shortly after a storm.

the critical amounts vary from region to region, any heavy, intense snowfall of several hours duration should be considered potentially hazardous from the mountain traveller's point of view.

How Snowfall is Measured

Snowfall can be measured and recorded in several different ways, depending on how the results are to be used. Depth of new snow is useful for establishing how fast the snow is settling, while the intensity of snowfall is an indicator of how fast avalanche slopes are being loaded with new snow. An even better indicator of loading is the precipitation intensity, as it does not depend on the density of the snow. A summary of measurements commonly used, with units and typical values, is given below. These values will be less for drier interior ranges and greater for coastal ranges.

Measuring Snowfall	
Terms used	Units used
Snow Depth	10 cm of snow
Snowfall Rate	1 cm of snow per hour

Forecasting Snowfall

Hazard from direct-action avalanches is directly related to the amount and intensity of snowfall. For this reason, forecasts of snowfall amounts are important in areas where direct-action avalanches are a source of danger. In the past few years meteorological agencies in both the USA and Canada have developed systems to provide accurate snowfall predictions for selected areas for use in avalanche forecasting.

The National Center for Atmospheric Research in Boulder, Colorado, is among the leaders in the field of snowfall prediction. Even so, in these days of wildly fluctuating climate changes, forecasting snowfall to the accuracy required for avalanche forecasting is a hit and miss business. Check the accuracy of the snowfall forecast before heading out. If more snow has fallen than forecast, you need to consider whether the Danger Level has increased as well.

Increase of Snowfall with Altitude

It's common knowledge that in the lower ranges such as the European Alps and the North American mountains snowfall is greater at higher elevations. Why?

As moist air rises it cools, due both to expansion and to the decrease of temperature with altitude. Cooler air cannot hold as much moisture, so condensation occurs. If the condensation level is below the freezing point, snow will fall. Maximum precipitation occurs just at the base of the clouds, where there is maximum moisture and maximum condensation.

Over a period of time, the amount of moisture in an air mass is reduced, the condensation level rises and precipitation only occurs when the air is forced up to higher elevations. This process, which on average results in higher elevations getting a larger share of the available moisture, continues until either all the moisture has been used up or the moist air stops rising and passes over the range.

Maximum precipitation occurs just to the windward side of the range. This is probably due to the shape of the airflow as it crosses a mountain barrier, the lines of flow flattening out before the summit ridge. Once past the summit there is no more lifting and thus little precipitation.

Wind-drifted snow in the Canadian Rockies.
Photo Bob Sandford.

Wind

It is the subtle, eddying wind gently depositing snow in insignificant hollows that makes the small but deadly slab avalanche. It is the wind blowing hard across mountain ridges that builds up treacherous cornices—the natural trigger of many a slide. It is the wind gusting across mountainsides that moves and shapes the snow into gently rounded slabs so deceptively attractive to the downhill powder-hound. Wind plays a most important part in the development of hazardous avalanche conditions. The mountain traveller must understand how wind transports and deposits snow, and be able to recognize from ground features the results of wind deposition.

Prevailing Winds

These are the winds that predominate in a particular area—the high altitude winds which, as part of the main circulation, are responsible for the overall weather pattern. There may be one or more prevailing-wind directions in any geographical area. For instance, in western Canada southwest winds bring snowfall to the mountains and chinooks to the easterly plains, while southerly winds often herald fine, dry weather. These winds are usually well defined and form the basis for long-range meteorological predictions.

Local Winds

Local winds are much more unpredictable and depend on prevailing winds, terrain features, temperature and even the time of day. For information on local wind direction, the traveller must depend on observation in the field, which is one aspect of avalanche prediction where the tourer has an advantage over desk-bound hazard forecasters, who have to rely on meteorological forecasts and remote weather stations for their information.

How Wind Transports Snow

Wind speed across a mountainside varies as the wind passes over or between various terrain features. Snow is picked up where the wind is steady or where it accelerates and is dropped where the wind slows down. The amount of snow transported depends on the wind speed, the type of snow crystals and the looseness of the snowpack. Cold new snow is readily transported by moderate winds, whereas little snow will be removed from an old, settled snow surface.

Light winds tend to deposit falling snow on the windward side of trees and rocks, especially if the snow is wet. Over the mountains an even blanket of snow is deposited, with a tendency for slightly greater deposition on the windward side.

Prevailing winds are high-altitude winds blowing across mountain ranges. Closer to the ground, where wind direction is modified by terrain, local winds often blow parallel to the valleys. Background image courtesy Google Earth.

As the wind increases above 5 km/h, so the movement of snow begins. At first, activity is confined to the few millimetres above the snow surface as snow particles are rolled along by the wind. Little snow is actually transported in this manner, although the resulting rearrangement of snow crystals contributes to the toughness of the snow due to joining of the more closely packed grains.

Medium wind speeds will begin to pick the snow up off the ground and bounce the crystals along the surface. The airstream at this stage is still uniform and steady and most of the activity is confined to the first few centimetres above the snow surface. Although the wind is only of moderate strength, a considerable quantity of snow can be transported and loaded onto lee slopes and the lee sides of ridges to form extensive deposits of slab. Poles standing three metres clear of the snow surface on the headwall of Coire Cas in the Cairngorms of Scotland were completely buried during a snowfall of 15 cm accompanied by winds of 70 km/h, and in Colorado snow deposition rates as high as 45 cm/hour have been measured.

Eddies, or vortices, formed on the lee side of any windbreak are responsible for the deposition and packing of snow into cohesive slabs.

Snow-carrying capacity As the velocity of the wind increases, so does its snow-carrying capacity. Each time the wind speed doubles, the amount of snow it can carry increases by a factor of eight. At a certain velocity, depending on the terrain and the roughness of the snow surface, the wind no longer flows steadily over the snow but becomes turbulent. Turbulence is an uneven air flow which produces eddies, or vortices, both vertically and horizontally. These eddies do not occur in one location but are continually moving, building up and dying down, producing an extremely complex pattern of air currents at the snow surface. Strong eddies will create a scouring action in the snow and cause erosion. An example of this are scour holes around trees and buildings. Where wind speeds are moderate, snow is usually deposited by the eddies. Snow fences rely on eddies reducing the wind speed behind the fence to create snowdrifts. In turbulent air conditions snow particles are held in suspension, by upward air currents, from a few centimetres above the snow surface to a considerable height. Very large volumes of snow may be transported in this manner.

Effect of Wind on Snow Crystals

Modification of snow crystals, both in the atmosphere and after they reach the ground, is an important factor in the development of avalanche hazard.

High winds will cause crystal collisions in the atmosphere, breaking up the more delicate forms such as stellar crystals into smaller fragments. On reaching the ground, crystals may be dragged along the surface, bounced off the terrain or picked up and swirled around several metres above the surface before finally being deposited. High wind speeds — 90 km/h or more — will scour the snow, reducing the size of cornices and etching the windward side of drifts.

Windblown snow tends to be tougher, more closely knit, denser and more cohesive. Snow deposited by high winds loses its crystalline characteristics and appears duller—wind slab is often described as chalky white in appearance. As a general rule, wind-carved snow formations are usually safe, while snow deposited by wind is often unsafe.

How Wind Creates Cohesive Slabs

The exact mechanism by which cohesive slabs are created is not fully understood. There is no doubt that wind plays an important part in slab formation, although I have seen storm-slab avalanches in the Yukon during and shortly after an apparently windless, but heavy snowstorm. It is also thought that high humidity enhances slab formation, as snow particles remain in suspension in the air for longer distances without subliming when the humidity is high. High humidity also allows a greater buildup of rime on the individual crystals.

Two actions of the wind appear to help in forming slabs. First of all, wind breaks up the more delicate crystals into smaller particles—as small as 0.1 mm—and second, the action of the wind physically packs the snow crystals closer together. Because individual snow crystals tend to be broken into small particles, the snow becomes small-grained and more rounded. Because of greater sintering due to close grain contact, the snow is stronger for a given density. (See **sintering** on p. 50.)

Deposition of Slabs and Cushions

The greatest danger to the skier is from either storm slab or wind slab avalanches. Such slabs are deposited by local winds according to wind direction and terrain features. Certain terrain features enhance the formation of slabs.

Think of air flowing over a bare, rounded ridge (see illustration above). The wind is approaching the ridge at a uniform speed and at a constant pressure. Because of pressure restraints, the same amount of air is forced through a narrower space at the top of the ridge, with the result that the air on the windward side is forced to accelerate, reaching maximum velocity at the crest of the ridge. Snow on the higher windward slope will be picked up by the accelerat-

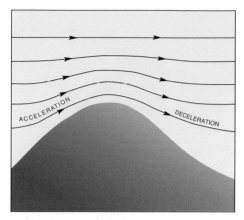

Airflow over a rounded ridge.

ing wind, thus denuding the windward side of snow. Once over the ridge the air can expand downward, which has the effect of reducing the wind velocity. The reduction in wind speed allows the snow which has been carried over the ridge to be deposited. Because flow over rounded ridges is often a steady flow and cornices may not form, other signs must be used to determine wind direction.

Cornices

As the ridge becomes sharper, so the accelerating and decelerating effect of the wind is intensified to such an extent that eventually the flow on the lee side of the ridge is turbulent with accompanying vortices, or circular swirls. In moderate wind speeds of about 25 km/h, cornices begin to form (see next page). As more snow is transported over the ridge the cornice grows and may eventually overhang the lee side of the ridge with many tonnes of snow. Cornices overhanging steep lee slopes are often very unstable due to lack of support. In the long run, high winds tend to erode a cornice, reducing its size. Sometimes a mound of soft slab called a **snow cushion** forms immediately below a cornice; in some cases the whole slope is covered in soft wind slab. These cushions are extremely dangerous during and for some time after formation.

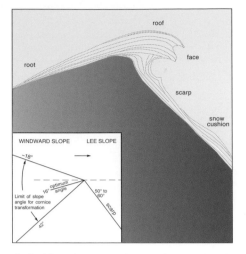

The buildup of a cornice, showing the critical angle of the windward slope for cornice formation. The maximum angle of the scarp is approximately 60°.

Notches or cols in mountain ridges are natural avenues for the wind, the terrain again accelerating the wind as it passes over the col and slowing it down on the other side where areas of slab are then deposited. Often, prevailing winds will blow over the gap while at the same time local winds, blowing at an angle along the mountainside, distort the deposition pattern (see diagram below).

In the mountains local winds often blow along valleys rather than across them, irrespective of the direction of the prevailing winds. When valley winds blow across a series of mountain ridges they will pick up snow on the windward side and deposit it on the lee side. Higher wind speeds, usually above treeline, will deposit smaller areas of hard wind slab in isolated pockets.

Some of the most subtle and insidious deposits of soft wind slab occur below changes in terrain steepness (see below) and it is these small areas of slab which can so easily catch the skier unaware. Note how succeeding layers of snow steepen up the slope and how the potential fracture line moves down the slope as the season progresses. Large areas of relatively flat terrain above such a slope can be the source of a considerable amount of snow during fair-weather drifting.

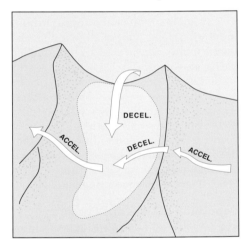

Effect of wind across a mountainside and across a gap in a ridge. After *The Avalanche Handbook.*

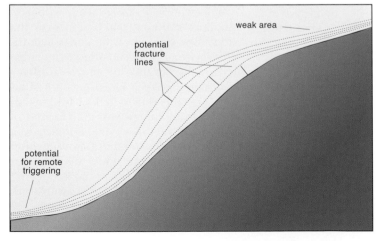

Relatively small changes in terrain steepness may develop dangerous wind slabs. Often referred to as wind rolls.

Extensive areas of slab have formed across the whole mountainside. The slide at the bottom right was triggered by a group of skiers traversing at about mid-slope. The other slides are natural releases.

Mountain Winds

Certain wind patterns peculiar to mountain regions influence the snowpack:

Air cooled by long-wave radiation drains down from the ice cap into the valley below. Background image courtesy Google Earth.

Katabatic winds Air lying over an elevated plateau area such as a glacier or icefield will become denser due to cooling by long-wave radiation on a cold, clear night. This denser air will then drain down the mountain slopes under gravity and into the valleys below. These katabatic winds are usually moderate breezes of 15 to 20 km/h, strong enough to form wind slab below rolls in the terrain

In some locations, however, where the air is cooled as it moves across a large snowfield and then drains down through narrow, constricted valleys, it can reach very high speeds. This normally occurs along the coasts of Alaska, Greenland and Norway and off some of the world's larger icefields such as Antarctica.

In parts of the world where these winds are especially severe they have been given local names such as the Bora, which brings cold air down from the Austrian Alps to the warmer Adriatic, or the Mistral, which sweeps down from the French Alps to the Mediterranean.

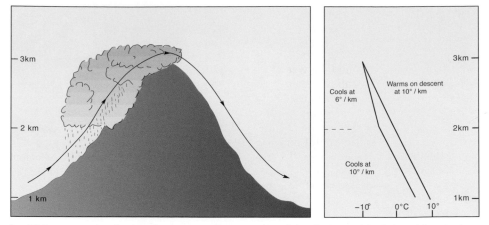

In addition to warming the air as it passes over the range, chinook winds also push back the cold arctic air, thus allowing a substantial rise in temperature.

Chinook and foehn The chinook and its European counterpart the foehn are both warm, dry winds blowing on the lee side of mountain ranges. The chinook, which blows over the plains to the east of the Rocky Mountains in Canada and the United States, was named by early settlers who thought the wind originated in First Nations territory of that name. The Indians themselves called the wind the "snow eater" because of the startling way in which large amounts of snow can be evaporated by the warmth and dryness of the air. In addition to warming the air as it passes over the range, chinook winds also push back the cold arctic air, thus allowing a substantial rise in temperature. The "chinook arch" cloud marks the meeting of warm and cold air.

Chinooks are caused when prevailing winds carrying warm, moist air are directed against a mountain range. The forced ascent on the windward side causes clouds to form, often with resulting snowfall. During most of the ascent the air is cooled at the moist adiabatic rate of 6°C/km, and by the time the air reaches the mountaintop much of the moisture will have been removed.

The term adiabatic is used to describe the twin phenomena of decrease in temperature due to expansion of air and increase in temperature due to contraction of air. At the moist adiabatic rate, moisture changes phase—vapour to liquid—due to condensation, or alternatively from liquid to vapour due to evaporation. Latent heat—the number of calories released or used during condensation or evaporation—either heats or cools the air.

Condensation of moisture in order to produce rain or snow releases latent heat which is absorbed by the rising air over the mountain range. As the air descends the lee slope it is warmed at the dry adiabatic rate of 10°C/km, so that when the air reaches the bottom of the mountain it is both warmer and drier than the air on the windward side.

Temperature of the Snowpack

The temperature of the snowpack and snow surface changes as heat is transferred within the snowpack and between the snow surface and the air above. Changes in temperature and difference in temperature between layers has a considerable influence on the snowpack's character. Snow exists close to its melting point and any small changes in temperature will affect the strength of the snow and hence its stability. There are three possible areas where heat exchange can take place: the snow surface, the interior of the snowpack and the ground surface.

Heat Transfer at the Snow Surface

Heat may be transferred at the snow surface by conduction, convection, radiation, condensation or evaporation, and precipitation. Often two or more of these processes are present at the same time, making the measuring of snow surface temperature a complex problem. This is the reason why experienced cross-country skiers rely on the feel of the snow in their hand rather than a reading from a thermometer when waxing.

Conduction and Convection combine to transfer heat to or from the surface of the snow. The rate of heat transfer is increased in windy conditions. If the wind is both moist and warmer than the snow, heat will be transferred to the snowpack; the higher the wind speed, the greater the amount of heat transferred. On the other hand, if cold arctic air blows across the surface, the snowpack will lose heat to the air and, because of the added effect of evaporation, will cool rapidly and become colder than the air above.

Evaporation and Condensation are the source of large exchanges of heat at the snow surface. It requires 600 calories to convert 1 gram of liquid water to vapour without a change in temperature. To convert 1 gram of ice directly to vapour (sublimation) requires 680 calories, so you can see that a large quantity of heat, usually provided by strong, warm, dry winds, is required to evaporate moisture from the snow surface. Disappointed skiers on the eastern slopes of the Rockies will attest to the phenomenal ability of a chinook to remove snow. Relatively little evaporation takes place in the absence of wind.

It follows that condensation of water vapour directly on the snow surface will release 680 calories of latent heat to the snow. In this case there is an excess of water vapour present in the atmosphere. During the formation of surface hoar it is this additional heat that keeps the temperature difference between the snow surface and the air above large enough to allow the continued growth of surface hoar crystals.

Radiation The amount of incoming solar radiation that reaches the earth is dependent upon the seasons, the latitude and the aspect of the surface relative to the sun's rays. In northern latitudes, north-facing slopes receive little or no solar radiation in winter. Areas closer to the poles receive

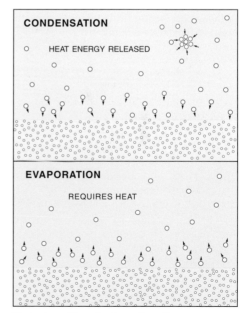

Heat gain and loss due to condensation and evaporation.

no direct radiation at all during the winter months, and even on clear days the snow will lose heat to the atmosphere.

While the atmosphere is virtually transparent to light radiation from the sun, it is relatively opaque to heat radiation from the earth, so only a small percentage of the radiated heat is lost to space; the remainder is absorbed by the cloud cover or by the lower layers of the atmosphere.

Snow is an excellent radiator of long-wave radiation. In fact, it is one of the best "blackbody" radiators known. A blackbody radiator is a material capable of giving off the maximum amount of radiation at a given temperature. On a clear night, snow may emit enough long-wave radiation to cool the surface by 15 to 20°C or more. Many climbers have suffered frostbitten feet due to snow cooled in this manner. On a cloudy night, if the atmosphere below the clouds is warmer than the snow, the snow will gain heat.

In the daytime, new snow reflects 80–90% of the short-wave radiation falling on it, so that even on a clear, sunny day the snow can still lose heat to the atmosphere from an excess of long-wave radiation. This is one reason why the sparkling layer of surface hoar formed during a clear, calm night will persist unchanged through clear, cold weather.

In spring, the snow becomes less reflective, due to melting and dust on the surface, and with the sun higher in the sky the process is reversed and incoming short-wave radiation exceeds the long-wave radiation from the snow surface. The maximum warming from radiation usually occurs with a partly cloudy sky where solar radiation and long-wave radiation from warm clouds combine in the most efficient manner.

Because a large portion of the available short-wave radiation is required to melt the snowpack, air temperatures do not rise significantly in an area until all the new snow has melted.

Precipitation Rain in small quantities contributes little to the transfer of heat at the snow surface. Because it requires 80 calories to convert 1 gram of ice to 1 gram of water without a change in temperature, large quantities of warm rain are required before melting at the surface occurs.

Average energy balance at the earth's surface. At higher latitudes heat loss exceeds heat gain during the winter months.

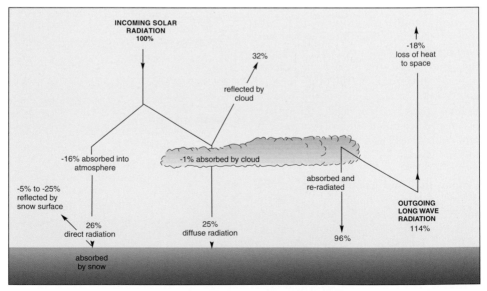

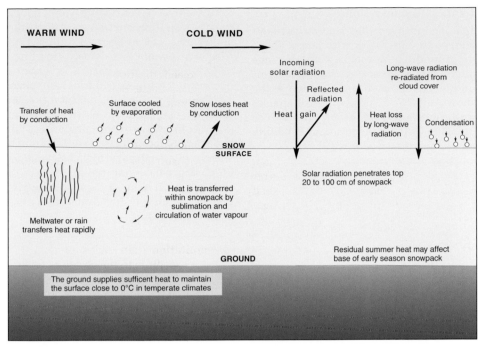

Modes of heat gain and loss at the snow surface, within the snowpack, and at the ground surface.

Heat Transfer within the Snowpack

Conduction, the transmittal of heat through grain-to-grain contact, is the primary mechanism for transmitting heat through the snowpack. The rate of transmission depends on snow structure, density and depth.

In dry snow conditions very little heat is transferred within the snowpack. This is one of the reasons why such large temperature differences can be found between various layers. Some heat transfer occurs due to sublimation and to circulation of water vapour through the pore spaces.

Conversely heat may be transferred very quickly in the wet snowpack when meltwater or rain percolates through the snowpack. Free water within the snowpack quickly raises the overall temperature to freezing point even though the rain will cause little actual melting. Water, freezing within the snowpack, releases 80 calories of heat per gram to the snowpack.

Heat Transfer at the Ground Surface

The amount of heat transferred to the snow from the ground is also small. Heat stored within the surface ground layers after the summer months may affect initial snowfalls, as the earth gives off enough heat to melt about 1 cm of snow a year. In temperate climates the main effect of the earth's heat is to keep the ground surface temperature from falling much below 0°C.

Decrease of Temperature with Height

Within the lower atmosphere, which varies in thickness from about 9 km above the poles to 16 km above the tropics, there is normally a gradual decrease in temperature of approximately 6.5°C for every 1000 m of height gain. Do not confuse this decrease in temperature with the temperature changes associated with rising parcels of air. The dry adiabatic rate for rising air is 10°C/1000 m.

Temperature Inversions

Temperature inversions occur when the air temperature increases with height above the ground. They occur over a wide range of climatological scales, from inversions in the first few millimetres above the snow surface to large-scale differences in air mass temperature and can produce dramatic variations in local snow stability within an area.

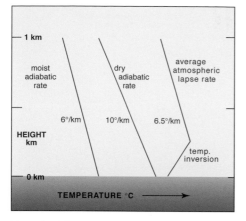

Atmospheric lapse rates.

When the snow surface has been losing heat due to long-wave radiation, temperature differences as large as 6°C have been measured between the snow surface and the air only 1 mm above. As any winter camper who digs a hole in the snow for their tent will find out, cold air settles in hollows during the course of a still night. Sleeping platforms in igloos and snow caves trap warm air in the top of the structure, while cold air settles in the doorway well.

U-shaped mountain valleys are often subject to temperature inversions. On a cold, clear night the earth's surface cools by radiating more heat than it receives, the heavier, colder air near the cooling ground surface sinking to the valley floor. A common indicator of this condition is the cloud or fog layer which sometimes forms at the junction of cold and warm air.

If the valley is below treeline you'll notice that the heavily frosted trees low down the slopes give way to trees with no sign of frost at a very obvious demarcation line.

Large-scale temperature inversions occur when warm, dry air tries to displace a previously well-established continental arctic air mass. Like the establishment of a warm front, the warm air pushing up over the colder air mass results in much warmer temperatures at higher elevations. Most skiers have had the experience of skiing at 2000 m in −5°C sunshine while the temperature at lower elevations has been −20°C or less.

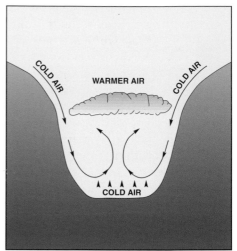

Temperature inversion in a U-shaped valley. Cold air drains down the mountainsides and builds up in the valley bottom. The warmest point is at the base of the cloud layer.

Snow

Travelling above snow line in winter and summer has many attractions: the tranquility of the frozen landscape, the dazzling whiteness of high alpine snowfields, the almost tangible silence when fresh snowfalls blanket forests and meadows.

Snow can hasten or hinder your progress. In good snow conditions, it's possible to travel many kilometres a day; in poor conditions of crust or rotten snow, progress is frustratingly slow. Firm, well-consolidated snow allows an easy ascent of steep mountain slopes; loose snow in gullies is a major danger of winter mountaineering. A metre of unconsolidated powder, while enticingly beautiful, creates impossible trail breaking for those on foot.

The shape of snow crystals and their temperature influence how well your skis glide and how well your climbing waxes hold. Safety from avalanches depends upon a countless number of minute physical changes which begin from the first moment the snowflake touches the ground.

It is important when evaluating avalanche hazard and slope stability to consider the various forms of snow, how snow changes on its way to the ground and how the snowpack builds up in successive layers during the course of the season.

A sparkling layer of surface hoar covers the snow, hiding the intricate changes that take place in the snow-pack underneath. Photo Leon Kubbernus.

The Three States of Water

If you want to learn more about how snow forms in the atmosphere and how it changes on the ground, read the following section, which explains the basic physical concepts governing the three states of water: gas, liquid and solid (vapour, water and ice). Otherwise, turn the page and resume reading at "Snow in the Air."

Water Vapour

Think of water vapour as individual molecules of water dashing around the atmosphere in a state of rapid but random motion. Each molecule consists of one blob of oxygen with two "eyes" of hydrogen attached.

Dew Point

Imagine a large number of molecules of water vapour floating along quite happily in their own cubic centimetre or so of air space. As they are propelled by the prevailing wind landward over the ocean more molecules, freed by evaporation, rise up to join them. Eventually they reach land and are swept upward over high ground. As they rise the air expands and the molecules slow down, their kinetic energy reduced. The more the air expands, the cooler the molecules become and the closer together they huddle, until at a certain temperature, known as the **Dew Point,** they condense into water droplets.

When this occurs the air is said to be **Saturated**. It contains as many free molecules as it possibly can at that particular temperature. The lower the temperature, the fewer molecules the air can hold before condensation takes place.

Water

Water is formed of molecules sliding over each other but held together at the same time in a loose liquid form by the attraction of one molecule to another. Because water molecules form strong bonds, a very large amount of energy is required to convert water to vapour. In fact, the evaporation of water requires approximately 540 calories to change 1 gram of water to vapour without a change of temperature. This is known as the **Latent Heat of Vaporization**. Conversely, condensation releases the equivalent amount of heat to the atmosphere.

Supercooled Water

If water vapour molecules encounter a temperature below freezing before they condense, the clouds that form will be composed of minute droplets which remain in the liquid state below the freezing point. The purer the water, the more the droplets can be cooled. But there is a lower temperature limit: at −40°C water droplets freeze instantly.

Vapour Pressure

Some molecules attain enough speed to break away from the surface of water. The higher the temperature, the more active the molecules and the greater the evaporation. Many of the molecules that break free remain in the form of an atmosphere of free-moving molecules hovering over the surface of the water. A concentration of these molecules is called **Vapour Pressure**. As the temperature falls the vapour pressure becomes lower.

Ice

Ice is a state of matter where the molecules are firmly joined and their movement is restricted to vibrations. However, as in the case of water, molecules are able to break away from surface of the ice and form an atmosphere of vapour.

Vapour Pressure over Water and Ice

For a given temperature below freezing the vapour pressure over water is greater than the vapour pressure over ice. This is because the molecules are able to escape more readily from water than from ice. This concept, and the concept of **Supersaturation**, are most important in the formation of ice crystals, both in the atmosphere and on the ground.

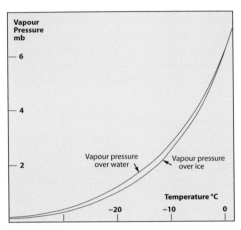

Saturation vapour pressure is higher over super-cooled water than over ice.

Condensation

Condensation happens when a large number of molecules join together to form a water droplet. If there is no foreign surface on which to condense, the molecules can only come together by accidental collisions, which may require a high degree of Supersaturation, especially in the case of slower-moving molecules at lower temperatures. If a sufficient number of molecules get together, then the droplet will continue to grow rather than evaporate away. In the atmosphere this is achieved by the presence of foreign particles such as dust and salts, called **Condensation Nuclei**, which provide a surface on which water molecules can begin to condense.

Supersaturation

Consider a glass of ice water. If the humidity is high enough it will soon become coated on the outside with condensed water droplets. Like the molecules around the cold glass, high-flying molecules in the atmosphere need some surface on which they can begin to condense. In the absence of such a surface, in the very clean air conditions at higher altitudes, it is possible for many more molecules to crowd together before condensation occurs. This higher moisture content is called **Supersaturation**.

Sublimation

Sublimation is the ability of water molecules to change from ice to vapour and back again without passing through the liquid stage. A warm, dry wind blowing over an ice surface will carry off water molecules, and because the vapour pressure over the ice is momentarily lower, more molecules will be encouraged to break away from the surface, thus hastening evaporation.

Saturation with Respect to Ice

If the atmosphere over a particle of ice contains the same concentration of water vapour as that given off by the ice, it is said to be **Saturated with Respect to Ice**. If the vapour concentration in the air is higher than the vapour pressure over the ice, it is said to be **Supersaturated with Respect to Ice**, and some molecules condense onto the ice surface (below).

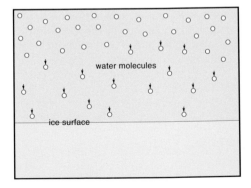

Snow in the Air

Snowfall

Snowfall occurs when moist air, rising to a level where it is cooled to below freezing, forms ice crystals that eventually fall to the ground as snow. The intensity, or rate of snowfall (measured in cm/hour), depends on how much moisture is available in the atmosphere and how fast the moist air rises. Many serious avalanche cycles are associated with higher than usual rates of snowfall.

Formation of Snow

In order for ice crystals to form, foreign particles are needed around which supercooled water droplets can crystallize. These are called **Freezing Nuclei** and are generally composed of clay particles and biological particles such as bacteria from plants. The colder the temperature, the more Freezing Nuclei become active, to the point where, at −40°C, supercooled water droplets freeze instantly. Once the initial crystallizing into ice has taken place it is possible that splinters of ice, breaking off from other crystals, may also act as freezing nuclei.

Eventually, a state is achieved where the cloud is composed of both ice crystals and supercooled water droplets. The difference in vapour pressure between ice and supercooled water allows the ice crystals to grow at the expense of the supercooled droplets because the cloud, which is only saturated with respect to water, is super-saturated with respect to ice. Molecules of water vapour are constantly migrating from higher-pressure regions over the water droplets to the lower-pressure ice surface. The transformation into snow crystals gives travelling molecules the opportunity to finally achieve an orderly existence. The crystals continue to grow until they are heavy enough to escape from updrafts in the cloud formation and begin their journey groundward.

Snow Crystals

If you look closely at falling snow you'll notice that it's usually composed of bright crystalline particles of ice, either alone or matted together to form larger snowflakes. These snow crystals are six-sided and vary from very thin hexagonal stars and plates to long columns or needles. Although the chance of two snow crystals being alike is remote, they do form a number of fairly consistent types as shown in the table below. The basic form of a snow crystal is determined by the temperature at which it forms. Its size and any subsequent change depends on the amount of moisture available. To a lesser extent the degree of super-saturation modifies the crystal form and controls the rate of growth. Most crystal types form within a very small temperature range. For instance, the beautiful classic stellar crystals only grow between approximately −12 and −16°C.

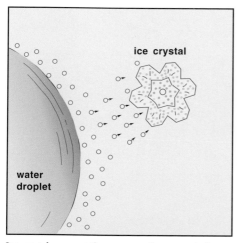

Ice crystals grow at the expense of supercooled water droplets.

Crystal Types	
Type of crystal	Temperature range at formation
Thin hexagonal plates	0 to −3°C
Needles	−3 to −5°C
Hollow prismatic columns	−5 to −8°C
Hexagonal plates	−8 to −12°C
Stellars and dendrites	−12 to −16°C
Hexagonal plates	−16 to −25°C
Hollow prisms	−25 to −30°C

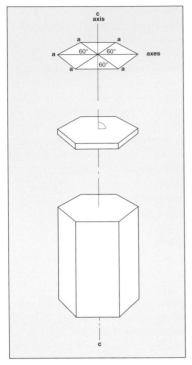

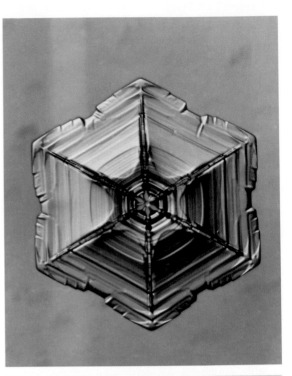

The crystal form of ice. Crystals may grow either along the a-axis to form plates and dendritic crystals or along the c-axis to produce columns and needles.

Above right: Plate crystal about 1 mm in diameter. Photo Y. Furukawa, The Institute of Low Temperature Science, Sapporo.

Right: Dendritic crystal about 2.5 mm in diameter. Photo Y. Furukawa, The Institute of Low Temperature Science, Sapporo.

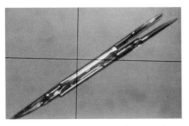

Needle crystal approximately 3 mm long. Photo Y. Furukawa, The Institute of Low Temperature Science, Sapporo.

A cluster of bullet-shaped crystals. Photo Ron Perla.

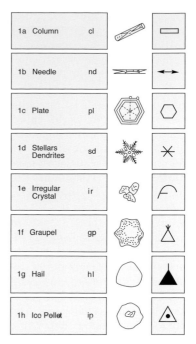

1a	Column	cl		
1b	Needle	nd		
1c	Plate	pl		
1d	Stellars Dendrites	sd		
1e	Irregular Crystal	ir		
1f	Graupel	gp		
1g	Hail	hl		
1h	Ice Pellet	ip		

International classification for precipitation particles. International Association of Scientific Hydrology.

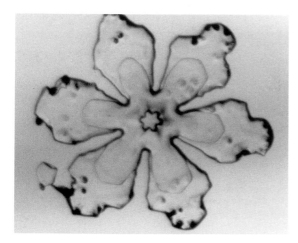

Left: Segmented crystal about 1 mm in diameter. Photo Ron Perla.

Falling Snow Crystals

The changes which take place in the form of snow crystals after their initial formation and before they reach the ground are important in evaluating avalanche hazard.

There are many factors that affect the crystal on its way to the ground: atmospheric conditions such as wind, turbulence, the temperature and moisture level in various layers of the clouds, coupled with the original form of the crystal and the total depth of the cloud. These factors can cause the crystal to either grow or evaporate away, melt into rain or break up into fragments from physical collisions.

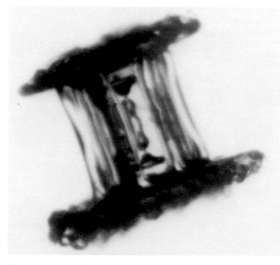

Capped column. Photo Ron Perla.

Of particular interest is the way crystals grow after their initial formation. There are three basic ways.

Snowflakes are formed when individual crystals collide with other crystals in warm, moist conditions to form conglomerates. The largest snowflakes are often composed of stellar crystals, although other crystal types can mat together in the same way.

Rimed star-shaped crystal about 2 mm in diameter. Photo Y. Furukawa, Institute of Low Temperature Science, Sapporo.

Riming The second way in which crystals grow has a significant effect on new-snow stability and the development of hazard. This is riming, or growth by collision with supercooled water droplets that instantly freeze on contact with the crystal. While most snowfalls have crystals with some degree of rime, the more turbulent the air in the upper atmosphere, the more rime a crystal collects, and in some cases, with thick clouds and strong updrafts, the original crystal form becomes totally unrecognizable. In these stormy conditions the snow formed is known as **Graupel**. Graupel is often associated with the passage of a cold front. Dry **Granular Snow**, occasionally encountered at high altitudes or in very cold conditions, is usually composed of clusters of moderately rimed crystals such as plates, bullets and columns. It has a dry, powdery appearance and is prone to forming cohesive slabs even when there is very little wind.

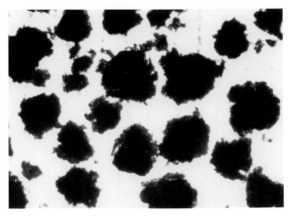

Heavily rimed star-shaped crystal. Photo Ron Perla.

Crystal growth The third form of growth is the continued growth of the original crystal to give larger and more intricate crystals.

Graupel about 2 mm in diameter. Photo Ron Perla.

Feathery crystals of surface hoar seen against a red jacket.

Other Forms of Snow or Ice

Different types of crystals, similar to snow crystals, form close to the surface of the earth under certain conditions of temperature and humidity. They are called **Non-Precipitated** forms of snow and ice.

Hoarfrost

Hoarfrost is a bright, sparkling, crystalline growth of crystals which can be found on, above or in some cases beneath the snow surface. It is formed in much the same way as snow crystals and could be considered the snow equivalent of dew.

Hoarfrost is responsible for the fern-like patterns on windows and the delicate, glittering tracery on vegetation.

It forms when daytime radiation allows the air above the snow surface to hold a substantial amount of water vapour. On a cold, clear night when the snow surface is cooled by loss of heat to the atmosphere, the air becomes supersaturated with respect to the ice, and water vapour condenses on the snowpack to form a delightfully crisp, crystalline surface on which to ski known as **Surface Hoar**. In cold northern latitudes surface hoar will remain unchanged during clear, sunny days in midwinter. When new snow falls on a layer of surface hoar the surface hoar forms a weak layer that can persist in the snowpack for a considerable period of time. This weak layer signifi-

cantly reduces the bond between the old snow and the new snow above. We will be discussing buried surface-hoar layers in the section on snow stability.

Weak layers of buried surface hoar are a concern for skiers and boarders in some regions. Layers such as this one can persist in the snowpack for many weeks. Photo Jim Bay.

Another variety, **Crevasse Hoar**, can be found in spaces around rocks and trees, inside crevasses and in ice caves where, over a period of several weeks, large crystals may form. The crystal illustrated in the upper photograph overleaf is approximately 7.5 cm long and 5 cm across the open cup.

A very large crevasse hoar crystal found in an ice cave at the snout of the Saskatchewan Glacier, Canadian Rockies.

Rime

Rime is formed when droplets of super-cooled water impinge on any object in their path. It has a dull white, non-crystalline appearance and is found deposited on the windward side of rocks, vegetation and sometimes whole mountainsides. Rime is a good indicator of wind direction. A ski pole standing outside overnight will often be found next morning with a feathery deposit of rime growing into the wind. The amount of fresh buildup can be related to wind speed; the longer the feathers or thicker the buildup, the higher the wind speed.

Snow Crystals and Avalanche Hazard

Crystal type Because of differences in shape and density, some types of snow crystals have a greater tendency to create hazardous avalanche conditions than others.

Delicate stellar crystals and clusters of bullet-shaped crystals with little or no riming have some initial cohesion due to interlocking of the crystal branches. Because it usually has a density of less than 70 kg/m^3, this form of snow sluffs off steeper slopes within a few days and doesn't form dangerous storm slab.

However, if the crystals are broken into fragments by moderate or strong winds they will pack together and form stiff, wind-drifted slabs that are potentially very dangerous.

Needle and plate crystals falling in windless conditions produce almost immediate hazard from loose-snow avalanches. If followed by a snowfall of crystals with greater cohesion, they will form a weak, sliding layer within the snowpack.

Effect of rime Rime builds up on snow crystals as they fall through the atmosphere. It not only increases the density but also gives more contact points, allowing adjacent crystals to more readily bind together. See **sintering** on page 50. In other words, the likelihood of slabs forming increases with the degree of riming.

Although partially rimed crystals allow greater initial stability, the condition can lead to a buildup of thick layers of snow before a slab releases. High intensity snowfalls of heavily rimed crystals deposited in strong winds form tough, hard and unpredictable wind slab. Rimed needles in particular will form dense, compact slabs up to 300 kg/m^3.

Because of its high density (up to 250 kg/m^3) and relatively low tensile strength, graupel readily forms slab when deposited in thick layers of 15 cm or more.

Feathers of rime growing into the wind are good indicators of past wind direction.

Snow on the Ground

Snow on the ground consists of many layers of solid precipitation modified by wind, sun or rain. These layers can be distinctly separate or can merge imperceptibly with one another. Weak layers, or lack of bond between layers, form sliding surfaces within the snowpack. The thickness of identifiable layers may vary from many centimetres of new snowfall to a millimetre or less of recrystallized grains.

Because of continuous changes in temperature and pressure within the snowpack caused by varying meteorological condi-tions, the physical composition of the snow is constantly changing until it either melts, evaporates or, in areas of permanent snow, consolidates to become glacier ice.

Use a magnifying glass to examine a sample of old, consolidated snow from 20 to 30 cm beneath the surface. If tem-peratures have been moderate you will see little trace of the original crystals. Instead there will be a mass of rounded ice particles called **Ice Grains** and a lot of vacant spaces called **Pore Spaces**. The grains may be connected to each other by **Necks** of ice: the thicker the necks, the stronger the snow structure.

Most avalanches slide at a weak layer in the snowpack or on a hard, smooth layer. An understanding of the layered composition of the snowpack is essential for evaluating avalanche hazard.

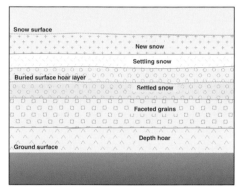

Snow on the ground builds up in many layers.

The cross-section below shows wind-toughened snow near the surface, a thin, fragile layer with partially settled snow below with a density of 180 kg/m³. Photo E. Akitaya, The Institute of Low Temperature Science, Sapporo.

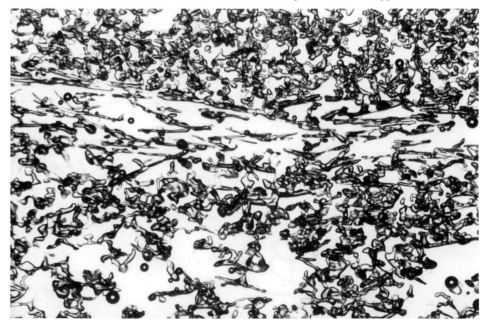

How Snow Is Deposited

In windless conditions snow falls uniformly over the mountains and, depending on temperature, can range from fluffy down-like stellar snow crystals to large, wet, heavy snowflakes. The initial properties of a snow layer depend on the crystal type, the amount of modification to the crystals and the meteorological conditions of wind and temperature near the surface of the ground at the time of deposition.

Snow accompanied by wind gives a different form of snowpack buildup. Snow tends to be deposited on the lee side of ridges or in gullies where the wind velocity drops. Over large areas the snow forms cohesive slabs of varying degrees of hardness, while smaller, isolated slabs develop wherever there are minor changes in slope angle or orientation of terrain.

Snow can also be deposited by wind alone, blown from the windward side of a ridge to the lee side. The amount of snow and the speed of buildup should not be underestimated.

An unusually high rate of new snowfall, or a rapid deposition of recent snow by wind, will cause a rapid increase in stress within the snowpack. Consequently there is a greater chance of weak layers within the snowpack failing.

The Ground Surface

The temperature of the ground in temperate climates remains close to 0°C. This is due in part to the residual heat in the earth's surface but is mainly due to the insulating properties of fresh snow. Even in colder climates, where the ground is several degrees below freezing, there can be considerable temperature difference between the snow surface and the ground surface in cold weather. This difference in temperature has considerable significance in cold climates when the snowpack is shallow.

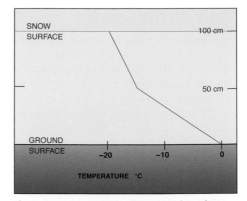

The temperature gradient often varies throughout the snowpack. In this simplified diagram the upper portion has a temperature gradient of 10°C/m, while the lower section is 30°C/m.

Temperature Gradient

The temperature gradient is the difference in temperature between two snow layers or between a snow layer and the ground, expressed in degrees Celsius per metre of depth. For example, consider 1 metre of snow lying on a ground surface whose temperature is 0°C. If the air temperature drops to −20°C there is a difference of 20°C in 1 metre of snow depth, or 20°C/m.

Because the temperature gradient influences the movement of water molecules within the snowpack, it has a significant effect on changes in snow structure within the snowpack.

The Effect of Temperature

Snow is an unusual and unpredictable material. It possesses the same properties as most common engineering materials, but because it exists close to its melting point and responds rapidly to small changes in temperature, these properties are difficult to measure. The temperature range at which we usually encounter snow is very small, from −20°C to just above 0°C. Above freezing, snow becomes wet and soggy, eventually melting; below −20°C there is little observable change from day to day.

Because the strength of a snow layer tends to decrease as the temperature rises toward the freezing point, it follows that a sudden rise in temperature will usually result in a decrease in stability. In practice, any sudden rise of 4° or 5°C is one of the major avalanche warning signs.

Density of Snow

The density of snow (the proportion of snow to air spaces) varies tremendously, from light fluffy snow deposited under moderately cold, calm conditions to hard, old, wind-deposited slabs and eventually, if it does not melt first, to green glacier ice.

Snow layers on the ground contain a considerable amount of air. The density of a layer is measured by weighing a known volume of snow and expressing the result in one of two forms: either as a weight of snow per cubic metre (kilograms per cubic metre) or by specific gravity, which has no dimensions. Specific gravity is a ratio between the weight of snow and the weight of an equal volume of water. In the case of snow it will always be less than one.

Typical Density of Snow Layers

Type of snow	Density kg/m³	Specific gravity
Wild snow	3	0.003
Light new snow	30	0.03
New snow – no wind	100	0.10
Wind-deposited snow	250	0.25
Cornice snow	400	0.40
Firn snow	600	0.60
Glacier ice	800	0.80

Adapted from a table by Marcel Roland de Quervain

Liquid Water Content

The amount of water in the snowpack is of considerable interest to the backcountry traveller, as any snow with a discernible liquid water content may have a significant effect on stability, either from the additional loading of the wet snow disturbing the equilibrium balance or from weak, cohesionless grains formed beneath the wet layer by water seeping from above, creating a sliding layer.

Strength of Various Types of Snow

Snow type	Strength	Variation with time
Recently deposited snow	Low to very low	Decreases with time although some forms of snow crystals will have initial strength because of interlocking of crystal branches.
Broken, wind-packed particles	Medium to high	Rapid strength increase due to close packing and rapid sintering.
Settled snow with rounded grains	High to very high	Increases with time and density. Offset by a decrease in strength with increasing grain size.
Settled snow with a high proportion of faceted grains	Medium	Decreases with increasing growth rate and grain size.
Depth hoar	Low to very low	Decreases with increasing growth rate and crystal size. Increases with increasing density.
Surface hoar	Extremely low	May exist in fragile state for long periods when buried in cold snow.
Melt–freeze snow	High when frozen	Strength increases with number of melt–freeze cycles. As liquid content increases, snow turns to slush with little strength.

Liquid water content may be estimated by trying to form a snowball. Moist snow (less than 3% water) will form a good snowball. Wet snow (3–8% water) will form a hard, solid snowball, but you will be unable to squeeze water from it. If you can squeeze water out, the snow is termed "very wet" and contains 8–15% free water.

Strength of Snow

The strength of a snow layer is its ability to resist stresses exerted on it. Strength varies according to the type of stress applied (compressive, tensile or shear), the rate at which the stress is applied, the amount of deformation (strain) and the rate at which the snow deforms.

Because snow is not a homogeneous material, its strength is dependent upon the density of the layer, the type and size of snow particles in the layer, and the temperature. Generally the strength of a layer increases with density; a layer of old firn snow may be 1000 times stronger than a layer of recently settled snow.

The table above gives typical strengths of various types of snow and how the strength of the snow may change over time.

Snow overhanging a rail shows the tensile strength of a cohesive mass of settled snow.

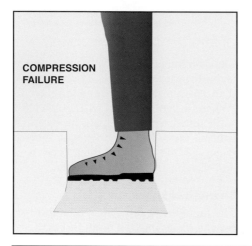

COMPRESSION FAILURE

Creep & Glide

Snow can be both brittle and viscous at the same time. If you place your foot in cold snow, the snow will fail by fracturing under the sudden load. On the other hand, snow lying on a steep roof will flow (creep) under gravity like a liquid, deforming under its own weight to hang over the edge. Cracks may form higher up on the roof as the snow fails in tension. The whole layer may move slowly and steadily (glide) down the roof or one layer may slide off on another—a shear failure between layers.

If the snowpack is lightly and slowly loaded it will deform gradually and settle due to the rearrangement of water molecules among the ice grains. If the snowpack is loaded rapidly, by a heavy snowfall or by strong wind deposition, the stresses in the snowpack result in a buildup of elastic energy that may, when released, result in the propagation of cracks at the base of a slab and the triggering of a slab avalanche (page 64).

Left: If you step down into snow, it will fail in compression due to brittle fracture of the connections between ice grains. The depth of penetration is an indication of the settling and strengthening of the snowpack.

Below: Snow sliding down a roof demonstrates both tensile and shear failure. Creep and glide tend to increase the tensile forces within an inclined snowpack.

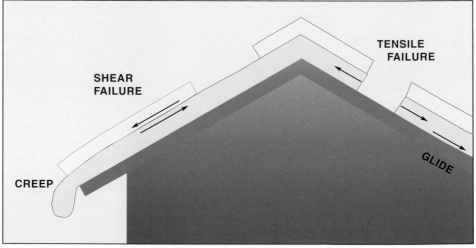

TENSILE FAILURE

SHEAR FAILURE

GLIDE

CREEP

Hardness

Hardness is the resistance to penetration of an object into snow. When we poke our fist or fingers into the wall of a snowpit, we are measuring hardness. The measurement of hardness is subjective and depends upon what instruments we are pressing into the snow. Poking a fist into the snow is a measure of very low hardness, while poking a glove, four fingers, one finger, or a pencil or knife will indicate increasing hardness of a snow layer. There is a direct relationship between hardness and strength.

Grain Shape and Size

The shape and size of ice grains found within the snowpack have a direct bearing on snow stability. Grain shape has been classified into a number of distinct types such as rounded, faceted, cup shaped. In the next section, on how the snow changes over time, we will be discussing the significance of the various grain shapes and how these shapes change from one type to another due to changes in temperature and temperature gradients within the snowpack. As the shapes change so does the size of the grains.

The Snow Surface and How It Changes

The snow surface is constantly changing. If temperatures remain below freezing and the surface is deprived of sun, conditions can remain constant for many days. Unfortunately there are several changes in weather conditions which will turn the ideal snowpack into something less than desirable.

Fresh, new snowfall leaves a bright, highly reflective surface which bounces most of the sun's heat back into the atmosphere. As the snow crystals break down, the surface becomes duller and the snowpack absorbs more of the sun's heat. Dust particles settle from the atmosphere, further dulling the snow. Later in the season, depressions called **Sun Cups** appear in the surface. Wind will form ripples much like sand on a beach; stronger winds will scour and redeposit snow or form areas of dull, chalky-white, hard-packed wind slab.

Simple observation of the snow surface can tell you a lot about past, present or potential avalanche hazard.

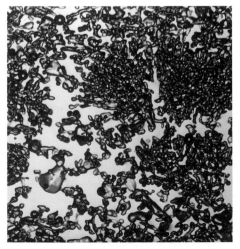

The recent snow in this picture contains a significant amount of graupel (the clusters of grains). Density 270 kg/m³. Photo E. Akitaya, The Institute of Low Temperature Science, Sapporo.

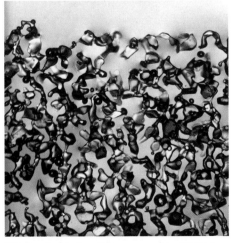

Wind-packed grains at the snow surface. Density 380 kg/m³, scale 15:1. Photo E. Akitaya, The Institute of Low Temperature Science, Sapporo.

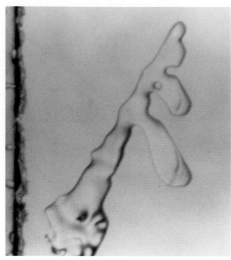

Wind-broken crystal fragment. Photo Ron Perla.

Wind-etching of the snow surface.

Surface Roughness

The shape and depth of irregularities in the snow surface caused by wind, rain, uneven evaporation or uneven melting is a useful indicator of past weather conditions. For example, convex furrows running down-hill in the snow surface is an indication of rain, with the depth of the channels giving a rough idea of the amount and duration of the rainfall.

Surface Penetration

Noting the amount of surface penetration by a person either on foot or on skis is a good indication of how much new snow has fallen and how fast it is settling. If you are breaking trail in fresh snow to mid-calf depth (about 30 cm) you should be concerned about the stability of the new snow on steep slopes.

Effect of Wind

One of the major forces altering the character of new snow is wind. Wind alters the snow layers you ski in by breaking up the crystals as they seek a place to settle, by battering them across the snow surface (saltation) and by redistributing them once they have settled. In addition, wind allows rapid evaporation from the snowpack by transporting water vapour away from the surface of the crystals.

The major effect of wind on the snowpack is the rapid loading of lee slopes with wind-blown snow. Large amounts of snow deposited by strong winds results in a rapid change in the equilibrium between the additional load of newly deposited snow and the strength of the bond between critical snow layers. The snowpack can only adjust to an increase in stress at a certain rate. If that rate is exceeded, then failure will occur. In practice, a steep slope loaded by wind-blown snow may release several times during a storm.

Wind Crust, formed by the action of wind blowing across the surface of snow, is a hardened, crusted layer that forms a discontinuity in the snow on which further snowfalls can slide. When neither deep enough nor hard enough to support a person's weight, wind crust creates extremely tiresome travelling conditions.

Effect of Sun

On a sunny day after new snowfall, the snow will begin to develop a crust called **Sun Crust**. A minute amount of melting in the first few millimetres beneath the surface forms a slightly icy, cohesive layer that gradually spreads down through the surface layers, changing what were perfect skiing conditions one day into tricky, crusty conditions the next.

Sun crust should not be confused with the sleek, shiny ice glaze found on some slopes after a period of cold, clear weather in spring and early summer.

A few days of hot, still weather in spring will result in a pitted snow surface. This type of crust, known as **Perforated Crust**, is formed by differential melting by the sun's rays. The portion of the ice grains which receive the greatest amount of radiation melt first, leaving minute hollows in the snow which are enlarged as time progresses. The shape of the hollows depends on the direction of the sun's rays and the angle at which the sun strikes the snow surface; wind and sun can combine to create many beautiful patterns. If the snow beneath is firm and the hollows not too big, perforated crust provides an excellent skiing surface.

Sun and wind combined to form this perforated crust near Mount Assiniboine, Canadian Rockies. Photo Bob Sandford.

As the snowpack settles through spring into summer, the process of differential melting continues and the hollows get bigger and are known as **sun cups**.

Effect of Rain

Rain forms an icy crust on the surface that may develop into an impervious layer when covered by further snowfall. November rainfall across Western Canada has been responsible in many years for a rash of avalanche accidents ranging all the way from Whistler ski area near Vancouver to Banff in the Canadian Rockies.

Sun cups provide ready-made steps for these climbers on Mount Sir Sandford.

Ice Glaze

Ice glaze is caused by deposition of rime on windward slopes. It often occurs within a specific altitude range and provides an excellent sliding layer when buried by fresh snowfall.

Settlement and Strengthening

Skiers automatically recognize a number of different types of snow conditions and classify them according to the ease or difficulty of travel. Snow conditions, particularly changes in snow conditions, may be related to the development of avalanche hazard.

Think of a fresh fall of cold **new snow** in relatively windless conditions. (The term "new snow" refers to snow immediately after it has fallen and before it has materially changed from its initial snow crystal condition.) Soon after it has fallen, depending on the temperature, it will begin to settle. Thirty centimetres of new snow, initially containing 85–90% air, may settle to 20 cm, so that instead of sinking knee deep, the skier will only leave tracks a few centimetres deep. What causes these changes and what is their significance for the recreational skier?

Metamorphism

Metamorphism means "change of form" and is the name given to changes in the structure of snow within the snowpack and also to changes in the snowpack itself due to the temperature of the snow and the difference in temperature between the various layers.

A small temperature gradient (page 42) will result in the rounding of ice grains and growth of the larger grains at the expense of the smaller ones. A large temperature gradient will result in a recrystallization process resulting in faceted crystals, and in extreme cases hollow, cup-shaped crystals of depth hoar. These processes have in the past been known as Equi-Temperature & Temperature Gradient metamorphism and are now referred to by the scientific community as **Equilibrium forms** or **Kinetic Growth forms**.

We will refer to the form of the snow particles as **rounded** or **faceted**, and to the processes involved as **rounding** and **recrystallization**.

The Process of Rounding

When outside temperatures are moderate or the snowpack is deep, the temperature gradients within the snowpack will be small. Snow will then change by a process known as "rounding." The natural process of minimizing surface area breaks down the intricate crystalline snow structure of the ice crystals into smaller, more rounded ice grains. At the same time, because of the

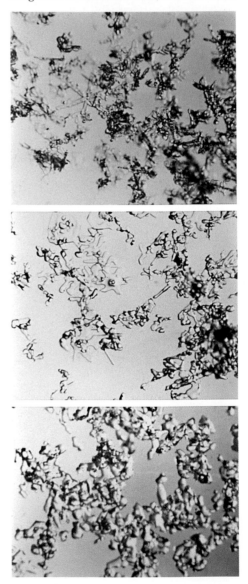

Three stages in the process of rounding. From top to bottom: new snow; rounded ice grains showing little evidence of original crystalline form; and well-sintered grain. Photo Ed LaChapelle.

reduction in volume of the snow particles, the snowpack consolidates and settles. When snow is first deposited it is light and fluffy, the crystal branches interlocking to form a cohesive mass. The snow during this period is stable and will remain plastered on steep slopes and rockbands. After a period of time, water molecules are transferred by vapour movement from the extremities to the body of the crystal, and the destruction of the interlocking branches results in a critical period during which the snow becomes unstable. Eventually the ice grains lose all sign of their previous crystalline structure and become more and more rounded. The larger ice grains grow at the expense of the smaller particles, resulting in a uniformity of size within each snow layer.

At temperatures close to freezing (0 to −5°C) change is rapid, the snow layers consolidating and becoming denser, stronger and more stable in a relatively short period of time. As temperatures drop, the process slows down, until at −40°C it is almost non-existent.

When the snow falls from trees you know that settlement and strengthening of the snowpack is taking place. Large, dense clumps of falling snow are called **tree bombs** and can trigger an avalanche.

Powder snow is snow that has undergone the first stages of rounding. It has lost its initial fluffy crystalline character and is beginning to settle, becoming duller and less cohesive.

Metamorphism, speeded up by the weight of additional layers of snowfall, produces **settled** snow. This is the light, cohesive snow beloved by the telemark skier or snowboarder; it's easy to turn in, yet firm enough to easily initiate turns. The best powder snow conditions occur when a snowfall starts out in relatively warm conditions and gets colder as it progresses. This results in denser snow at the base of the layer for the skis to carve turns in, and light powder at the top to billow up around you as you descend.

It is interesting to note that strengthening due to the additional weight of further snowfalls does not take place as rapidly on a slope of 30° as it does on level ground. This is because the vertical force varies with slope angle, and so snow on steeper slopes is often not as well consolidated. This is one reason why you must examine small slopes of the same steepness when evaluating a suspect avalanche slope.

A stellar crystal, with some riming, showing initial rounding. Photo Chris Stethem.

How Snow Gains Strength

You've probably noticed that a trail broken in soft new snow the previous day will harden overnight. This packing and hardening process, where the snow gains strength by the joining together of ice grains, is called **Sintering**.

In the case of the ski trail, the snow crystals or ice grains are forced together by the weight of the skier. However, over a period of time the natural settlement of the snowpack and the weight of additional layers will also result in the ice grains being pressed together. This pressure creates stresses at the boundary where the grains press together, resulting in the migration of water molecules in the area of the grain bond to form boundaries (necks) between grains. At temperatures just below freezing, the grain boundary grows, forming stronger bonds between ice grains. On rewarming, the necks between ice grains will be reduced, weakening or destroying the bond between grains.

In the absence of appreciable wind or extremes of temperature the process of settlement and strengthening makes an ideal snowpack, with light, unconsolidated snow near the surface gradually getting denser and more firmly packed as the depth increases.

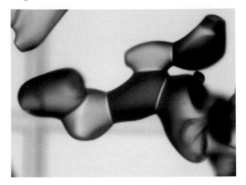

Sintering: Grains are joined by necks forming between ice grains forced into contact with each other. Photo Ron Perla.

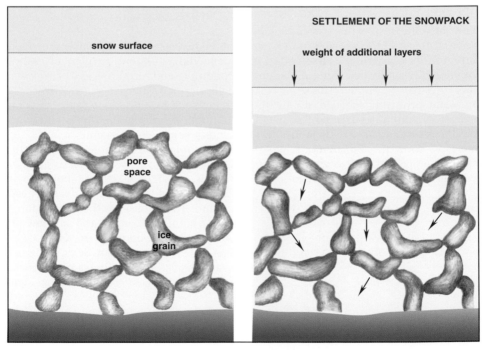

The snowpack gains density and strength by a combination of rounding and the weight of additional layers of snowfall.

Changes Due to Cold

Crystal Growth

Crystal growth is the result of a relatively large temperature difference between two layers within the snowpack. For instance, the loose sugar-snow found in shallow, early-season snowpacks in some snow climates is the result of large temperature differences between the ground surface and the snow surface. In other cases, layers of loose snow grains may be found in the upper layers of buried crusts formed by a large temperature gradient between the warmer crust and the colder snow above.

Growth occurs because of an upward movement of water molecules within the pore spaces in the snowpack: the rounded ice grains formed at more moderate temperatures begin to take on a more angular form as water molecules move from the top of a grain and are deposited on the bottom of the grain above. This process is called **recrystallization**.

The Significance of Recrystallization

Recrystallization leads to a weakening of snow layers within the snowpack. Such layers can be microscopically thin—and difficult to detect—or can consist of a metre or more of large, cup-shaped crystals which have very little strength and become cohesionless when disturbed.

Recrystallization due to steep temperature gradients is prevalent in colder climates early in the winter when the snowpack is both shallow and unconsolidated. Extreme growth occurs when temperatures are very cold—below −20°C.

In denser snow, where smaller pore spaces allow little space for the growth of individual crystals, steep temperature gradients result in faceted grains. In very dense snow, with small pore spaces, faceting may not occur.

While we normally think of recrystallization occurring vertically within the snowpack, large temperature differences between objects such as rocks buried in the snow and the surrounding snow can

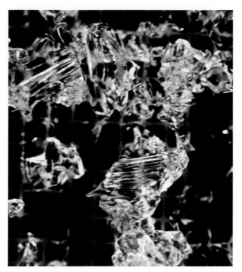

A collection of 4 mm depth hoar crystals. Photo Ron Perla.

result in recrystallization horizontally from the object, leading to localized weakening. See the discussion on **Weak Areas** on page 183.

Grain shape classification recognizes several stages of the recrystallization process. The two main ones are faceted grains and cup-shaped crystals (depth hoar). For practical purposes we will discuss the two separately, but remember that it is the same process at a different stage and taking place under different conditions of temperature gradient and snow density.

Depth hoar crystal 4 mm long. Photo Ron Perla.

Faceted Grains

The formation of faceted grains marks the beginning of crystal growth, which is characterized by the development of angular grains with flat crystal faces, or facets, just like the faces on a cut diamond. As long as there is sufficient temperature difference between individual grains in the snowpack, crystal growth due to the temperature gradient will successfully compete with the tendency for rounding. If the size of the initial ice grains is large enough and the pore spaces big enough, the process of crystal growth will continue and large cup crystals with well-developed, stepped surfaces will form. These large crystals are called **depth hoar**.

Faceted grains can develop at the base of the snowpack, in layers within the snowpack and even in the surface layers of the snowpack. It is the layers buried within the snowpack that are of most concern to the backcountry traveller, as in many instances they are very hard to detect.

Faceted grains. Photo E. Akitaya, The Institute of Low Temperature Science, Sapporo.

Typical Faceted Layers

At the base of the snowpack. In cold weather some faceting occurs in the lower layers of almost all shallow snowpacks. How much the process will weaken the snowpack depends on the temperature, the temperature gradient and the density of the snow. As temperature gradients moderate as a result of further snowfall or warmer temperatures, the process of rounding will prevail and the snowpack will be strengthened due to sintering. However, if cold conditions continue, and the snow is not too dense, depth hoar will form, substantially weakening the base of the snowpack.

Thick layers within the snowpack The temperature difference between a thick layer of cold new snow falling on an old, warmer snow surface may be sufficient for a relatively thick layer of faceted crystals — 10 to 40 cm thick — to develop within the snowpack. Such a layer may remain in a weak state for many days waiting for a sudden change in temperature to reduce its internal cohesion sufficiently to release the snow layers above.

Radiation recrystallization On clear, dry days during the winter and early spring, slopes with a southerly exposure will absorb enough of the sun's heat for a thin freeze–thaw crust to form a centimetre or so below the surface even though the temperature of the snow surface may still be well below freezing due to infrared cooling. The difference in temperature between the cold surface snow and the warmer snow beneath allows recrystallization of the snow on top of the smooth freeze–thaw crust. These thin layers of recrystallized snow form weak, poorly bonded layers when buried beneath further snowfalls.

Areas which are susceptible to this phenomenon are described as having a "radiation snow climate." A good example is the San Juan Range of southwest Colorado.

In order to achieve this form of recrystallization a delicate radiation balance is required; too much solar radiation or too little infrared cooling will lead either to Firnspiegel or to melting and suncrust formation. Unfortunately, radiation recrystallization is difficult for the tourer to detect and usually can only be surmised after careful examination and testing of the snowpack. This is not the same as surface hoar, as it is recrystallization of the old snow at the surface rather than a new deposit.

Surface layers of faceted crystals At high altitudes and in polar regions, a significant layer of faceted crystals may form in the top layers of the snowpack after a protracted cold spell −25 to −30°C for a week or more). Described by early ski runners in the Alps as resembling "raw rice," these large, loose, faceted crystals are the result of recrystallization in snow grains which have undergone normal settling. Because the size attainable by faceting depends upon the initial size of the ice grains and the open space around them, these grains rarely exceed 3 mm in diameter.

When covered by subsequent snowfall they form weak layers in the snowpack which are often responsible for avalanches at higher elevations.

While forming an ideal surface layer for skiing down, climbing up through this type of snow on skis can be frustrating and usually requires a low angle of ascent to get any reasonable grip.

Thin layers within the snowpack If new snow falls on a snowpack warmed by sun or rain, it will initially bond to the old snow. However, if it is very cold for the next few days, the steep temperature gradient will allow recrystallization of the grains at the bottom of the new snow layer, weakening the bond with the older snow surface. This effect is intensified if there was a sun or rain crust on the old snow surface, and results in a layer of faceted crystals above the crust. These layers are very difficult for the backcountry traveller to detect.

Recrystallization may also occur on top of a deeply buried crust such as a sun or rain crust. This occurs due to a steep temperature gradient between the surface of the crust and the snow layer a few millimetres deep above it.

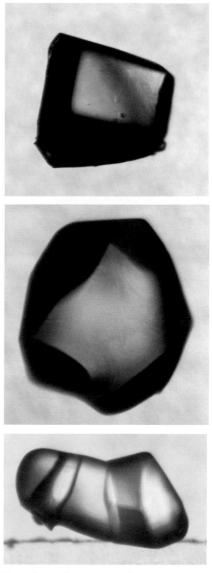

Faceted crystals approximately 1.5 mm in diameter. The bottom two crystals show evidence of rounding. Photo Ron Perla.

The subsequent thin layer of faceted crystals leads to **deep slab instabilities** such as those that resulted in numerous avalanche fatalities in 2002–03 and 2007–09 in Western Canada.

Depth Hoar

When there's a large temperature difference between grains and relatively large spaces between grains, a more advanced type of crystal growth takes place. This process forms delicate, hexagonal, cup-shaped crystals known as depth hoar, or sugar snow. As new, individual, cohesionless crystals are created, the former bond between the ice grains is destroyed, thus weakening the bottom layers of the snowpack considerably. Most extreme early in the season, depth hoar not only makes an unstable base for future snowfalls, but also makes for extremely tiresome travelling conditions in which the tourer breaks through into bottomless sugar snow with each step.

If cold temperatures persist, the process of crystal growth works its way up through the snowpack, with layers as much as one metre thick not unknown in the Canadian Rockies. The size of depth hoar crystals typically varies from 4–10 mm long, although larger crystals may form in extreme conditions. The largest crystals

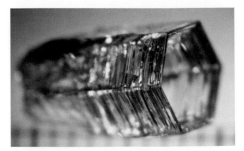

Columnar depth hoar cup crystal approximately 10 mm long. Photo Ron Perla

Depth hoar crystals with a density of 290 kg/m³, scale 15:1. Photo E. Akitaya, The Institute of Low Temperature Science, Sapporo.

are found at the bottom of the snowpack and around the base of trees and rocks. As the crystals grow larger, the lateral bonds between grains disappear, resulting in a snowpack composed of large, cup-shaped, striated, hollow crystals arranged in columns—very fragile snow that has almost completely recrystallized.

The final stage in the growth of depth hoar at steep temperature gradients in low-density snow is the development of very large (10–20 mm) columnar crystals which have their c-axis (page 36) horizontal. Some bonding occurs as a result of packing due to the weight of snow layers above, and there is some strengthening of the snow layer. Depth hoar crystals are a very durable crystal form and once formed will often be present at the bottom of the snowpack for the remainder of the season.

During the early part of the season, if the snowpack remains shallow during extended cold spells, the snowpack may be composed entirely of faceted and depth hoar crystals. Trail breaking is very tiresome, and the whole snowpack will avalanche down to the ground, with the cohesionless crystals running freely around rocks or trees. A surprising number of people are caught in small depth hoar slides in December and January in the Canadian Rockies. Most of them are able to stand up, brush off the granular crystals, and carry on skiing or boarding. However, some ski mountaineers have taken long, and usually fatal, rides over cliffs or into crevasses from very small depth hoar slides.

As the season progresses, the weight of additional snowfalls will result in a toughening of the depth hoar layer due to packing and sintering. The larger depth hoar crystals at the bottom of the snowpack do not necessarily form the weakest layer any longer; many avalanches are the result of failure at the interface between the depth hoar and faceted layers above.

Although the bottom layer of depth hoar gains some strength during the season, it take little change in weather conditions to destroy the fragile bonds. Old depth hoar becomes incredibly rotten if the snowpack warms up quickly due to percolating water or very warm weather in the spring, resulting in impossible travelling conditions. Descending from the high mountains with heavy packs one April, we fell waist deep, right through to the ground, every few metres for the last 2 km back to the highway.

Snowpack Metamorphism

Throughout the season in many climates, the snowpack alternates between rounding and faceting, with rounding predominating as spring approaches. In certain conditions both types of metamorphism may be present in the snowpack at the same time, although one will usually predominate. This can happen after a fresh fall of snow in cold weather; in the surface layers rounding will be busy breaking down the original intricate shape, while at the same time faceting will be taking place at the bottom of the snowpack. To complicate matters even further, rounding can occur in recrystallized layers, for example, the rounding of edges of large faceted crystals as they develop.

Snow at Higher Temperatures

The Melt–freeze Process

When the sun is sufficiently strong to melt the top layers of the snowpack during the day, and when nighttime temperatures fall below 0°C, cycles of freezing and thawing will occur. In this process, called **Melt–freeze Metamorphism**, smaller grains will melt before larger ones, and so during the course of a number of melt–freeze cycles larger grains will grow at the expense of smaller ones. The meltwater wetting the surface of these larger grains eventually refreezes and firmly cements the grains together. Melt–freeze grains have a tendency to freeze together in clusters, leaving large pore spaces within the snowpack.

During the melting cycle enough water may be produced to percolate through channels and pore spaces into the lower layers where it can form lubricating layers adjacent to the ground or impervious layers within the snowpack or freeze into areas of ice called ice lenses.

The major cause of melting of the snowpack is heat from the sun, which is greatest at noon when the sun is highest. This implies that the most dangerous time for wet snow avalanches is between noon

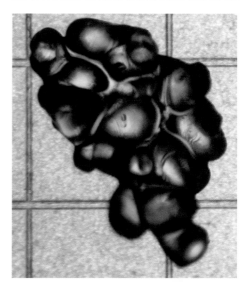

A refrozen melt–freeze cluster shows the strength of a frozen layer.
Photo Ron Perla.

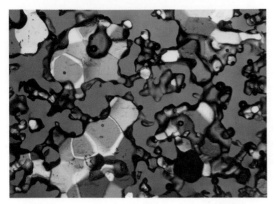

Melt–freeze grains. Larger grains grow at the expense of smaller ones, grains group together and pore spaces are enlarged. Photo E. Akitaya, The Institute of Low Temperature Science, Sapporo.

Clusters of melt–freeze grains. Note the large pore spaces between clusters. Photo Ron Perla.

and early evening when freezing begins again. Of course, this rule does not apply if the overnight air temperature remains above freezing. This point is well illustrated by a report of an early-morning wet slab avalanche: *On Easter Sunday at 8:30 the Glory Bowl in Teton Pass, Wyoming, released. More than half of the large bowl fractured 3 feet deep and buried the highway below 25 feet deep and 240 feet in length. Two skiers had put tracks in the path earlier in the morning, and another group of five skiers were preparing to ski the bowl. The avalanche released while they were sipping tea at the edge of the bowl.*

The process of melt–freeze metamorphism results in a number of familiar snow conditions:

Spring Snow is the name commonly used for softened melt–freeze grains. This form of snow varies from small, early melt–freeze grains to large, well-formed grains which, when wet, slide over each other with very little friction. The best skiing conditions occur shortly after melting begins and last until the snow, finally saturated with meltwater, becomes heavy and soggy. Spring snow takes several days to develop from new snow, and during this interim period sun crust may make skiing impossible. Try moving to slopes of a different orientation; follow the sun around.

Rotten Snow Rotten snow is common in late spring in climates which favour the formation of appreciable amounts of depth hoar during the winter. When old depth hoar layers become saturated, they lose any mechanical strength they may once have possessed. One result of this condition is the wet-snow avalanching in spring which cleans off the snow right down to the ground. Travel, especially in late afternoon, can be exhausting, with the tourer sinking thigh-deep in heavy, wet snow which then collapses inward on top of skis or snowshoes, burying them.

Meltwater Crust Meltwater crust is formed when snow melted during melt–freeze metamorphism refreezes in the top layers only, leaving wet, unfrozen grains underneath. Such a crust may easily bear the weight of a skier in the early morning, but later on as the day warms up, it will weaken to create frustrating, leg-breaking conditions.

Firnspiegel Firnspiegel, or firn mirror, is the result of subsurface melting due to intense solar radiation during cold, clear weather in spring or summer. The meltwater eventually forms a thin surface layer of clear ice that acts like a green-house, allowing melting of the snow just beneath — a highly reflective background for climbing or skiing photographs given the right slope angle and good lighting.

The bright, mirror-like surface of firnspiegel is an excellent texture, giving a firm bite to the ski or board as it is turned.

Older Forms of Snow

So far, I've been describing new snow in the season it has fallen. However, there is a limit to the amount of densification which can occur due to rounding alone, and once the ice grains have achieved a uniform, more or less spherical shape, two other processes are needed to cause a further increase in density. One of these, the melt–freeze process, has already been covered. The other process, known as **Pressure Metamorphism**, is the primary mechanism in the formation of glacier ice. The separate grains are deformed and pressed together by the weight of additional snow layers until finally the pore spaces within the snowpack are so closed up that they no longer allow free movement of water vapour through the snow.

Firn Snow Firn snow can be defined either as snow which has passed through several cycles of melting and freezing or as snow which has survived the spring thaw to become part of a permanent snowpatch or glacier. During the day it takes a lot of energy to break its dense structure down into loose grains, which consequently freeze at night into a solid mass again.

Some Unusual Forms of Snow

Wild Snow Wild snow is snow that has fallen in complete calm at very low temperatures. Resembling goose down, it's extremely light (it contains 97 to 99% air) and lies very loosely, with the crystals hardly touching each other; you can walk or ski through it and feel no resistance. Wild snow I've seen in the Canadian Rockies appears to be made up of fine spatial dendrites, thin needles and a small proportion of whole stellar crystals. It's extremely unstable and will flow almost like a liquid down steep slopes. Although the avalanches it generates are usually harmless, large, destructive avalanches have been reported in the Alps when great depths of wild snow gained additional density during the descent. Very often the frequent sluffing that occurs during and shortly after a fall of wild snow has a stabilizing effect on the fresh layer.

Diamond Dust Diamond dust is another form of ice crystal that occurs in very cold, clear conditions. They're often seen early in the day as tiny, glittering crystals floating in the atmosphere a few metres above the ground. It's believed these minute crystals are formed during a temperature inversion when air a short distance above the ground is warmer than the air next to the ground.

Slab avalanches on all sides. Photo André Roche.

Avalanches

Avalanches fall when the weight of accumulated snow on a slope exceeds the forces within the snowpack or between the snowpack and the ground which hold the snow in place. The balance between these forces can be changed by further snowfall, by internal changes in the snowpack or by the weight of a single skier. The often small force required to start the snow sliding is called an **avalanche trigger**.

There are two main types of snow avalanches: **loose-snow avalanches** that originate in cohesionless snow and that start from a single point, gathering more and more snow as they descend; and **slab avalanches** that start when a large area of cohesive snow begins to slide at the same time.

Both types occur in wet and dry snow. Slab avalanches are further classified according to how they are formed: storm slabs and wind slabs, or by the location of potential weak layers: persistent and deep persistent slabs.

Size of Avalanches

Avalanches vary tremendously in size, from small sluffs a few metres high to the giant avalanches of the Himalaya where millions of tonnes of snow fall many vertical kilometres. However, it is relatively small avalanches that cause most fatalities.

The smallest slides, which only bring down a few cubic metres of snow and are not large enough to bury a person, are called **sluffs**. Even so, a small sluff is quite enough to dislodge a climber from a precarious position and carry them into danger.

Mountaineer Frank Smythe, writing in *Kamet Conquered* about a sluff which carried him down a steep slope, says: *As an avalanche it was so small as to be scarcely worthy of the name, yet it had carried me helplessly down the slope, and, had the fates not been kind, would have killed me. It is not the spectacular snow avalanche weighing tens of thousands of tons that causes mountaineering disasters, but the small, apparently inoffensive slide, that buries the mountaineer in the depths of a crevasse or casts him over a precipice.*

Sluffs

A small loose-snow avalanche is called a **Sluff**. It can be dry loose snow, falling from steep terrain during or shortly after a storm, streams of near faceted crystals released by skiers or boarders on extremely steep slopes, or small, wet point avalanches on open slopes. Though rarely the direct cause of burial, sluffs can deposit the unwary in terrain traps or carry them over cliffs. Unless well managed, sluffs may result in a high-speed fall for those riding extremely steep terrain.

In mid-November a size 1.5 slab avalanche occurred at Ranger Creek in Kananaskis Country, an ice-climbing area known for avalanche hazard. A sluff that started above two of the routes flowed over the climbs and triggered a wind slab up to 40 cm deep. The debris ran into a gully and surprised an ice climber who was walking up to the base of the route. The flow ran up to his knees but he was not buried.

A small slab avalanche that buried and killed a skier at Aspen only ran for 30 m down the slope, which many people would not consider dangerous. Photo courtesy Dale Gallagher, US Forest Service.

Solar-triggered loose wet snow slides on the left side and a cornice-triggered wet slab on the right.
Photo Kananaskis Country Public Safety.

Any slide that releases enough snow to bury you is considered to be an avalanche.

There is no better example to illustrate the point that the small avalanches are often the killers. The snow ran for only 90 feet — yet it was able to bury the victim sufficient to suffocate her. So concludes the official report about an accident at Aspen ski area, Colorado.

On Mount Foraker, in Alaska, an 8 cm deep new-snow slab released on a sheet of blue ice and carried four climbers several thousand feet to their death.

Statistics show that a large proportion of backcountry avalanche accidents involve relatively small slides that have been triggered by the victims themselves.

Slab avalanches with an average crown fracture line greater than 15 cm deep are potentially dangerous. The depth of fracture lines can vary from a few centimetres to over 10 metres; even in the relatively low-lying Cairngorms of Scotland, crown fracture lines of 8 metres have been reported. The huge avalanche which killed seven helicopter skiers in the Purcell Mountains of British Columbia on Valentine's Day in

Size of Avalanches			
Size	Description	Typical path length	Typical mass
1	Relatively harmless to people	10 m	10 t
2	Could bury, kill or injure a skier or snowboarder	100 m	100 t
3	Could bury a car, destroy a small building or break a few trees	1000 m	1000 t
4	Could destroy a railway car, large truck, several buildings or a forest with an area up to 4 hectares	2000 m	10,000 t
5	Largest snow avalanches known; could destroy a village or a forest of 40 hectares	3000 m	100,000 t

1979 is reported to have had a fracture line which extended over a kilometre around the mountain and which, in places, was 3 metres deep. Sometimes crown fracture lines run for several kilometres around an entire mountain cirque.

One method of classifying avalanches by size, useful to both the amateur and those engaged in avalanche control work, is shown in the table above, adapted from the original work of Dave McClung. Omitted from the table are typical impact pressures, which range from 1 kPa to 1000 kPa.

The Avalanche Path

The avalanche path is the entire area in which an avalanche moves. It has three parts:

Starting Zone

The starting zone is the area where unstable snow breaks loose from the snowpack and starts to slide. In the case of a slab avalanche this zone extends from the crown line to the stauchwall.

Track

The slope or channel down which snow moves at a more or less uniform speed is called the track. It may be non-existent in a small slab avalanche or, conversely, can extend for several kilometres in a very large snow slide.

Runout Zone

The runout zone is the portion of the avalanche path where snow slows down and comes to rest. The area where the bulk of the snow accumulates is called the **deposition zone**. Sometimes this is surrounded by an area of deposited airborne snow dust called the **wind-blast zone**. In high mountains, where avalanche

Parts of an avalanche path.

tracks are long and steep, you should be aware that runout zones can extend for considerable distances across relatively flat terrain.

A massive avalanche that fell some 3000 m off the south face of Mount Logan and raced across the flat Icefield in front of Mount McArthur for a distance of about 1.5 km. Photo Clair Israelson.

Significant Layers in the Snowpack

Layer type	How formed	Significance
Crusts		
Sun crust	Melting of snow surface by solar radiation	Only forms on sunny slopes. If still wet, new snow bonds well. In cold, clear weather, can grow thin layer of facets, becoming a persistent weak layer if buried.
Rain crust	Refreezing of rain-wetted snow surface	Covers all aspects below freezing level. If crust is frozen, new snow bonds poorly. When buried, is an impermeable layer conducive to facet formation.
Recrystallization		
Surface hoar	Deposition of water molecules on the snow surface to form a fragile, feather-like layer	Formed in areas sheltered from wind. May exist in a fragile state for long periods when buried in cold snow. Weakened by further recrystallization.
Radiation recrystallization	Recrystallization of snow crystals above a thin layer of melt–freeze crust formed just below the surface by solar radiation	Forms on sunny slopes and is more common in southerly latitudes. When buried, can form a persistent weak layer that is hard to identify.
Thick facet layer at surface	Formed at high altitudes or in polar regions during protracted cold spells as a result of the recrystallization of settled snow grains	Found after long spell of very cold (−25°C or lower) weather. Makes for difficult skiing conditions, and when buried, forms a weak layer while it remains cold.
Facet layer within snowpack	Thick layer of cold new snow falling on a warm snowpack followed by cold weather	Constantly changing with the temperature gradient. Delays settlement and strengthening. Hard to identify.
Very thin facet layer above or below a buried crust	Cold new snow falling on a snowpack warmed by sun or rain, often with a crust, then buried	Along with buried surface hoar, recrystallization above and below crusts in both old and new snow is the usual cause of most persistent weak layers.
Depth hoar	Formed in shallow snowpacks when there is a steep temperature gradient between the ground and the snow surface.	Remains in a shallow snowpack for most of the season. Gains strength slowly as snowpack depth increases. Allows early-season avalanches to run right to the ground. Results in rotten snow during the spring thaw.
Rimed crystals		
Heavily rimed crystals	Formed by the collision of supercooled water droplets with snow crystals in the atmosphere	Most common in maritime climates. Forms hard slab when deposited by strong wind. Stabilizes quickly as a result of its already rounded structure.
Graupel	Heavily rimed crystals caught by updrafts in turbulent air form spherical pellets	When deposited in warm conditions, can remain in the snowpack for a long time. In colder conditions, it tends to roll off steep slopes and collect in isolated areas where it can remain a hazard for several days.

The Layered Snowpack

This section presents a summary of significant layers in the snowpack and how they affect avalanche hazard. Other than avalanches that occur in new snow shortly after a heavy snowfall, most avalanches slide on a layer, or combination of layers, that are unusually hard (strong) or unusually soft (weak).

In favourable conditions, weak layers of surface hoar, loose, cohesionless facets and thick layers of depth hoar can persist in the snowpack for many weeks and initiate several avalanche cycles before finally disappearing. These are known as **persistent weak layers**.

Because these layers sometimes get buried quite deep in the snowpack they are very difficult for the backcountry skier or boarder to detect. The usual tests for snow stability that are practical in the backcountry do not reach down far enough into deeper layers. So it is important to follow the buildup of the snowpack early in the season by reading professional forecasters' opinions on the existence of persistent weak layers.

Persistent weak layers are the usual cause of avalanches that release in old snow layers, usually with clearly defined fracture lines. The resulting avalanche may step down into weak layers beneath. This type of instability is referred to as **deep-slab instability**.

Avalanche Triggers

The most important natural trigger is the rapid loading of snow slopes by additional snowfall, rainfall or wind-drifting of snow onto lee slopes. A sudden temperature rise will also cause increased stresses within the snowpack, because snow is weaker and deforms more easily at higher temperatures and because temperature-induced pressure changes within the snowpack may result in a weakening of the bonds between ice grains. Long cold periods allow recrystallization to take place, further reducing the strength of loose, weak layers. Other natural triggers are small sluffs of loose snow, snow falling off trees (tree bombs), falling cornices and occasionally earthquakes.

Artificial triggers can be explosives or sonic booms, but most commonly it is the additional weight of a skier or climber on the snow surface which adds sufficient stress to the snow to release the slide.

On a few occasions it's been suspected that vibration from a passing helicopter was the final catalyst. There's the story of the four Irishmen in Scotland which has elements of farce but no happy ending.

It really began when a climber fell from the Carn Mor Dearg/Ben Nevis arête and was taken to the CIC hut to be picked up by helicopter. As the helicopter was coming in, it passed just below a group of four climbers who were taking a stroll around the bottom of Carn Dearg to look at some ice. They had no intention of climbing that day; heavy snowfalls followed by strong winds and a thaw had made conditions too dangerous. As the helicopter passed, they stopped to dig out their cameras from their packs; here was a chance to get a photograph of the chopper when it returned.

Helicopters are widely used for avalanche control and rescue. In extremely unstable conditions it is possible that vibration from the aircraft is sufficient to trigger avalanches. Photo Chris Stethem.

At that moment, a huge slab avalanche, the largest ever seen on Ben Nevis—the debris covered an area 150 metres by 250 metres—broke from Castle Gullies and Raeburn Buttress and swept them away down a rocky hillside. It was quite unexpected, as the noise of the helicopter had effectively masked any sound the avalanche may have made. Two of the climbers, suffering minor injuries, came to rest on the surface and were able to dig out a third companion with a fractured skull. Evacuation was speedy: the helicopter on its return journey was waved down and the three casualties were put aboard. The fourth man wasn't found for three days; he had landed in a gully and died instantly of a broken neck.

Types of Avalanches

Prior to the development of skiing in the Alps, snow avalanches were classified as Ground avalanches that left the slope bare, or Superficial avalanches that slid off on an underlying layer of snow or ice. In 1921, Arnold Lunn in his classic book *Alpine Ski-ing at All Heights and Seasons* took the classification a little further and divided avalanches in the Alps into four main classes: Dry powder, Wet new snow and Wet old snow avalanches, and Snow slabs.

These days the avalanche community has settled on a number of avalanche types that reflect the problems presented to the backcountry traveller by an unstable snowpack. Modern avalanche forecasts feature **avalanche problems** and offer advice on how to recognize and deal with them (page 107).

There are two different types of avalanches, with significantly different characteristics: loose-snow avalanches and slab avalanches. A fresh dump of cold, dry snow may result in **Loose Dry** avalanches in steep terrain. As the snow settles it initially loses cohesion and sluffs off cliff bands and down steep couloirs. As time goes on it becomes more cohesive, and will settle and bond to the snow layers beneath. If it is moderately windy when the snow falls it becomes a **Storm Slab**. If driven by strong wind and deposited on the lee side of terrain features it becomes a **Wind Slab**.

This same layer will eventually be covered by settled layers deposited by later storms. If there is a weak layer beneath it that still persists, the layer becomes a **Persistent Slab**. If the snow is deposited on a rain or sun crust, the crust may develop a layer of facets above it and the slab becomes a **Deep Persistent Slab** that may end up relatively close to the bottom of the snowpack. Very cold temperatures in regions with a shallow snowpack may change the snow grains at the bottom into depth hoar that also results in the snow layer above becoming a **Deep Persistent Slab**.

With rising temperatures and stronger solar radiation, surface layers will become saturated and release **Loose Wet** avalanches. A cohesive layer of snow with a sliding layer beneath it may release as a **Wet Slab** avalanche.

The next section will define these avalanche types and look at the main problems each type presents. Later in the book, on page 168, I will present some guidance on how to manage these different problems when you are out in the mountains.

A skier triggered this size 2 avalanche by jumping on the slope from a 3-metre-high cornice. He managed to ski out of it. Photo Parks Canada.

Loose-snow Avalanches

Loose-snow avalanches, sometimes called point avalanches, start at one point on the snowpack and grow in size as they descend. They occur in snow with very little internal cohesion when the steepness of the slope exceeds the angle at which snow will cling to the snowpack. The critical angle, the angle formed by snow that is on the verge of sliding, is called the **angle of repose**. Two types of loose-snow avalanche are recognized: **Loose Dry** and **Loose Wet**. Small loose-snow avalanches are called **Sluffs** (page 60).

Release is progressive and starts with a small, initially insignificant wedge of snow breaking away. Maybe the snow has collapsed internally because of surface

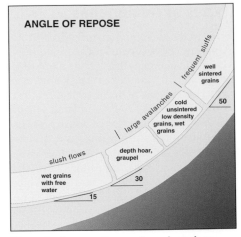

The angle of repose of a snow layer depends on grain size and shape, temperature and the wetness of the snow.

Loose-snow avalanches are often triggered by snow falling from rocky outcrops above. Photo Jan Uttl.

melting or maybe it has been disturbed by some external force such as sluffs falling from the rocks above. There is no definite fracture line, and the bed surface—the layer on which the snow slides—is not usually identifiable.

Dry, loose, new-snow avalanche danger persists until the new snow begins to settle—usually within a day unless the weather is very cold.

Like loose dry avalanches, loose wet avalanches start at a point and entrain snow as they move downhill. While they generally move more slowly than loose dry avalanches, their higher density generates forces that you will be unable to fight against. Loose wet avalanche danger persists as long as temperatures and solar radiation remain high.

Occurrence Loose-snow avalanches can be observed at all times of the year in the mountains, but they most frequently cause problems during the winter snow season.

Loose dry avalanches often fall as numerous small sluffs during or shortly after a storm, removing snow from steep upper slopes and either stabilizing lower slopes or loading them with additional snow. More rarely they can occur in old surface snow that has faceted after extended periods of clear, cold weather.

Wet loose-snow avalanche down a gully in the Canadian Rockies. Photo Alf Skrastins.

Loose wet snow avalanches usually occur in late winter, spring and summer in all mountain ranges when wet new snow or wet surface snow loses cohesion and starts moving downslope. Melting may be caused by warm temperatures, solar radiation, rainfall or a combination of these factors. Loose wet avalanches caused by solar radiation heating are influenced by aspect and slope angle, and potential danger on a given slope will change as the sun moves around during the day.

Slope angle The slope angle required for loose snow to slide depends upon the temperature and the type of snow lying on the slope. Four conditions, acting either alone or in combination, may lead to loose-snow avalanching.

- Very light, fluffy snow deposited under windless conditions will initially cling to slopes of 50 to 55°, but because the snow lacks internal cohesion, it will eventually slide off as harmless sluffs before any great depth can accumulate.

- Cold, dry, granular snow and graupel will bounce and roll off steep slopes, falling as a constant stream onto easier-angled slopes below.

- Dry or slightly damp powder snow deposited in light winds will develop enough cohesion to adhere to slopes of 50° to 60°. After a period of time, depending on temperature, changes in the structure of the snow will reduce internal cohesion and release small sluffs.

In areas such as the Pacific Coast Ranges snow from warm, moist air plasters steep walls and faces, where it stays in significant deposits.

- Wet, granular snow lubricated by meltwater or rain has very low internal friction and will slide on slopes as flat as 25°.

Size Dry loose-snow avalanches are generally small and tend to involve only small portions of the avalanche path. However, in the case of high mountain faces with large collection zones, a considerable amount of snow can be involved, leading to large, destructive wind-blast avalanches.

Wet loose-snow avalanches are also generally small. However, late in the season, large avalanches of this type, lubricated and weighed down by meltwater or rain,

can travel a long distance and have tremendous destructive power. Fortunately most people have switched to summer activities by this time.

Hazard Although dry loose-snow avalanches are relatively small, they can easily dislodge you from a safe stance and take you for a ride over cliff bands or into a crevasse. Most winter ice climbers are familiar with fresh snow cascading down the climb from above; in these conditions you should be particularly careful when negotiating steep snow slopes between pitches. Snow falling from steep upper slopes can either stabilize the lower slopes, load them with an additional weight of snow, or in some cases trigger persistent slab avalanches from the old snow layers.

Wet loose-snow sluffs, although not dangerous in themselves, are a hazard that both winter recreationists and summer climbers should be aware of. Even a small sluff can carry you over a cliff, force you into a terrain trap or plaster you against a tree. Ice climbers in gullies during periods of warm weather or intense solar radiation should be concerned. Use sluff management techniques in extreme terrain. Because these sluffs contain cohesionless wet, slushy snow, they set up like concrete, and even if only your legs are covered it will take an ice axe to dig you out!

Triggering Typical natural triggers are sluffs from steep ground above, rockfall and tree bombs. Loose-snow avalanches are usually triggered at the point where the snow is initially disturbed (hence the term "point avalanches"). They can be triggered by skiers or climbers traversing steep terrain and are often pulled loose when descending very steep terrain.

Wet loose-snow avalanches are naturally triggered by rising temperatures, strong solar radiation or rain. Small wet snow avalanches can be triggered when travelling on relatively low-angled slopes winter or summer.

Sluffs of loose snow create problems for ice climbers. Raymond Jotterand on Bourgeau Left-hand, Canadian Rockies. Photo Gregory Spohr.

A small slab avalanche on a wind roll in the Esplanades, British Columbia.

Slab Avalanches

A slab avalanche occurs when a large area of cohesive snow begins to slide on a weak layer within the snowpack (page 63) or on smooth ground. The consistency of the snow can vary from soft powder which loses all its cohesion on release, to tough, hard snow which deposits blocks measuring many cubic metres at the bottom of a slope. Slab avalanches are readily identified by the usually well-defined fracture line at the point where the moving mass of snow breaks away from the rest of the snowpack.

Slab avalanches are the worst hazard you are likely to encounter. Because of the initial stressed condition, slab release is very rapid. In many cases there will be initial settling of the snow at the moment of fracture, then the whole slab will start breaking up. The settlement and loss of internal cohesion as the slide starts throws any but the best skier off balance, and

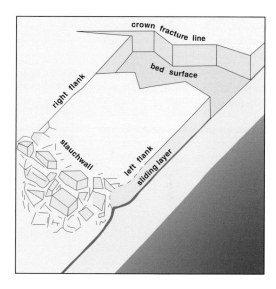

once downed the skier may be inundated by successive waves of snow from above.

Soft slabs are easily released, though not necessarily by the first skier or boarder. As slabs become harder their behaviour becomes more unpredictable; they may allow several people to cross or descend a slope before releasing.

Types of Slabs

For forecasting the avalanche community recognizes six slab avalanche problems:

- Storm Slab
- Wind Slab
- Persistent Slab
- Deep Persistent Slab
- Wet Slab
- Glide Slab

Slabs are susceptible to rapid temperature changes, both sudden warming and sudden cooling. Rapid warming is one of the reasons for weak layers within the snowpack to fail. On the other hand, it's been calculated that for normal-density settled snow a drop in temperature of 10°C would cause a snow slope 300 m wide to contract 2 cm. Early ski mountaineers in the Alps noticed that avalanches sometimes occurred when shadows struck a previously sun-warmed slope.

Slope angle Slab avalanches release most frequently on slopes of between 30 and 45°. On slopes of less than 25° snow tends to fracture and settle without sliding. Sometimes slab avalanches occur on steeper slopes when there is a high rate of deposition in collection areas such as bowls and gullies.

These two photographs of a skier-released avalanche are excellent examples of quick slab release. Note how the snow fractures, cracks and starts moving all at the same time. Read the discussion on **Weak Areas** on page 183 and take another look at these pictures. Photo Rudolf Ludwig.

Large, naturally released storm-slab avalanches on the Gaudergrat above Davos, Switzerland. Avalanching has occurred on almost all the slopes that are steep enough to slide. Photo André Roch.

Storm Slab

Storm slab forms over widespread areas during heavy storms, and is associated with moderate wind speeds, high humidity and, in some cases, rimed snow crystals. Whether the new snow develops into a slab depends on the weather during the storm and on the surface of the old snow.

If the temperature remains about the same during the storm, winds are light and the old snow surface is free of surface hoar or crusts, the new snow will bond to the old snow and settle and strengthen to become a new layer in the snowpack.

Formation New snow can form a slab when one or more of the following are present during a storm.

- Light to moderate wind, especially eddying winds, will pack the new snow crystals together, breaking them up and speeding up the strengthening process.
- A substantial (>15 cm) layer of new snow on an old snow surface with a weak or sliding layer will settle and strengthen into a slab. The new snow may release

during the storm or the slab remain touchy for several days.

- The weather warms up during or shortly after a storm. Typically this leads to a denser, more cohesive layer of consolidated slab over colder, less cohesive snow. Conversely, if the weather cools down after a warm storm, the snowpack will stabilize fairly quickly.

Hazard Storm-slab avalanches can occur naturally during and shortly after intense snowfalls accompanied by atmospheric conditions conducive to slab formation. Storm-slab problems typically last between a few hours and a few days depending on the temperature. They are usually quite soft compared to other slab types, and riders may not realize that a very soft slab has failed until well after it is running. Usually only the new snow layer releases.

Fortunately, storm slab problems are predictable; the old rule of never travelling in avalanche terrain until a few days after a storm still holds. However, remember that any significant new snowfall will add load to the snowpack and may activate a previously buried weak layer.

Triggering Storm slabs are easily triggered by skiers and boarders and by other disturbances such as loose-snow avalanches from steeper ground above, cornice falls and even tree bombs.

Storm-slab avalanches can propagate over large areas, and the resulting avalanches are often larger than expected. They are not usually triggered remotely.

Wind Slab

Wind slab forms when strong winds deposit snow in localized areas where wind typically erodes snow from the upwind sides of terrain features and deposits snow on the downwind side. Wind slabs are more common at higher elevations at and above treeline, although they can occur anywhere strong wind is able to move snow.

The density of wind slab can vary from soft to very hard. Slab deposited during a storm by moderate winds over extensive areas is usually considered to be storm slab.

Formation The wind-deposited snow can be new falling snow or snow scoured from the existing snow surface. Wind slab commonly forms on the lee side of ridges, bowls and gullies, on the downhill slopes of steep drop-offs and rollovers, and even downwind of stands of trees. See **How Wind Creates Cohesive Slabs,** page 23.

Appearance Freshly deposited wind slab with no new snow on top often has a distinctive appearance. Because wind slab is formed by snow crystals broken into small particles and packed together by the wind, the snow surface will look duller than the snow in areas without slab. Areas of slab will look smooth and rounded and may be referred to as cushions or pillows.

Frequently, hard slabs are underlain with a layer of softer snow which, over time, settles beneath the slab and which accounts for the characteristic hollow feeling and the drop of a few centimetres when the slab fails.

Hazard Wind slab can be hard to detect, especially if it is buried under new snow. A ride in a wind slab avalanche may be made more hazardous by large blocks of very hard snow. In high mountains slab occurs at all times of the year. How long it lasts depends on the temperature.

Like any other avalanches types, failing wind slabs may trigger underlying persistent weak layers, resulting in a larger than expected avalanche, and may themselves become a persistent weak layer in the future.

Triggering Recently formed wind slabs, although rarely releasing naturally, can be triggered by the weight of a single person. With harder windslab, release becomes unpredictable. A slab may be triggered by the first person on it, the last person or any of the party in between. It may also be triggered remotely or may release when someone is halfway down, exposing them to snow from above the trigger point.

A classic skier-triggered wind slab released from a cross-loaded gully. Photo Parks Canada.

A slab avalanche releases from a fracture line up to 4 m deep, stepping down into layers beneath.
Photo Tony Salway.

Persistent Slab

Persistent slab avalanches are avalanches caused by a cohesive slab within the upper to middle layers of the snowpack losing its bond to the underlying layer. Persistent slabs may remain unstable for extended periods of time and be the cause of an avalanche long after they were buried. As further layers build up the snowpack there may be several weak layers that wake up at different times.

Formation Persistent slab forms when a cohesive slab sitting on a persistent weak layer becomes buried by storm snow or wind slab. Persistent layers include surface hoar, sun/rain crusts and near surface facets. Persistent slab crusts may result in deep persistent slab problems when a layer of faceted grains develops on top of the crust. In continental snow climates depth hoar forms a persistent weak layer at the bottom of the snowpack and the slab may be referred to in the forecast as deep persistent slab.

Hazard Persistent slab is a major hazard facing backcountry recreationists in the dry, cold ranges during early winter and in all areas during low snowfall years, simply because they are so difficult to predict. The snowpack may appear to be stable once new storm snow instability has subsided, only to have the ticking time bomb of a weak layer primed for human triggering. Such avalanches have claimed many lives in the mountains of Western Canada.

Triggering Persistent slabs are so potentially dangerous because triggering is unpredictable, especially as the slab and its underlying weak layer become more deeply buried in the snowpack. To make things more uncertain, remote triggering from weak areas (page 183) by a single rider is always a possibility, and a release on one slope may propagate over to adjacent slopes. As the weak layer gets buried deeper, triggering becomes less likely but any resulting avalanche will be larger.

A number of weather conditions are believed to increase the likelihood of a persistent weak layer being triggered.

- Heavy snowfall (>30 cm).
- Deep deposits of wind-driven snow.
- Rain.
- A rapid rise in temperature, especially above 0°C.
- Strong solar radiation.

Persistent weak layers may also be triggered by unusually large forces such as cornice fall, icefall or the stresses induced by snowmobilers highmarking.

Deep Persistent Slab

Deep persistent slab problems occur when a persistent weak layer of facets or depth hoar forms near the base of the snowpack. This typically occurs adjacent to an ice crust buried early in the winter, or when depth hoar forms at the bottom of the snowpack.

When crusts become buried under layers of new snow they will be bonded to some extent to the layers above and below them. These crusts are not a problem until the weather changes. Then, vapour flow within the snowpack due to large temperature gradients allows the development of faceted crystal immediately above or below the crusts or the formation of depth hoar in the snow close to the ground. The layer of faceted crystals becomes a weak layer. In shallow snowpacks buried crusts may be responsible for cycles of avalanches several times during the season.

While the name "Deep" persistent slab implies that instability only occurs in deep (>2 m) snowpacks, this is not so. A recent study of seven years of forecasting avalanche problems in Canada found that the most frequent mention of deep persistent slabs has been in the shallow snowpack of the Canadian Rockies.

The potential hazard, probability of triggering, and management of the problem are different depending on the snow climate and the depth of the snowpack.

When interpreting avalanche forecasts for the region where you plan to ride, you need to be aware of the differences outlined below.

Formation In shallow snowpacks the deep layer is often depth hoar on an early-season rain crust. Such instabilities, deep only in relation to the total snowpack, can lead to avalanches that fail right to the ground at any time during the season.

In deep snowpacks crusts can be buried several metres deep. Multiple storms build up the snowpack on top of the crust over many weeks, leaving it deep relative to the depth of the snowpack.

Hazard In some areas a deep persistent layer is present for most of the winter, lying dormant most of the time but waiting to be woken up. In shallow snowpacks the early-season avalanches tend to be small, the main danger being that of getting carried over cliff bands or strained through trees, rather than being buried. Later in the season the weak layer tends to toughen, but can easily be woken by rising temperatures. Deep persistent slabs are harder to trigger in a deep snowpack, but when triggered they usually lead to large, destructive avalanches.

Triggering In regions with a shallow snowpack, deep persistent slabs may be triggered from shallow areas, weak spots on rocky slopes, and on steep, convex, unsupported rolls in the terrain.

Any change at the surface such as heavy new snow, rain or significant wind loading may increase the likelihood of triggering, as may rapidly rising temperatures and strong solar radiation.

In deep snowpacks triggering of deep persistent slabs is completely unpredictable. The failed layers are usually deeper than stresses from riders or even snowmobiles penetrate. Rapid rise in temperature and/or strong solar radiation is believed to reduce the strength of the weak layer.

Forecaster's Comment

Note the shallow depth of the crust in this deep persistent slab forecast.

The dominant issue in the snowpack is the November 12 crust (down 30–70 cm). This crust is evident throughout the region and has started to become reactive especially on South aspects just above tree line.

The forecaster was right! On the same day, at a danger level of Medium, a ski cut triggered a large avalanche on a southerly aspect at a weak point in the shallow layer next to a protruding rock. The crown ranged in depth from 30 to 55 cm and slid on the crust layer from November 12th.

Wet Slab

A wet slab avalanche is the result of a cohesive slab losing its bond with the lubricated layer below. This can result in the entire snowpack sliding directly on the ground, especially where the ground surface is smooth rock or vegetation. Because of the high water content of the snow, heavy wet slab can be very destructive.

Occurrence Wet slabs are usually a problem after a prolonged period of warm weather, particularly when overnight temperatures remain above freezing. They tend to occur soon after the snowpack becomes isothermal (0°C throughout), and can be a serious problem in maritime climates during high-temperature rain-on-snow events.

Short periods of high temperatures and intense solar radiation on a cool snowpack usually result in loose wet avalanches.

Slope angle Wet slab avalanches release most frequently on slopes between 30 and 45°. On slopes of less than 25° snow tends to fracture and settle without sliding.

Hazard Wet slab avalanches are generally slower moving than dryer slab types and tend to flow in channels. Release is difficult to predict and impossible to test for. The initial slab can feel solid and stable, only to become a semi-liquid mix of wet, slushy snow that flows downslope to set up like concrete when it stops. There are no air spaces to keep you alive while someone chips you out! Fortunately, backcountry travel has usually become too onerous for most people by the time wet slab season starts.

Triggering Potential for triggering depends on the depth and nature of the weak layer. Movement of liquid water through snow is influenced by the structure of the snowpack. Coarse-grained snow allows easy drainage and results in a relatively stable snowpack. Fine-grained snow inhibits drainage and leads to more rapid avalanching.

When weak layers are close to the surface and are lubricated by liquid water, a wet slab avalanche can be triggered by relatively light loads such as skiers, snowmobilers or a small cornice fall. Weak layers farther down in the snowpack require larger loads for triggering, such as large cornice falls or avalanches from steeper slopes above or avalanche that step down to a deeper layer. As with persistent slab

Wet slab avalanche triggered by partial cornice fall, showing typical snowball-like appearance of the debris and large destructive blocks. See complete photo at page 8. Photo Alf Skrastins.

there are a number of weather conditions that make triggering more likely.

- Loading at the surface by heavy wet snow.
- Extended periods of rain.
- An isothermal snowpack, especially when temperatures remain above 0°C overnight.

Glide Slab

A glide slab is a phenomenon where the entire snow cover creeps downhill on steep grass or smooth bedrock slabs. They are uncommon in most snow climates and tend to be confined to specific, well-known terrain features. As the snow creeps downhill, full-depth glide cracks form. Many glide-cracked slabs never result in avalanches.

Release When glide slabs release, the whole snow cover avalanches down to the ground. Glide slab avalanches consist of well-settled snow which may vary from dry to wet. The snowpack often breaks into large blocks. Release is usually initiated when water from rain or snowmelt reduces the friction holding the snowpack to the ground. They don't necessarily release during the warmest part of the day.

Hazard Because the time between crack formation and avalanche release can vary widely, glide slab avalanches are highly unpredictable.

Triggering Glide slab avalanches are unlikely to be triggered by a person, but they could possibly be triggered by a cornice or snowmobile. Predicting failure is virtually impossible.

The photographer rode this 2 km-long wet slab avalanche for a considerable distance. Note the down-to-the-ground scouring action. Photo Jim Buckingham.

This wet-snow slab slid slowly for about a week until it gained sufficient speed to release. Keep away from such areas showing cracking and compression lines. Photo Leon Kubbernus.

Photo Kananaskis Country Public Safety.

Cornices

Cornices are overhanging wind-sculptured snow formations that form on the lee sides of ridges, usually above treeline. They range from small soft-snow wind features on the downwind side of terrain features to massive overhangs of hard snow.

Hazard Cornices present the backcountry traveller with several problems:

- Cornices can be difficult to detect when you are travelling along a corniced ridge, especially in poor light or misty conditions. They can break off without warning and often break back farther from the edge than one would expect.

- The hard, dense snow of a falling cornice is enough to injure a person. Beware of people above you kicking off cornices.

- The large mass of a cornice fall has the potential to trigger loose snow or slab avalanches on slopes below. Large avalanches can result from a relatively small cornice fall.

Cornice falls Recently formed storm-snow cornices tend to fail during or shortly after their formation when the mass of snow becomes too heavy to support itself. Older cornices that have been formed by strong winds transporting snow from windward slopes have smaller grains with strong bonds, are more persistent, and can fail long after they are formed.

Triggering Cornice fall may be triggered by:

- Wind loading of recently formed cornices during or shortly after a storm.

- Temperatures rising above freezing, especially a rapid rise in temperature.

- Strong springtime solar radiation.

- Rain, which adds weight to the cornice as well as weakening the bond between ice grains.

- People kicking cornices off from above. Yes, it does happen!

An ice avalanche falls onto the popular route leading to Bow Hut in the Canadian Rockies. The skiers in the foreground, overtaken by the dust cloud, were out of range of the debris, which stopped just short of the leader of the party. Photos Kevin Cronin.

Climax Avalanches

Climax avalanches bring down the accumulation of several snowfalls or even the whole of the season's snowpack right down to bare ground. They are usually the result of a significant change in the weather such as a warming trend or additional snowfall. Early-season climax cycles are difficult to predict. Learn to recognize weather conditions that might lead to instability, and keep off steep slopes at such times. Most climax cycles occur in spring, when the whole snowpack, or significant layers of it, become isothermal. Isothermal means equal temperature throughout. In avalanche terminology the term **isothermal slides** refers to slides that occur when a layer of snow becomes isothermal at a temperature of close to 0°C. The first occasion in spring when temperatures remain above freezing for several days and nights is the time to be wary. Keep an eye on indicator slopes—those which get the greatest amount of radiation—for the first sign of avalanching. If you think a cycle of climax avalanching is about to occur it's best to stay out of the mountains until conditions improve.

Ice Avalanches

As a glacier flows down a steep, uneven slope, it often splits open into a chaotic zone of crevasses and unstable ice blocks many metres high called séracs. Although it's the movement of the glacier which causes the séracs to topple, air temperature changes and melting within the séracs play a part too; it appears that ice avalanches are more active during the late afternoon. Because of their unpredictability, ice avalanches are extremely dangerous.

The photographs on the opposite page show an ice avalanche mixed with powder snow falling over a cliff onto a well-travelled route leading to Bow Hut on the Wapta Icefield (Canadian Rockies). Although it looks as if the skiers are about to be overwhelmed, they were only caught in the accompanying cloud of snow dust and not engulfed by the avalanche itself.

A party of 6 guides and 23 climbers on Mount Rainier were less lucky. While stopped in a supposedly safe place near Disappointment Cleaver, part of the icefall created by the junction of the Ingraham and Emmons glaciers broke away and came sweeping down to bury 11 victims under 20 metres of car-sized blocks.

So what can you do to minimize the danger? Your only defence is to move fast and don't stop until clear of danger. On no account camp below an area of séracs on a glacier or below a cliff topped with an ice wall.

Sérac fall, consisting of blocks of ice and powder snow, can be a significant source of avalanche hazard for climbers and ski mountaineers in glaciated areas.

A Weekend of Avalanches

The 21st and 22nd of February was not a good weekend to go ski touring in the Canadian Rockies. A long spell of cold, clear weather at the beginning of the month had given way to a series of storms coming in from the west. Across the Columbia Trench, in the Purcells, 180 cm of snow had fallen in the previous ten days. Farther east, in the Rockies, more moderate snowfalls accompanied by strong winds had created treacherous pockets of wind slab on all lee slopes. Surface hoar produced by the cold spell was now sandwiched like a loose filling of feathery crystals 45 cm below the new-snow surface. As the weekend approached, snowfall became light to intermittent and the temperature rose to a relatively mild −5°C during the warmest part of the day. Slopes were now in prime condition to slide; all they needed was a trigger.

It was Saturday around noon. Four experienced ski tourers traversing the Wapta Icefield became concerned about the increasing hazard, and rather than carry out their planned route, they decided to abort down Glacier des Poilus and Waterfall Valley to Yoho Valley. Bad routefinding led them into a narrow ravine only a few kilometres from the top of Twin Falls. The first man had just made it safely through when he heard a swooshing noise behind him and on looking round saw the second skier being pushed down into the creek by a small slab avalanche and buried under 8 metres of snow. A rescue beacon search revealed nothing, despite the digging of a huge pit in an effort to reduce the tremendous depth of snow between themselves and the victim. Probing with short ski poles proved equally useless in the circumstances. It was a long way to the nearest road and the cry for help wasn't received until 10:00 that night. On Sunday at about 10:30 am a Parks Canada rescue group, using fine probing, located the body lying face down in the creek; he had been pinned there by the weight of snow and drowned.

While the recovery operation was going on, the mountains were busy claiming two more victims. Thirteen kilometres away across the same icefields, three climbers were attempting to climb Mount Thompson on skis. All three were relatively inexperienced in winter mountaineering and certainly knew nothing about the danger from avalanches or they would never have chosen the route they did. They had read the high hazard warning at the Banff warden's office when they picked their hut permit but didn't take it seriously. So there they were, starting up a steep bowl in the centre of the face. At the last minute, the third man decided it was easier and quicker to scramble up the rock ridge to one side and wait for his companions above the bowl. When they didn't turn up he climbed up and down the ridge a bit, thinking they had either gone on ahead or had decided to follow his route after all. Still nothing. He then descended the bowl and was lucky to be caught by only a small avalanche which gave him a ride to the bottom of the slope. After extracting himself, he noticed there were other slides about, but not realizing their significance, he returned to the hut feeling sure he would find his friends waiting. Of course they weren't there either and he must have spent many anxious hours wondering before rushing off to get help.

That same afternoon, many kilometres nearer to Banff, four cross-country skiers had finally made it up the long, steep trail to Bourgeau Lake. After lunch the two women returned to their car while the men carried on beyond the lake toward a small pass. Although the first skier was carrying a shovel, they seemed unaware of the high avalanche hazard and had chosen a route which crossed a small, rather shallow gully below in which old avalanche debris was still visible. The combined weight of both men on the slope was sufficient to release the slab which carried them down. By swimming, the second man managed to stay close to the surface. Finding no sign of his companion, he limped back down to the road on one ski to raise the alarm. The rescue group, hardly recovered from their morning's exertions, were at the scene within three-quarters of an hour, but despite a dog search and careful probing, the body wasn't found until late that evening, lying face down with an ice crust around the head.

This small slab avalanche was remotely triggered by a touring party about 50 m from the foot of the slope at a time of High avalanche danger. It produced enough debris to bury a fallen skier or boarder.

For the weary, dejected searchers it was a long ski in the dark down to the road; the welcoming news that two climbers were missing on Mount Thompson was hardly guaranteed to raise their spirits. It was too late to do anything that night, but at first light they were all gathered on the Wapta Icefield helping in the recovery of two more bodies. That wasn't the end of it: the same afternoon, a report came in that three heli-skiers had been buried by a large avalanche in the Purcell Mountains and would they stand by.

In times of instability, good travel practices and careful routefinding are required for travelling safely in avalanche terrain. Cariboo Mountains, British Columbia. Photo Alf Skrastins.

Avalanche Terrain

The ability to read terrain so that you can recognize and avoid avalanche-prone slopes is the most important skill to develop if you wish to travel safely in the winter backcountry. On a downhill run in challenging terrain it is the judicious choice of route—avoiding convex rollovers, staying away from weak areas, keeping away from terrain traps—that will reduce your risk to a minimum. If you are backcountry ski touring you need to be able to recognize avalanche slopes so you can stay away from them or cross the runout zones quickly.

If you are going to spend much time in avalanche terrain you will need to:

- Consider how you will use avalanche terrain in your chosen activity.

- Recognize **Avalanche Paths** and estimate the angle of steep slopes above your route.

- Recognize a variety of terrain features and how they affect avalanche hazard.

- Identify features that are potential **Terrain Traps** in the event of an avalanche.

- Know which areas of an avalanche slope are possible **Trigger Points**.

- Learn how slope **Aspect to Sun and Wind** can influence snow stability.

Users of Avalanche Terrain

Before I delve into the intricacies of avalanche terrain I need to outline how various groups of recreational users become exposed to avalanche terrain, and also to clarify the terminology I use when describing user groups. The table below briefly describes how terrain is used by different "winter backcountry enthusiasts" (my collective term for anyone going into or near avalanche terrain) and their objectives.

Once I had set out the primary reasons why people venture into avalanche terrain it was obvious there were two major user groups: those whose primary purpose is to avoid avalanche-prone terrain while travelling in the winter backcountry, and those who seek out steep slopes to ski, board or highmark on. As a result I divided the backcountry portion of the book into two chapters: **Travel in Avalanche Terrain**, which stresses avoidance, and **Riding Steep Slopes**, which addresses local knowledge, slope stability, terrain configuration and safe skiing and boarding practices.

There are also a number of other users who put themselves at risk such as freeriders, ice climbers, ski mountaineers and summer climbers and scramblers. The risks for each of these groups are different. Some users, such as summer climbers and scramblers, have to assess the risk without any help from avalanche forecasts. Factors that affect these groups are scattered throughout the practical portion of the book.

Each group should understand what information they need to get from the avalanche forecast that is important for their particular pursuit. See **Interpreting Avalanche Forecasts** on page 109.

Users of Avalanche Terrain	
Users	**Objective and likely terrain use**
Backcountry tourers	Backcountry tourers are primarily concerned with avoiding avalanche terrain. Their primary objective is to ski up valleys, enjoy alpine meadows above treeline, ski to destinations such as lakes and cabins, and maybe traverse easy passes. Some backcountry tourers will seek to get in some turns, generally on moderately steep slopes of less than 30°.
Snowshoers, fat-bikers	Snowshoers and fat-bikers have similar goals to backcountry tourers. Modern equipment allows travel on moderately steep slopes and the possibility of being lured into terrain traps.
Backcountry skiers and boarders	Have alpine touring equipment and are looking for good snow for turns in steep to very steep terrain. They ski or board in the backcountry, often travelling through complex avalanche terrain to reach their downhill runs. They are able to assess snow conditions on the approach.
Out-of-bounds skiers and boarders	Skiers and boarders who access terrain outside ski area boundaries with or without approval from the ski area. Access is usually near the top of the area, and skiers and boarders head down the steepest part of the slope through the trigger zones of potential avalanches without the benefit of assessing snow conditions on the approach.
Freeriders	A name commonly applied to both skiers and boarders who seek random natural terrain such as chutes, rocky outcrops, cliff bands and snow cushions. This terrain is nature's terrain parks. Often below treeline, the terrain tends to be outside ski area boundaries or easily accessible from roads so as to minimize the approach with fat skis and heavy gear.
Extreme skiers and boarders	Extreme skiers and boarders have as their objective extremely steep slopes of 45° or more. They are descending chutes, couloirs, steep ridges and sometimes steep open faces.
Ski mountaineers	Ski mountaineers travel through difficult mountain terrain to reach summits or to complete multi-day traverses. They venture into terrain that may require them to take off their skis and don crampons, or find their way through steep and dangerous glacier icefalls.
Climbers/scramblers	Travel on foot at any time of the year for the purpose of alpine-style ascents. Snow in gullies or on ledges presents the most common avalanche hazard.
Waterfall ice climbers	Ice climbers, including mixed climbers, may ski or snowshoe through avalanche terrain to the start of their climbs. If the climb is threatened by avalanches from collection areas above, they will be exposed to hazard much longer than any other user of avalanche terrain.
Snowmobilers	Snowmobilers can travel long distances and access high mountain terrain above treeline. Of all the groups, they are the most likely to cross into several major aspects during the course of a day. High-marking of potential avalanche slopes is a common objective.

Avalanche Terrain Exposure Scale

Spearheaded by Grant Statham, in consultation with mountain guides and avalanche professionals, Parks Canada has developed a terrain rating system that evaluates the complexity of avalanche terrain and makes recommendations on the suitability of avalanche terrain for various users.

A major strength of the rating system is that the majority of backcountry destinations in Canada's national parks have been rated and lists of rated trips have been made available to the public. Waterfall ice climbs have also been rated for exposure to avalanches from above or on the approach (page 155).

The terrain rating covers specific backcountry trips. It does not rate individual slopes. It also assumes that backcountry tourers stay on the route used in the rating. Heading up a slope to get in some turns will negate the rating.

While it was developed initially to provide risk ratings for specific tours and backstop legislation for custodial groups, it has proved to be a powerful educational tool for winter backcountry enthusiasts, the public and the media. Grant Statham writes ...*it has become a useful tool that dispenses common sense and provides an important contribution toward understanding and communicating the principles of avalanche terrain.*

The table below is used to communicate the terrain rating to novice backcountry tourers, organized groups such as outdoors clubs, and the public. It is simple, elegant and effective. It is also used as a key component of the Avaluator, a trip planning tool developed by Avalanche Canada for backcountry enthusiasts with little experience of avalanche terrain (page 111).

A more detailed terrain rating model is available to experienced backcountry recreationists as a rating guide and as an educational tool.

Parks Canada has also issued some guidelines outlining the experience needed to undertake trips in the three classes of terrain, which are worth repeating here.

Simple terrain requires basic winter travel skills and the discipline to respect avalanche warnings. Simple terrain is usually low avalanche risk and is ideal for novices gaining backcountry experience. However, these trips may not be entirely free from avalanche hazards, and on days when the danger level is Considerable or High you may want to rethink any backcountry travel that has exposure to avalanche danger—stick to groomed cross-country trails or stay within the boundaries of a ski resort.

Challenging terrain requires skills to recognize and avoid avalanche-prone terrain—big slopes exist on these trips. You must also know how to interpret the public avalanche forecast, perform avalanche self-rescue and basic first aid, and be confident in your routefinding skills. You should take an avalanche course before travelling in this type of terrain. If you are unsure of your own or your group's ability to navigate through avalanche terrain, consider hiring a certified guide.

Avalanche Terrain Exposure Scale		
Description	Class	Terrain criteria
Simple	1	Exposure to low-angle or primarily forested terrain. Some forest openings may involve the runout zones of infrequent avalanches. Many options to reduce or eliminate exposure. No glacier travel.
Challenging	2	Exposure to well-defined avalanche paths, starting zones or terrain traps; options exist to reduce or eliminate exposure with careful routefinding. Glacier travel is straightforward but crevasse hazards may exist.
Complex	3	Exposure to multiple, overlapping avalanche paths or large expanses of steep, open terrain; multiple avalanche starting zones and terrain traps below; minimal options to reduce exposure. Complicated glacier travel with extensive crevasse bands or icefalls.

At first glance this might appear to be simple terrain, but note wind-slab avalanches on all of the steep roll-overs where snow has been deposited by wind. Photo Leon Kubbernus.

Detailed Avalanche Terrain Exposure Scale

	1 – Simple	2 – Challenging	3 – Complex
Slope angle	Angles generally less than 30°.	*Mostly low-angle, isolated slopes greater than 35°.*	*Variable with large percentage of slopes greater than 35°.*
Slope shape	Uniform.	Some convexities.	Convoluted.
Forest density	Primarily treed, with some forest openings.	Mixed trees and open terrain.	Large expanses of open terrain. Isolated tree bands.
Terrain traps	Minimal. Some creek slopes or cutbanks.	Some depressions, gullies and/or overhead avalanche terrain.	*Many depressions, gullies, cliffs, hidden slopes above gullies, cornices.*
Avalanche frequency	1 equal to or greater than size 2 every 30 years.	1 every year less than size 2. *1 every 3 years equal to or greater than size 2.*	1 every year less than size 3. *1 every year equal to or greater than size 3.*
Start zone density	Limited open terrain.	Some open terrain. Isolated avalanche paths leading to valley bottom.	Large expanses of open terrain. Multiple avalanche paths leading to valley bottom.
Runout zone characteristics	Solitary, well-defined areas. Smooth transitions spread deposits.	Abrupt transitions or depressions with likelihood of deep deposits.	Multiple converging runout zones. Confined deposition area. Steep tracks overhead.
Interaction with avalanche paths	Runout zones only.	Single path or paths with separation.	*Numerous and overlapping paths.*
Route options	Numerous. Terrain allows multiple choices.	A selection of choices of varying exposure. Options to avoid avalanche paths.	*Limited chances to reduce exposure. Avoidance not possible.*
Exposure time	None; or limited exposure crossing runouts only.	*Isolated exposure to starting zones and tracks.*	*Frequent exposure to starting zones and tracks.*
Glaciation	None.	*Generally smooth with bands of crevasses.*	*Broken or steep sections of crevasses. Icefall or sérac exposure.*

Where an item is in italics, the factor described will dictate the rating even if the other factors indicate a lower rating.

Complex terrain demands a strong group with years of critical decision-making experience in avalanche terrain. There may be no safe options on these trips, forcing exposure to big slopes. A recommended minimum is that you, or someone in your group, should have taken an advanced-level avalanche course and have several years of backcountry experience. Check the public avalanche forecast regularly, and ensure that everyone in your group is up for the task and aware of the risk. This is serious country—not a place to consider unless you're confident in the skills of your group. If you are uncertain, consider hiring a certified guide.

It is important to remember that these terrain ratings are intended to be used in conjunction with other information. They are meant to help you choose a suitable trip for the prevailing avalanche conditions. If conditions are poor you should select conservative terrain. When conditions improve, then you could consider an outing in the next level of terrain.

A glacier icefall is tricky to navigate, as even a small sluff can take you into a crevasse and bury you. Cariboo Glacier. Photo Alf Skrastins.

Typical of Complex terrain, there is no safe alternative route to the col at middle left. Evidence of recent avalanching was enough for us to abandon the traverse and content ourselves with taking photographs.

Terrain Features

The mountainside is made up of bowls, terraces, gullies, steeply uniform slopes, convex and concave slopes, ridges, cliffs and so on. Some of these features provide routes safe from avalanches; others are death traps. The term **terrain traps** is used to describe small, often innocuous-looking terrain features that can snare the unwary winter backcountry enthusiast.

Steep, Straight Slopes

These are obviously potential avalanche slopes. On long open slopes it's difficult to predict where the starting zone for avalanches may be, though often they start at some discontinuity in the slope such as exposed rock outcrops.

Convex Slopes

Many avalanches start where there is some change in slope profile. The rounded top to a peak or ridge can be the trigger zone for slab avalanches. This is because creep due to the weight of snow down the steeper part of the slope sets up tensile stresses in the snowpack that are greatest in the rounded portion of the slope above. Any small disturbance is sufficient to relieve these stresses by the cracking of the snowpack and subsequent avalanche.

In some cases the crown line of avalanches on open convex slopes occurs at the point where the convexity straightens, indicating that the convex portion of the slope is influencing the formation of slab rather than setting up stresses leading to failure. The main danger of convex slopes is that they lead the traveller onto slopes of increasing steepness with a corresponding increase in the probability of avalanche release.

Concave Slopes

Concave slopes are generally considered to be safer than convex ones, but this is not always the case; a lee concave slope, with possibly a cornice at the top, can be just as deadly. There are several recorded incidents where a party, traversing on the safe-looking flat bottom part of the slope, triggered a slab avalanche and were buried by the mass of snow descending from above.

In the absence of soft slab, the snow at the bottom will tend to support the snowpack higher up. But if the lower layer of the snowpack is depth hoar there is a danger that any undercutting, by a ski track or by wind erosion for example, will bring the whole slope down (page 145).

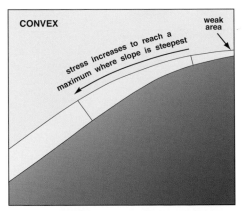

The most likely fracture point is where stresses are greatest. Terrain breaks such as cliff bands or rocks may also create lines of weakness or weak spots.

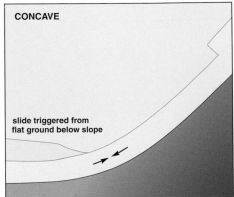

When instability is high, snow on concave slopes can be triggered remotely from flat ground below.

This avalanche on a typical convex–concave slope has cleaned off the snow down to the ground on the roll-over and deposited a significant amount of debris on the flat area at the bottom. Photo Jan Uttl.

Terraces

Terraces tend to prevent avalanching until later in the season when sufficient snow covers them over to form a continuous slope. Although early-season slides tend to end up partway down the avalanche path, retained on the terraced sections, these deposition areas can easily bury a fallen skier, so treat terraces with caution.

Terraces across an avalanche path allow enough snow to accumulate to bury a person. See also the comment about tent platforms on page 133.

Bowls

Bowls with rounded concave sides and straight slopes leading into them are among the most dangerous terrain traps. Their shape makes them susceptible to the deposition of slab and in addition they often have narrow, restricted outlets that allow the snow to funnel down and pile up many metres deep at the bottom. Unfortunately, such bowls offer tempting skiing in powder snow. Beware!

Rocky Outcrops

Many slab avalanches start among rocky outcrops on steep slopes below ridgelines. The rocks themselves create a weakness in the snowpack where they protrude above the surface, and below the surface they may allow recrystallization in the shallower area of slab. These outcrops are often on slopes of 40° or more. The sudden release of stress concentrations in one location can lead to extensive fracture lines across large areas of the slope. When the danger level is high, large avalanches can be remotely triggered from below, as well as by skiers and boarders descending between the rocks.

Gullies

For the purpose of discussion in this book, I am defining gullies and couloirs differently, although the terms are often used interchangeably. Gullies are steep valleys running down a hillside, created by water eroding the bedrock. They differ from couloirs (below) in that they often broaden out at the top in bowls or side slopes that act as steep collection zones for snow.

Steep gullies form natural deposition zones for slab and natural chutes for loose falling snow. Avalanche starting zones are difficult to pinpoint; there may be many different side branches higher up the main gully which can't be seen from down below. Collection zones above are often large, and again it's difficult to predict from below whether and how they become loaded with snow. There is usually little warning of the avalanche coming and often there is no escape. Keep away from shallow gullies on open slopes; the slight depression they make in the slope is an ideal location for slab to form.

Skiers and boarders are attracted to gullies because gullies tend to be sheltered from the wind and have the best and most consistent snow.

Many fatal accidents to winter climbers and scramblers occur in gullies, probably because they present the easiest way up or down the mountain.

The popular sport of waterfall ice climbing has been luring climbers into gullies that were formerly avoided. If you are contemplating an ice climb in a steep gully with a collection zone above, you should wait until you are sure the snow above has either released or become stabilized.

Couloirs

A couloir is a steep break in a cliff face or a steep gully descending directly from a ridge or col that contains snow or ice in winter—sometimes year-round. They are usually hemmed in by rock walls. Although they don't have large collection zones at the top, they frequently have big cornices.

This steep gully has multiple collection zones at the top and a popular waterfall ice climb at the bottom.

Polar Star Couloir. Mark Synnott writes in his
Baffin Island guide: *Possibly the best skiing couloir
on earth and worth a trip to the area on its own.
Defines perfect couloir skiing—long, narrow, turn-
able, steep, sheltered, straight and stunning. 1100 m
(3,640 ft.) of 45–50°*. Photo Andrew McLean.

While moderately steep couloirs with good runouts can be enjoyed by competent skiers, steep, long, twisty couloirs are the playground of extreme skiers and boarders.

There are many famous couloirs within bounds at ski areas, and some of the best couloir skiing in the world is on the east coast of Baffin Island, where they provide runs of 1400 m (4,500 ft.) at angles of 40 to 50°.

Trees

While not really a terrain feature, trees are, along with rocks and cliff bands, the most common source of injury in an avalanche. Many people wear a helmet when tree skiing. Open trees provide good tree skiing when visibility is bad or avalanche danger above treeline is high. However, avalanches can run through trees on any steep slope that is skiable. The presence of trees at the bottom of a steep, open slope should be considered when you ask yourself: What would happen to me if the slope should avalanche?

Where many years of avalanches have cut a swath through the trees, the edge of the trees is often referred to as the **trimline**.

Crevasses

Crevasses, especially bergschrunds—the crevasse where the glacier meets the steep slopes above—can be a significant terrain trap. If you are concerned about stability, try to stay above a section of the 'schrund that is filled in and covered with snow when you ascend the slope above. If you get avalanched above a crevasse and carried into it you have virtually no hope of survival.

Ridges

Wide, gently angled ridges offer the safest route of travel. Narrower ridges, although probably still the best route to a summit, can pose the problem of cornices, a problem compounded by bad visibility. Very often, because of the action of wind across the top of such a ridge, the windward side will give good, firm footing, whereas the opposite side, below the cornice, will be smothered in deep, soft snow in precarious condition. If the ridge is corniced on both sides you've got problems.

Cirques

Amphitheaters ringed by peaks or ridges can be the scene of extensive slab avalanching, the fracture line travelling rapidly round the whole cirque and releasing large volumes of snow, making escape virtually impossible. One example of this is the cirque below Mount Sir Donald and Uto Peak in the Selkirk Range of British Columbia; in heavy snowfall years, the cirque produces a large climax avalanche which fills the valley at the foot of Illecillewaet Glacier with some 10 to 15 metres of snow.

Canyons and Gorges

These features are natural depositories for avalanching snow. You should ask yourself: What kind of slopes feed in from above? How much snow is on them and is it stable? Even a very small slide can pile up enough snow in the bottom of a canyon to bury a person. This happened to a skier in Leeks Canyon, Wyoming. His presence on a 45° side slope above the canyon caused a small slab to fail and down he went to the bottom, buried up to his waist. He probably would have escaped unscathed if the first slide hadn't triggered a second one, which in turn triggered a third. He was found two days later under 3 metres of debris. It's sobering to realize that the slides ran less than 60 metres and the combined width of all three was less than 100 metres.

This old photo, taken during the search for the buried skier in Leeks Canyon, Wyoming, is a good example of a relatively small avalanche burying a skier in a classic V-shaped valley terrain trap. Photo courtesy Dale Gallagher, US Forest Service.

Snow Cushions

Cushions are accumulations of snow on rocky outcrops, down cliff bands, on boulder piles and even on trees. For freeriders they form nature's terrain parks. Cushion lines are series of cushions in steep terrain lined up to provide "a series of airs." Many good cushion lines can be found below treeline in areas safe from conventional avalanches. However, freeriders can get buried by large blocks of snow falling or being skied off, especially if they fall into moats that form between the rock and the snow. Where cushion lines descend gullies with significant streams there is also a danger of slipping down a moat into the streambed and drowning. Freeriders usually go out in groups and operate using the "buddy" system with lots of hootin' and hollerin'.

The route to Bow Hut in the Canadian Rockies leads up this narrow canyon. Fortunately, the slopes above this canyon rarely avalanche.

Flat Ground

When travelling or setting up camp it's important to consider the shape and length of runout zones in the event of an avalanche occurring. The outrun from large avalanches can travel many kilometres across flat ground; in a restricted valley avalanches can flow up the opposite slope, removing trees and depositing debris along the way.

Keep well away from the foot of steep slopes when hazard is high; there have been a number of cases of parties on seemingly safe slopes remotely triggering the steeper slopes above.

Terrain Traps

Terrain traps are features that:

- Are likely to lead to increased burial depths
- Reduce your chance of escaping from the sliding snow
- Speed up the flow of the snow, resulting in a higher chance of injury.

Left: Note the old fracture line on this steep side slope above the V-shaped valley below.

This short 30° slope occasionally releases enough snow to pile up 2 metres deep against the rock and trees at right.

This slab avalanche on the Zermatt Breithorn carried the skier across the bridged crevasse. Had the crevasse been open at this point she would have been swept in and buried under many metres of snow.
Photo Al Schaffer.

Consider what is below the slope you are crossing. Ask yourself: Where will I end up if it does slide?

In this case, you would probably end up at the bottom of the cliff.

Surface Roughness

The surface of the ground has a major influence on early-season avalanching. Roughness of surface determines the snow depth needed to fill irregularities, controls the amount of creep, and significantly affects the ability of the snow to avalanche to the ground in many regions.

Generally, the rougher the ground surface, the more snow depth is required before avalanching will take place. Broken terrain and boulder fields won't become avalanche slopes until sufficient snow has fallen to cover most of the rocks. On the other hand, smooth grass slopes, talus slopes and smooth rock slabs need little snow before avalanching occurs and will avalanche to bare ground frequently throughout the winter.

Professional hazard evaluators are using a figure of 30 to 60 cm, depending on location, as the minimum snow depth necessary to cover roughness of ground before natural avalanching occurs. This figure applies to many areas but should not be taken as an infallible rule of thumb. For instance, in the Canadian Rockies during the early winter of 1981–82, little snow and cold temperatures resulted in a snowpack that was almost entirely composed of recrystallized grains (depth hoar and faceted crystals). In many locations the snow had enough internal cohesion to enable it to form potential slab avalanches. Because rocks were showing through the snow, many skiers thought the slopes were safe to cross. The avalanches they released flowed round the rocks like granulated sugar; even slopes with as little as 15 cm of snow were avalanching right down to the ground. There were many lucky escapes.

A wet snow avalanche which slid on the smooth rocks of the Great Slab, Coire an Lochain, Scotland. Photo Rod Ward.

A down-to-the ground slab avalanche on smooth grass, Davos. Photo André Roch.

Effect of Vegetation

Another factor that influences avalanching is ground cover and vegetation. Grass provides an ideal sliding surface for snow. Willows and slide alder tend to stabilize snow early in the season, but later on, due to creep of the snowpack, they are bent over until they are lying parallel to the ground, thus becoming a much less effective barrier. In cold, dry climates, the air spaces provided by brushy ground cover like willows and alder allow the development of large depth hoar crystals that provide a weak layer at the bottom of the snowpack.

Light timber, defined as timber which you can ski through without too much difficulty, is no protection; slabs can form from wind eddies. Unless you have detailed local knowledge, pinpointing actual avalanche locations is very difficult. Heavy timber that is virtually impossible to ski through is usually safe, although abnormally large avalanches may break through from above.

Four skiers were killed in a massive avalanche in the Canadian Rockies during a major avalanche cycle in which 85 cm of snow had fallen in the past 24 hours. Skiing a popular ski trail, they had crossed the path near the very bottom and had probably stopped to get something out of their packs about 20 m into the heavy timber on the far side. A cornice break 350 m above the skiers triggered the huge snow-laden bowl. The airborne avalanche blasted into the timber, severing mature trees and stripping branches 10 m up the trunks of those left standing.

Deforestation and reforestation play a large part in avalanche development and control. Areas recently deforested may show no sign of previous avalanche activity, which doesn't mean they are safe to ski. Treat such areas with caution, assessing snow conditions as you would for any other open slope.

Lightly timbered slopes such as this one are no protection against storm-slab avalanches.

Slope Aspect

A slope's orientation to sun and wind is very important. When considering their effect on north and south slopes and on lee and windward slopes, don't forget that slopes with other aspects will exhibit characteristics somewhere between the two extremes and that a heavy, uniform, windless fall of snow may make windward slopes just as avalanche prone as lee slopes. In certain conditions of wind, temperature and humidity, storm slab can form over an entire mountainside.

Orientation to Sun

Heat gain and loss from a snow surface is dependent on the angle of the slope, the direction it faces, its latitude and the season. In midwinter, when the sun is low in the sky, south-facing slopes receive sun almost at right angles to the surface, thereby obtaining the maximum possible radiation. During the same period, north-facing slopes receive almost no radiation. As an example of the way latitude affects avalanche characteristics, consider the Canadian Rockies and the southern Colorado Rockies. Although these two areas have similar snowfall, with cold temperatures and clear nights enhancing the formation of depth hoar, the difference in latitude between Colorado, which is 39°, and the Canadian Rockies, which is 52°, results in much greater radiation on south slopes during the day in Colorado and the subsequent formation of layers of recrystallized snow. This tends to build up layers of firm, well-settled snow separated by thin layers of weak crystalline snow that are potential sliding layers.

South slopes Because south-facing slopes receive the most solar radiation, rounding proceeds more rapidly than on other slopes; stabilization and settlement is faster. Although south-facing slopes, not taking into account other factors such as wind direction and terrain features, tend to be the safest during mid-winter, they're often **indicator slopes**; that is, they are the first to release avalanches during and shortly after a storm. If there's enough radiation available for melting, sun crusting will occur. As spring approaches and the days get warmer, melting results in snowballs or wet snow avalanches. Previously safe slopes now become dangerous.

North slopes North slopes receive little or no sunlight in mid-winter and thus are subject to maximum cooling by outgoing long-wave radiation. Because the snow tends to be cooler and rounding slow, avalanche danger extends for longer periods after a storm. Lower temperatures also provide optimum conditions for the formation of depth hoar, which is likely to persist as a weak layer in the snowpack for a greater part of the season. By spring, conditions are reversed: north slopes may provide a route safe from wet snow avalanches, while south-facing slopes are dangerous.

Orientation to Wind

Lee slopes Lee slopes can be very dangerous: they are subject to a rapid accumulation of snow during a storm or during fine but windy weather. Such slopes are often overhung by cornices that can break off and trigger an avalanche on the slope below. It's important to remember that the aspect of a lee slope can vary around a mountainside, depending on local air currents. To complicate matters further, both lee and windward slopes can form on the same side of a mountain. Individual ridges, stands of trees or outcrops of rock will also have their own, localized lee slopes. The majority of avalanche accidents involving backcountry enthusiasts take place on lee slopes.

Windward slopes Slopes exposed to wind tend to receive less snow deposition. The resulting shallow snowpack may result in the formation of depth hoar, but usually the snow is more firmly compacted by wind action. Rime deposits on windward slopes give an indication of wind direction as do formations such as sastrugi and etched layers.

Slope Angle

The basic terrain feature necessary for avalanching is a steep slope. How steep and how can you judge the steepness? Studies of slab avalanches have shown that the majority release on slopes between 30 and 45°, although the critical angle for slab avalanches can range from as little as 25° to 55° or greater. Wet snow avalanches have been reported on slopes as shallow as 15°. On such shallow slopes, wet snow avalanches move very slowly, though they may move long distances, and they are unlikely to be dangerous to the traveller provided no other hazards such as cliff bands are present. Loose snow slides on slopes in the same angle range as slab avalanches do. The angle of repose depends on the type of snow crystal: it's low for wet, slushy snow and becomes higher as the snow becomes grainier and well sintered. Usually, loose, dry snow sluffs harmlessly off steeper slopes during or shortly after a storm. In the highest mountains and in coastal areas such as the Cascades and the Scottish Highlands, snow can be plastered on very steep faces, with slab forming on slopes of up to 60°.

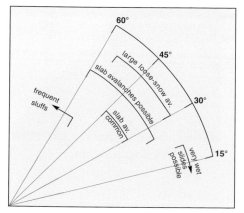

Most frequent slope angles for avalanches. Many slab avalanches trigger on slopes of 38 to 40°.

The table below defines the terms I use in this book to describe slope steepness.

Slope Steepness	
Term used	Slope angle
Moderately steep	25 to 30°
Steep	30 to 35°
Very steep	35 to 45°
Extremely steep	over 45°

A Litany of Gully Accidents

Scotland, which is renowned for its fine gully climbs (the term "gully" being rather loosely defined sometimes—the bottom section of Zero Gully is a 400-foot vertical corner bulging with overhangs), has seen an alarming increase in the number of avalanche accidents. In the winter of 1982 four separate avalanche accidents killed three people within an hour or two of each other on the Ben Nevis massif. Three of the accidents occurred in gullies. The day was sunny and calm, hardly a harbinger of tragedy, but prior to that the weather had been stormy and falls of heavy snow accumulating on a thawed and refrozen old-snow surface had created ideal avalanche conditions. In the first accident a tier of snow sliding from a terrace on the buttress above swept a party of five climbers almost 200 metres to the bottom of Castle Gully. The two uninjured climbers dug out their companions but by that time only one was alive.

Half an hour later a 19-year-old girl standing at the foot of Gardyloo Gully died from an avalanche presumably triggered by her two companions above. One survivor was uninjured; the other broke a femur when the rope, which had wound round his legs, snagged on a boulder and came to a sudden stop. Not long after this, two climbers were swept down No. 2 Gully and another group triggered a slab avalanche while descending the Carn Mor Dearg Arête. Somehow, both parties escaped with only minor injuries.

Common Trigger Points

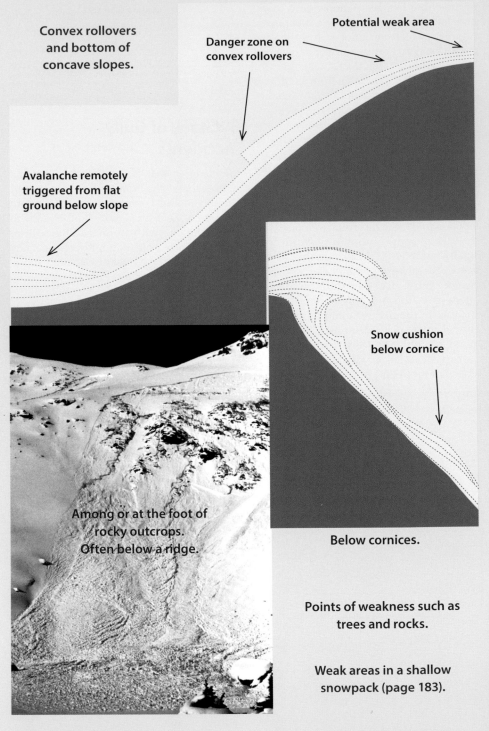

Convex rollovers and bottom of concave slopes.

Danger zone on convex rollovers

Potential weak area

Avalanche remotely triggered from flat ground below slope

Snow cushion below cornice

Among or at the foot of rocky outcrops. Often below a ridge.

Below cornices.

Points of weakness such as trees and rocks.

Weak areas in a shallow snowpack (page 183).

Trip Planning

Improvements in public avalanche forecasting in the past 10–15 years have firmly established the Public Avalanche Forecast as the primary trip planning tool for the winter backcountry enthusiast. Built around the Avalanche Danger Scale and containing information on the forecaster's primary concerns, backcountry travel advisories, and snowpack and weather information, the Public Avalanche Forecast will allow you to decide on the complexity and steepness of the terrain that is appropriate for both the current snowpack conditions and your personal level of risk. **Planning for every backcountry trip should start with a review of the current Avalanche Forecast.**

Before you begin to consider a trip you should:

- Assess your personal **tolerance for risk**.

- Be able to interpret the **Avalanche Danger Scale** and obtain the most pertinent information from the **Avalanche Forecast**.

- Plan a backcountry trip and the **route** you will take.

- Choose suitable **companions** and/or assess the **trip leader**.

Wet snow avalanches in the Monashees of British Columbia.
Photo Alf Skrastins.

Avalanche Forecasting

The major achievement of the professional avalanche community in the last twenty years has been the increased sophistication and accuracy of avalanche danger forecasting. If you evaluate avalanche accidents over the past few years you will find that the forecaster was usually right on in the assessment of the **Danger Level**.

Avalanche professionals in every major area where people ski or board in avalanche terrain in North America and Europe produce regular Avalanche Forecasts (some call them Advisories or Bulletins). You can access them through avalanche.ca for Canada, avalanche.org for the US and avalanches.org (avalanches with an "s") for links to Europe's alpine nations.

Depending on their funding, there is considerable variation in coverage, frequency and sophistication among avalanche centres across North America.

Most avalanche forecast centres are making their forecasts available by phone, email, instant messaging, podcasts and RSS feeds as well as online. They are also using social media to get their message out in the form of iPhone and Android apps and Twitter and Facebook pages. Many local radio and TV weather reports broadcast advisories when danger levels are high. There is little excuse for backcountry enthusiasts to be uninformed.

Forecasts are built around the **Avalanche Danger Scale**, a five-level indicator of avalanche danger for a specific region. Danger levels are established after expert assessment of vast amounts of weather and snowpack data from weather forecasts and automated weather stations, combined with information from field observers, ski patrollers, highway safety personnel, commercial ski operations and guides, along with reports from backcountry skiers. They predict snowpack stability at various terrain elevations and aspects and the probability of an avalanche being triggered.

Avalanche Danger Scale

International co-operation has resulted in the standardization (almost) of Avalanche Danger Scales used in North America and Europe. The danger scale uses five progressively decreasing danger levels: Extreme (called Very High in Europe), High, Considerable, Moderate and Low. The new scale, implemented for the 2010/11 season, now gives basic travel advice in the form of recommended actions in the backcountry, the likelihood of an avalanche occurring, how avalanches might be triggered and their potential size and distribution. It is a compromise between those who wanted a minimalist scale for the general public and others who felt it should give more-experienced backcountry users more specific information.

However, the wording accompanying the danger scales is still very brief, and some explanation of each level is warranted. In particular, the transitions between levels, signs of instability at each level, and the implications of slope angle, aspect and elevation need discussing.

Extreme

Extreme danger levels are rare and usually the result of unusually large amounts of new snow. The snowpack is weakly bonded and unstable. Numerous large avalanches are likely. The weight of the new snow can trigger avalanches on layers buried deep in the snowpack. Natural avalanches can release on slopes of less than 30°.

Backcountry touring is not recommended and often impossible. Avoid all avalanche terrain and keep well away from avalanche path runouts.

High

Conditions have become dangerous, most often as a result of significant amounts of new snow, snowfall accompanied by wind or the snowpack becoming isothermal and threatening wet snow avalanches. The snowpack is poorly bonded over large areas

Danger Level		Travel Advice	Likelihood of Avalanches	Avalanche Size and Distribution
5 Extreme		Avoid all avalanche terrain.	Natural and human-triggered avalanches certain.	Large to very large avalanches in many areas.
4 High		Very dangerous avalanche conditions. Travel in avalanche terrain not recommended.	Natural avalanches likely; human-triggered avalanches very likely.	Large avalanches in many areas; or very large avalanches in specific areas.
3 Considerable		Dangerous avalanche conditions. Careful snowpack evaluation, cautious route-finding and conservative decision-making essential.	Natural avalanches possible; human-triggered avalanches likely.	Small avalanches in many areas; or large avalanches in specific areas; or very large avalanches in isolated areas.
2 Moderate		Heightened avalanche conditions on specific terrain features. Evaluate snow and terrain carefully; identify features of concern.	Natural avalanches unlikely; human-triggered avalanches possible.	Small avalanches in specific areas; or large avalanches in isolated areas.
1 Low		Generally safe avalanche conditions. Watch for unstable snow on isolated terrain features.	Natural and human-triggered avalanches unlikely.	Small avalanches in isolated areas or extreme terrain.

Safe backcountry travel requires training and experience. You control your own risk by choosing where, when and how you travel.

and human triggering is likely on steep slopes (steeper than 30°). Remote triggering is likely and large natural avalanches are to be expected.

Stay on slopes that are flatter than 30° for any part of the slope and be aware of the potential for avalanches from slopes above. If you do decide to ski or board on less steep slopes, be very aware of the surrounding terrain to avoid inadvertently crossing the bottom of steeper slopes or cutting down a steep convex rollover.

Usually this level of hazard is only present for a few days at a time. The smart backcountry traveller will stay in simple terrain until conditions improve. If you are caught out on a multi-day trip, you may have to dig in and wait for travel conditions to improve and the avalanche danger to lessen.

Considerable

Conditions have become much less favourable. The snowpack is only moderately or poorly bonded over a much larger area of the terrain. Human triggering is possible by a single skier on steep slopes and aspects mentioned in the Avalanche Bulletin. Remote triggering of avalanches is also possible, so the maximum steepness of the slope you are on should be used when deciding whether you want to continue.

Instability indicators mentioned under Moderate danger below will likely be present. Backcountry touring at this danger level requires good routefinding skills and experience in recognizing dangerous terrain and evaluating slope stability.

Keep to slopes of less than 35°, especially slopes at the altitude and aspect indicated in the Avalanche Forecast. Remember that remote triggering is possible. Typically the talus fans at the bottom of gullies start out at around 30° and the slope steepens as it gets higher. Keep off such slopes at this hazard level.

The remarks about **persistent weak layers** in the next section on Moderate danger level also apply to this danger level.

Moderate

This is the most difficult danger level for backcountry skiers and boarders in assessing snow stability. Many of the usual indicators such as cracks, settling, whumpfing and signs of recent avalanche are absent, especially at the lower end of the Moderate level. Key indicators are any recent snowfall, and wind deposition. Snowpack tests may help assess stability.

Conditions are generally favourable for travel, providing routes are chosen carefully. The snowpack is only moderately bonded on some steep slopes. Areas of danger are usually restricted to certain types of terrain such as bowls and gullies. The altitude, aspect and type of terrain where danger can be expected are usually detailed in the Avalanche Forecast. Remote triggering is unlikely.

Human-triggered avalanches are possible. Ski or board carefully, one by one, in suspect terrain and avoid high loading of the snowpack by spreading people out on the uphill track. Carefully evaluate the stability of very steep slopes (steeper than 35°) and aspects identified as potentially dangerous in the forecast.

Be especially careful if the higher elevation band in the forecast, or the danger on other aspects, is Considerable. There is a significant difference in instability between Moderate and Considerable. Don't get sucked onto higher, steeper and more dangerous slopes.

Although naturally triggered avalanches are not expected, ice climbers should watch out for the sun warming steep collection zones above their climbs.

If **deep-slab instability** due to a persistent weak layer is mentioned in the forecast, you need to pay careful attention to the terrain. Avalanches from such a layer are not only likely to be large and extensive, they are also completely unpredictable. Unless you have specific local knowledge, keep off large open slopes at this danger level.

Low

Travel is generally safe. The snowpack is well bonded and natural avalanches will not be seen except for small sluffs on extremely steep slopes. Human-triggered avalanches are unlikely except in isolated locations in extreme terrain. The danger will usually be from wind-driven snow in gullies and chutes or deposited across very steep open slopes near ridgelines. Ski or board one by one as smoothly as possible without falling if you suspect the formation of wind slab. Be aware of shaded north to east aspects where the danger may be transitioning to Moderate. There are few fatalities at this danger level.

Avalanche Forecasts

The terms Advisory, Bulletin, Forecast and Report are used interchangeably in North America. Avalanche Canada uses Forecast, except for areas where they have little data. Avalanche Canada is experimenting with Hot Zone Reports based on users MIN reports (page 108). They use Advisory for basic danger information and travel advice for the media. Canadian national parks use Bulletin (as does EAWS, the European Avalanche Warning Services), while most of the agencies in the US use Advisory.

Most avalanche forecasts have three major sections:

- The current danger rating and the anticipated rating for subsequent days. See graphic on opposite page.

- The avalanche problems presented to the backcountry traveller by an unstable snowpack.

- Information on recent avalanche activity, the condition of the snowpack and a forecast of the weather for the period of the bulletin. Standardized terms are used. A glossary of terms may be found at avalanches.org.

In addition to indicating danger levels at various elevations, many forecasts contain a Travel Advisory or highlight the "bottom line" for backcountry users.

The format of avalanche forecasts varies widely. Some agencies provide consistently structured forecasts with eye-catching graphics, while others report in plain text. Some of the more common components of avalanche forecasts are discussed below along with their significance to various backcountry users.

In the following section I am describing the format, and reproducing the graphics, used by Avalanche Canada. The Canadian mountain parks use the same basic format with a few tweaks of their own. The major avalanche centres in the US use a similar format but with different graphics.

Preliminary Information

Versions Forecasts come in a number of versions: computer, mobile or as apps. Advances in Internet programming allow for one version that can be scaled to fit all sizes of screen.

Forecast area Each forecast will be headed by the name of the forecast area. In North America, especially in Canada, most avalanche danger warnings and accompanying forecasts are issued for large geographical regions, some larger than small European countries.

Backcountry users in many western Canadian areas must do their own assessment of the level of danger and the risk of avalanches for their local area using the information in the forecasts as a starting point.

In spite of these limitations you should never think of venturing into the backcountry before consulting your regional Avalanche Forecast. If you are heading out on a multi-day trip, look through past forecasts to get a sense of how the snowpack has developed.

Date of issue All forecasts contain the date issued, how long it is valid for and sometimes the date and time of the next scheduled update. The forecaster's name is usually given. For Avalanche Canada forecasts, click on the area name for full-screen, which makes it easier to read on tablets.

Confidence Most forecasts express the confidence level of the forecast. This can be critical information, especially when a low confidence level is due to uncertainty in the weather forecast leading to the possibility of substantial changes in the snowpack.

Opening statement A well-written opening statement should give you a quick overview of the state of the snowpack in the forecast area. Don't skip it.

Forecast layout Avalanche Canada and Parks Canada present the three sections — Forecast, Problems and Details — using slightly different tab layouts and headings as in the screenshot below.

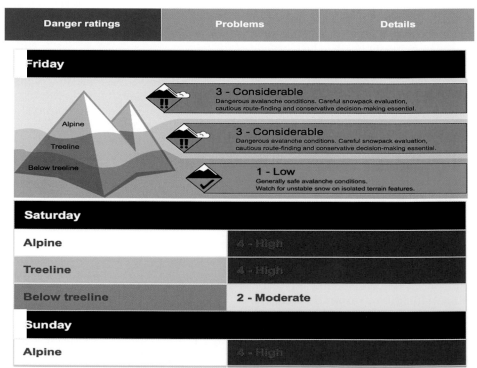

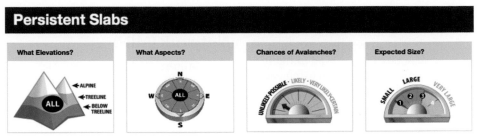

Persistent Slabs

| What Elevations? | What Aspects? | Chances of Avalanches? | Expected Size? |

We're still dealing with a highly variable early season snowpack and several persistent weak layers have been reported from across the region including surface hoar, crusts and facets.

Travel and Terrain Advice

Now is a good time to dig a snow profile (or two) and figure out how the snowpack changes with aspect and elevation.Be aware of thin areas that may propogate to deeper instabilites.Early season hazards such as rocks, trees and stumps are lurking on or just under the surface

A typical Avalanche Problem display, with icons showing information related to the problem, followed by the forecaster's comments and terrain advice.

Avalanche Problems

The second major section, and the "meat" of the forecast, presents up to three avalanche types that are considered to present a **problem** for winter backcountry enthusiasts. For each avalanche type, four icons indicate where the problem exists and on which aspect, and the chance of an avalanche and how big it could be. See **Managing Avalanche Problems** on page 168 for more information on how to manage these problems when riding steep slopes.

Elevations may be shown in bands of feet or metres where most of the backcountry activity is on open slopes, or as "Alpine," "Treeline" or "Below treeline" for areas with forest cover at skiable elevations. The icon will show bolded information at the elevation bands where the problem exists.

Slope aspect The Aspect icon highlights which sectors of the mountain the particular problem is likely to be found in. In most forecasts, aspects where danger is considered to be most critical are also indicated in the text of the forecast.

Remember that shady slopes and sunny slopes are not necessarily the same as northern slopes and southern slopes. Depending on the angle of the sun, shady and sunny slopes can be present on several dif-

ferent aspects and at various times of day. Lee slopes (slopes that face away from the wind) and wind-loaded slopes mean the same thing: the likelihood of wind slab.

Critical terrain There is often mention of specific terrain that the forecaster is concerned about. It may be a particular aspect or terrain features such as large open slopes or steep bowls. Many backcountry users assume that terrain that is not explicitly mentioned has a danger level one lower on the danger scale. While this has proved to be a reasonable assumption, you should not make a go/no-go decision based on this assumption alone.

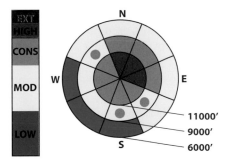

The AviRose, used by some US forecast centers, shows danger level on various aspects within elevation bands. The danger trend is indicated using a series of AviRoses. Graph courtesy of the Colorado Avalanche Information Center.

Chance of avalanche This icon indicates the likelihood of an avalanche, either naturally or human triggered. The chance of an avalanche can vary from unlikely to almost certain. It is important to remember that this likelihood only applies to the particular avalanche problem at a certain elevation and aspect. There may still be a very good chance of an avalanche of a different type at other elevations and aspects. You need to consider all the avalanche problems that are presented and combine the information before you decide on the safest slopes to ride.

Expected size The Expected Size icon gives a sense of how large an avalanche might be, if triggered. Your ability as a rider and your tolerance for risk will determine how large an avalanche you are willing to be exposed to.

Problem statement The short text following the icons is often the most useful part of the problem forecast. Read it carefully!

Terrain and travel advice is given as a number of short points on how to manage the avalanche problems in the backcountry. The number of messages are usually limited to the five or six most important ones over the whole forecast. For more on how to manage avalanche problems, see page 168.

Forecast Details

The third major section of the forecast has three parts:

- A discussion of recent avalanche activity. If you only read one of the detail sections, read this one.

- A discussion on how the snowpack is building up and what weak layers are present.

- The weather forecast for the day of the forecast and for the next few days. More-detailed weather forecasts are available elsewhere on both Avalanche Canada and Parks Canada websites.

Mountain Information Network (MIN)

The Mountain Information Network, developed by Avalanche Canada, allows backcountry users to submit Quick Reports using the Avalanche Canada app or via the website, and more extensive reports on Avalanches, Snowpack, Weather and Incidents via the website (although some of these report forms may be included in the app by now).

These reports appear as blue icons on the main Avalanche Canada map, which you can click to view the reports. Reports in a small area are grouped together, with the icon showing the number of reports until you click on it or enlarge the map. An icon with a red dot indicates an incident report is included. Once you click on an icon, a pop-up displays the report, and tabs at the top of it show available associated reports.

Inputting information on your smartphone for a Quick Report is an easy three-step process. After entering some basic information such as report name, date and time, and location, you are given the opportunity to upload photos directly from your smartphone.

The third step involves checking off predetermined options that allow you to specify riding quality, snow conditions, the kind of slopes you rode and what slopes you avoided, the weather that day and avalanche conditions.

Avalanche Conditions gives you four choices relating to observed slab avalanches, whumpfing, additional loading of the snowpack and rapid rise in temperature.

A final text area allows you to add comments to your report. If you have cellphone coverage, submit the report immediately; otherwise, save it and submit later.

If you select the Mountain Information Network tab on the Avalanche Canada website you will find information and videos on how to use the MIN as well as links to the apps.

Interpreting Avalanche Forecasts

Backcountry tourers and snowshoers—including climbers and scramblers accessing their climbs or descents—who do not intend to venture onto steep slopes are primarily concerned with the danger rating for their chosen altitude zone. The Avaluator (page 111) will give you guidance on what type of terrain is suitable for the forecast danger level.

If the danger rating is Considerable or higher, look for any indication of **persistent weak layers** (page 63) in the forecast, especially if a **warming trend** is also mentioned. Read the forecaster's opinion on the likelihood of significant **natural releases** from slopes above your planned route.

Backcountry skiers and boarders who are intent on making turns should use the danger rating as a starting point for further evaluation. Unlike tourers, riders are deliberately going into the starting zones of potential avalanches and need all the information they can extract from the forecast.

While most avalanche forecasts don't specifically mention slope angle, you can apply the danger rating to the Swiss Slope Angle Scale (page 171) as a first step in determining the risk of descending steep and very steep slopes.

Unfortunately, while deterring you from skiing or boarding very steep slopes when the danger rating is Considerable or higher, the Avaluator and the Swiss Slope Angle Scale use terms like "extra caution" and "elevated risk" in the fuzzy areas between the green and the red. You can miss out on a lot of good turns if you don't pay close attention to the finer points in the forecast.

The first thing to look for is the **confidence** of the forecaster in the forecast. If there is no confidence statement, you may want to ask around as to the track record of the forecast centre you are consulting.

Next, look for a Travel Advisory or a "bottom line" statement. This is a summation of the forecaster's local knowledge and the recent backcountry experiences of the forecaster's contacts — guides, friends and other avalanche professionals.

Pay particular attention to **terrain** where danger is considered to be most critical, in particular any mention of **lee slopes** and **wind deposition**, **north slopes** early in the season and **sunny slopes** as spring approaches.

Note any mention of **buried surface hoar** and sliding layers such as rain crusts. In some years **persistent weak layers** are a major problem in some areas and you should read the archived forecasts to get a feel for how the snowpack has built up during the season.

Finally, take note of whether the danger level is increasing or decreasing and of the weather forecast for the period when you will be in the backcountry.

The avalanche forecast can only give you an indication of whether to go out in the backcountry and what slopes to ski or board. Your final go/no-go decision will have to be made after assessing the conditions through observation and some basic stability tests on the snow. Take a copy of the forecast with you!

Out-of-bounds skiers and boarders differ from backcountry skiers and boarders in that they are usually descending into the start zone of an avalanche slope from above without having the opportunity of observing snow conditions on the approach.

You will have to rely on the forecast being correct and make careful note of reports of recent avalanching and of terrain the forecaster has concerns about. The risk at Considerable and High will be unacceptable to most people.

You will have to be more conservative than backcountry skiers and boarders because once you have launched yourself into an out of bounds area it may be very difficult to escape from if conditions turn out to be scary.

Local knowledge of the area and of all the escape and exit routes is essential. Don't ski or board out of bounds unless your are thoroughly familiar with the geography of the area and the character-istics of the terrain.

Freeriders should read the paragraphs concerning **Backcountry tourers and snowshoers** on the previous page. Your aims are similar — keep out of avalanche terrain while having fun. Remember that the landing from a kicker is usually on 35–40° slopes — prime avalanche terrain. Stay off big open slopes.

Extreme skiers and boarders rely heavily on local knowledge for safe descents. You should follow the forecasts throughout the season, and when the snow on your chosen descents begins to show signs of stabilizing, contact the forecast centre directly for more specific advice. You should be confident that the terrain will not avalanche, and should be fully cognizant of the finer points of sluff management.

Ice climbers, once at the foot of the climb, are concerned about natural releases from above. The nature of ice climbing means that climbers are exposed to danger for long periods of time — much longer than any other user of avalanche terrain.

If the danger level is High, and espe-cially if the aspect of the climb is singled out as having a critical hazard, then your decision is easy — do the climb another day. If the danger level is Considerable there is still a chance of natural avalanches. Look for mention of **wind loading** and of **warming trends**. Many releases above ice climbs occur when the sun hits the slope above the climb.

Note also the trend in the danger level. Is the forecaster predicting a higher danger level for the next day? Why? Is more snow forecast or is a warm front coming through? If the latter, when?

In the absence of local knowledge, it is best to wait until the danger level is Moderate or Low.

Ice climbers are encouraged to carry avalanche rescue gear, including transceiv-ers, probes and shovels.

Snowmobilers should use the avalanche danger rating and forecast as their pri-mary decision-making tool. Look for any mention of **persistent weak layers** in the snowpack when the danger level is Moder-ate or higher and note aspects which the forecaster considers more hazardous. Pay particular attention to the Travel Advisory or "bottom line" statement. Your machines are capable of taking you long distances into a wide variety of terrain and around many different aspects.

Don't even consider highmarking when the danger level is Moderate or higher.

When There Is No Forecast

Some years there is good skiing or board-ing at the end of the season after regular forecasting ceases. Well-settled snow remains in steep gullies, offering extreme descents, and it's prime time for high alpine and glacier traverses, with warm days and lots of daylight.

Consider the four main components of avalanche hazard used in most avalanche forecasts:

- The types of avalanche problem.
- Where in the terrain the problem may be found — above, at or below treeline.
- What is your likelihood of triggering an avalanche?
- How big could the avalanche be?

Then ask yourself: What is likely to happen to me if an avalanche occurs?

You should be familiar with the sec-tions of this book that deal with assessing the general danger level in the terrain, assessing the stability of specific slopes, recognizing signs of instability, and the techniques of safe travel in complex terrain.

The bottom line is you are on your own, just like in the old days when there were no forecasts. What is different now is that modern communications such as email and the Internet facilitate getting information and advice.

Trip-planning Tools

There have been many attempts to develop planning and decision-making tools that can be used by the informed backcountry recreationist. Unfortunately most of them have been developed in Europe and have been promoted for use in the countries where they were developed. Only one of the European tools has been translated into English, probably because they would need modifying before they would be applicable to North American conditions. The tools vary widely, from cards relating slope angle to danger level, to a calculating device that requires the user to answer 25 questions. The tools are partly rule-based—plugging in known factors—and partly knowledge-based. Critics claim the rule-based part is simplistic and the knowledge-based part is not suitable for novices.

Avalanche Apps

Avalanche apps have been around since about 2010, and more are appearing every year. Many of these apps allow you to receive the forecast and other information for your local region, and also, like the Avalanche Canada app, enable you to submit real-time reports on snow and avalanche conditions. Some apps feature terrain maps with marked descent routes and plots of your location on the routes via GPS. Users can update descriptions of their route and share them with others on social media.

These apps are getting more sophisticated and more reliable, and are a valuable addition to the planning and decision-making process. I am not going to attempt to review all the available apps—I don't have the space and the technology is evolving so quickly—the better ones will prevail. Stay tuned.

Note: Don't confuse these apps with ones that claim you can use your smartphone to search for a buried victim. More on this later.

Avaluator 2™

Avalanche Canada has taken some of the ideas from Europe and developed the Avaluator, a tool for trip planning and slope evaluation. It is accompanied by a booklet explaining the avalanche danger and terrain rating scales as well as basic recommendations on recognizing avalanche terrain and good travel habits. The Avaluator Trip Planner is discussed here. The slope evaluation tool, a separate card used during your trip, is discussed on page 130.

The Avaluator Trip Planner relates three types of terrain—Simple, Challenging and Complex (page 85)—to the Avalanche Danger Scale. It is an awareness tool that allows the user to make a suitable choice of terrain based on the forecast danger rating. It provides the first step in assessing the risk associated with a planned backcountry trip.

The Avaluator is proving to be a valuable educational took in recreational-level avalanche courses.

Using the Avaluator Trip Planner

The real strength of the Avaluator Trip Planner is the growing number of popular areas and trips that have been assigned terrain ratings by avalanche professionals and local guides. For western Canada, ratings are published online. They are also available as pamphlets from information centres and are starting to appear in guidebooks.

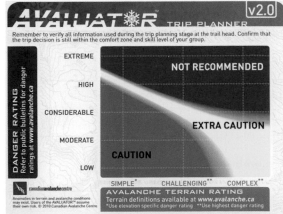

Avaluator 2™. Courtesy Avalanche Canada.

Trip Planner. Courtesy Avalanche Canada.

The Avaluator is designed to be simple to use. Obtain the danger rating from the forecast and the terrain rating from the above-mentioned sources. If there is no terrain rating available, use the Detailed Avalanche Terrain Exposure Scale on page 86 to make your own evaluation.

Danger levels are given for various elevation ranges. For Simple terrain use the elevation-specific danger rating. For Challenging and Complex terrain use the highest danger rating.

The intersection of the two lines selected above will land in one of three zones which indicate that either "Caution" or "Extra Caution" is required or that travel is "Not Recommended." For example, if the danger level is Considerable and the terrain is rated Challenging, the intersection of the lines is in the yellow "Extra Caution" zone. This indicates that you should be experienced in routefinding and navigation, stability evaluation and group management and have rescue and first-aid skills.

Remember

- The Avaluator is a trip planning tool, and does not predict the stability of a given slope.

- Just because you are in the "green" area of the Avaluator doesn't mean you are completely safe—25% of historical accidents have occurred in this zone. Be on the watch for isolated slabs.

- The terrain rating system used by the Avaluator does not address the needs of skiers and boarders who are looking for turns on steep or very steep slopes.

- How you use the Avaluator Planner will depend on your level of experience and the makeup of your party. Clubs are using it to select trips for outings and to decide whether to hire a guide. Some have a policy that a trip will not proceed if the indication of danger is not in the "green" zone. Parks Canada uses the terrain ratings to legislate custodial groups.

Online Trip Planner

At the time of writing, Avalanche Canada was reworking its online trip planner. It allows you to chose your activity and the terrain rating you feel is appropriate for the forecast danger level. The map will display clusters of trips that meet these conditions. You can view trip details and compare different trips. This will be a great tool for planning trips once they get it working again.

Planning Your Route

Being prepared is critical if you are to have a safe trip through avalanche terrain. If you have not done the tour or climb before, find out as much as you can about it beforehand. You need to:

- Ensure the route is within the capabilities of all of your party, and furthermore that the level of risk is acceptable to everyone.
- Be confident that you can follow your planned route in any conditions.
- Plan your route on a map, determining how far it is and how much time it is likely to take. Will you have enough daylight to allow a suitable safety margin?

Advice of Friends

Often the best information comes from experienced friends who are able to recollect and describe a route in detail. Get together over a beer with a map and guidebook and pick their brains. Caveat: there are some people who are hopeless at accurately describing a route, even if they have travelled it recently—you probably know who they are.

Guidebooks

Up-to-date guidebooks are a good source of information, though unless the author is particularly good you will probably have some questions after reading the descriptions. The key to really understanding the guidebook description is to follow it on a map, or on Google Earth if the resolution is good enough.

A good guidebook will indicate the popularity of an area and thus give an indication of how much it is used. The more an area is skied during the season, the more stable the underlying snowpack is likely to be.

Maps

United States The US Geological Survey (USGS) 7.5', 1:24,000-scale maps allow considerable detail to be shown and are ideal for trip planning.

Canada The 1:50,000 topographic maps covering the mountain areas have serious limitations for route planning. With contour intervals of 40 m (100 ft. on some older maps) there can be, and often are, cliff bands that don't show up at all. In many cases the maps have not been updated recently and roads and trails are shown incorrectly or not at all.

When viewing your route on a map you are looking for:

- The length of the route and the height gain and loss, an indication of how long the trip is likely to take.
- Alternative routes and potential escape routes.
- If the mapping is good, try to identify potentially dangerous sections of the route.
- At the 1:24,000 scale there are enough contour lines for you to calculate an approximation of the slope angle on the steepest portions of the route.
- Note the aspects traversed by the route and relate them to the Avalanche Forecast.
- Note the elevation of sections of the route. Which elevation bands on the Danger Scale will you be in?

Google Earth

Many areas are now covered in high resolution—good enough sometimes to see large rocks. Most areas are shown without snow cover, so you have to imagine what it will be like in winter.

If you have a GPS track log of your route in KML format, you can display the track on the satellite picture.

GPS Track Logs

GPS track logs for popular tours are becoming available on a number of websites. If you have a GPS receiver I suggest you log all your routes and upload them to the receiver every time you do the trip. They are especially valuable above treeline in bad visibility. You can also use mapping software to view the route in 3D. While still somewhat tacky due to poor elevation information, the 3D view can be quite instructive.

Trip Plan

Having planned the route, you need to plan the logistics of your trip.

Who is going? Are they capable of completing the trip and is the level of risk acceptable to them? I know I am repeating myself, but this is a very important point.

Safety equipment If you get into trouble, companion rescue is your only hope. Does everyone have a transceiver, a shovel and a probe as a minimum? Have they practised with the transceiver and do they know the rudiments of companion rescue?

Emergency Plan

In the winter backcountry you have to plan for emergencies. A night out, especially if you are injured and hypothermic, is a serious matter. The elements of an emergency plan are:

- Brainstorm how you would deal with an emergency such as an injury or broken equipment. What if?

- Everyone should carry enough warm clothes to survive a night out in some form of snow shelter.

- Someone should be delegated to bring a bivy bag. Ideally there should be one double bag for every two people — it's much warmer with two.

- For longer, more remote trips someone should carry a stove, pot and provisions to provide hot drinks. There are some very lightweight stoves and pots available.

- Discuss how you might communicate your predicament to the outside world. Depending on your location, the options are cellphones, satellite phones or GPS devices like the "Spot."

Assessing Personal Risk

A discussion on trip planning would not be complete without some mention of risk. Risk is about accepting the fact that you are exposing yourself to danger, and managing risk is about doing everything you can to minimize the risk.

Whatever your personal acceptable level of risk, the potential reward must always outweigh the potential consequences. In other words, don't stick your neck out for a run or two of lousy skiing. Save all of your "nine lives" (hopefully more) for those occasional perfect days.

Everyone has a different tolerance for risk, from the risk-seeker who skis steep slopes regardless of conditions, to the person with a low tolerance for risk who will only venture onto steeper slopes when the snowpack is indisputably stable.

When skiing with a large group or with companions who are better skiers, you should avoid being pressured into accepting more risk than you really want to tolerate. Be aware of your companions' attitude toward risk and make adjustments on the conservative side if necessary.

Travelling Alone

Don't travel alone off frequented trails in avalanche terrain. *A ski tourer travelling alone in the backcountry near Taos Ski Valley, New Mexico, triggered and was buried by a soft slab avalanche. Rescuers instantly spotted a ski tip sticking from the snow and made a quick recovery of his body from under two feet of snow. The victim had died of suffocation, a death that would have easily been prevented had he not been travelling alone.*

Your Companions

Your choice of skiing companions is an important factor in the pursuit of safe skiing. The riskier the skiing, the more critical it is to know their skiing ability and experience, their tolerance for risk and their potential behaviour in an emergency. Ideally you should ski with a small group of companions of similar ability and with similar tolerance for risk. If you ski with a large group you will have to be much more conservative in your choice of slope, as it is much more difficult to apply the principles of safe skiing to a big group.

The ideal group size is one that is small enough to be manageable and large enough to be effective in the event of an avalanche rescue. Four is a good number. Skiing alone leaves no margin for error and is not a good idea in avalanche terrain.

The correct speed of travel for any party is the speed of the slowest member. Bearing this in mind, select a party able to travel at approximately the same pace. Conditioning and ability may make up for lack of experience, or, conversely, sheer doggedness can balance lack of skiing ability.

On the whole, though, an inexperienced person out of condition and with little skiing ability will slow a party down considerably. I am not suggesting that this person should be left behind, but rather that the party should lower its objectives and allow more time for the trip.

Ability

Because a good skier making smooth turns stresses a slope much less than a falling skier, you should match your skiing ability with the steepness and stability of the slopes you ski. A skier who has a tendency to "crash and burn" on steep slopes should not ski steep powder of dubious stability. There are some who consider that to descend deep powder in marginal conditions you should either use a snowboard or be able to "parallel" ski, as "telemarking" puts greater stress on the snow!

Group Leadership

Outdoor clubs and similar organizations owe it to their membership to provide competent leadership for their outdoor activities. Records of avalanche accidents show that many of the so-called competent leaders used by clubs, experienced mountaineers even, had little or no knowledge of safe travel in avalanche terrain.

Anyone who proposes to lead large parties of mixed ability into the backcountry must have significant personal experience in the mountains, first-aid training and strong leadership skills. The following outline issued a few years ago by Banff National Park wardens for ski tourers describes the duties of a party leader. It's included here as a reminder to club leaders and also as a checklist for people who are deciding whether or not to go out on a trip with a certain leader.

- **Plan the trip thoroughly**, not only the route, but the equipment to be carried by the party.

- **Evaluate each member's capacity and ability,** adjusting the severity of the trip to the ability of the party's weakest member.

- **Minors** If you have young people in your group who are not accompanied by a parent, read the next topic. Even if you are not going to a Canadian national park, the principles behind their policies are worth considering.

- **Group size** Groups larger than five or six people are more difficult to manage and travel slower than smaller groups. If there is only one leader, you should try to limit the group to no more than 10 people. If you wish to accommodate more people, you need more leaders and should split the party into two or more independent groups based on ability and speed.

- **Check the personal equipment** of the party to ensure that everyone is adequately equipped.

- **Pace the travel speed of the party** so that no one becomes exhausted. Amateur leaders often try to burn off the rest of the group.
- **Keep the party together** but not too close in avalanche terrain. Large groups require a "tail-end Charlie." Frequent stops and counts of the party must be made, especially when skiing downhill.
- **Route selection** The leader should be experienced in route selection.
- **Snowcraft** The leader should have a thorough knowledge of mountain weather, snowcraft and avalanche hazard evaluation.
- **Navigation** The leader must be capable of travelling with map and compass or GPS in whiteout conditions.
- **Repairs** Ensure there are sufficient tools in the group to repair broken skis, skins and bindings. After late starts, broken equipment is the next most common indirect cause of accidents.
- **Rescue** The leader must be capable of organizing a backcountry avalanche rescue, applying first aid and keeping survivors alive until rescuers arrive.
- **Backcountry communications** Most backcountry locations in Canada don't have cell phone coverage. This means that emergency communication requires some planning. Figure out if the area you are heading to has cell phone coverage. Expect this only near highway corridors and townsites.

Satellite Messenger devices such as Spot and DeLorme inReach are becoming popular and reliable, and their cost is reasonable (page 123).

If you are going into really remote areas, consider renting a **satellite phone**. Although not 100% reliable, they will usually work from anywhere that has a reasonable view of the sky. It is best to write down the local emergency numbers and keep them with the phone. Make sure the batteries are fully charged before departure, and carry a spare.

Custodial Groups in Canada's National Parks

A "custodial group" is a group affiliated with any organization where there are minors participating whose parents aren't present. A group of friends or families that includes minors accompanied by their parents is not a custodial group.

Parks Canada Custodial Policies

Custodial group policies are based on Avalanche Terrain Exposure Scale (ATES) ratings (page 85) along with a list of over 250 rated trips in the mountain national parks that can be obtained from any Parks Canada information centre.

- **Simple terrain** Custodial groups are not required to travel with a licensed guide. Parks Canada recommends that custodial groups avoid backcountry travel entirely when the forecast avalanche danger is High or Extreme. Anyone who leads a group into the backcountry should be a competent leader as described in the previous section, **Group Leadership**.
- **Challenging terrain** Custodial groups must be led by a licensed mountain or ski guide with a valid custodial permit. Group size must not exceed a total of 10. They should travel on avalanche terrain only when the licensed guide rates the slope-specific snow stability as Good or Very Good.
- **Complex terrain** Custodial groups will not be permitted into Complex terrain under any conditions.

It is important that any organization considering taking minors into the backcountry in Canadian national parks consult the Banff National Park webpage pc.gc.ca/eng/pn-np/mtn/securiteenmontagne-mountainsafety/gardiens-custodial.aspx and view the public safety information on custodial groups.

Avalanche Gear

This short section covers equipment specifically related to travelling in avalanche terrain. Most of the items are emergency equipment for use in the case of an avalanche accident. While it is important to carry the appropriate equipment, particularly **Beacon**, **Shovel** and **Probe**, it is more important to make informed decisions to avoid being caught in an avalanche in the first place. How often do we hear in the media that the deceased "...was experienced and had all the right equipment"?

Avalanche Rescue Beacons

Avalanche rescue beacons, interchangeably called **Avalanche Transceivers**, are electronic devices capable of both transmitting and receiving an audible electronic signal. When travelling in avalanche terrain each person carries one of these devices switched to transmit. Because power usage is minimal, transceivers are usually left on all day, so that if someone gets buried by an avalanche, the rescue beacon will carry on transmitting its signal. Their companions will immediately switch their own units to receive and begin a predetermined search pattern. Typically, if the victim is buried 1 m below the surface and the searchers are 50 m away at the start of the search, it should be possible to find and dig out the victim in less than 10 minutes.

There is no doubt that modern avalanche rescue beacons offer the fastest and most reliable method for locating a buried avalanche victim. They have been credited with saving many lives and have the potential for increasing the depth at which live recoveries are made. **No serious mountain tourer, skier or snowboarder goes into avalanche terrain without one.**

Avalanche Beacon Technology

Improvements in transceiver technology have resulted in avalanche beacons that are more reliable and easier to use. All new receivers use digital technology to process the analog signal from more than one antenna.

The latest transceivers have three antennas. They are the ultimate point and find receivers.

Receivers with two antennas, however, are still functional, and if you practise regularly, you can find a buried person just as fast as with a three-antenna receiver.

Although a few single-antenna analogue receivers still exist, I do not advise buying one. They have some advantages in the hands of a skilled operator, but they are harder to use and require more practice.

Which Beacon Should You Buy?

You should buy the best digital transceiver you can afford.

I recommend you buy one of the latest three-antenna transceivers. They are easier to use in the pressure and excitement of a rescue, and if they save someone's life, they are worth the extra cost.

There are at least five manufacturers that make transceivers for the North American market. All of them make good, reliable instruments, the difference being the variety of features each manufacturer emphasizes to attract your attention. Here are some pointers:

- Look for a unit with a simple, foolproof method of switching on and off, and of switching from transmit to receive. Some beacons will automatically switch back to transmit if there is no activity for a certain length of time.

- Don't get caught up in the multiple-burial debate. There have been very few true multiple burials in Europe or North America—victims have been far enough apart to be considered single burials when searching.

- Be wary of manufacturer's gimmicks that may add to the complexity (and price) without adding much to ruggedness and simplicity of use.

- Avalanche transceiver technology has changed so fast over the past few years, that I advise you to compare the latest models before buying. At the time of writing there is an excellent website for such research, called **beaconreviews. com**, run by Steve Achelis, a software engineer and former rescue team commander.

Care of Avalanche Rescue Beacons

Modern avalanche beacons are sealed in injection-moulded plastic cases that are rugged and reasonably moisture proof, although condensation can still be a problem. In spite of the electronics being reliable and well protected, avalanche rescue beacons are potentially fragile and should be treated with respect.

- Try not to drop them and don't throw them around. If you break a ferrite rod antenna the unit will still transmit but the frequency won't be correct, the reception of other signals will be noisy and the range may be significantly reduced.

- Keep the battery terminals clean. If they become oxidized there will be a high-resistance connection between the battery and the electronics, resulting in the unit working erratically or not at all.

- Remove the batteries at the end of the season. Make sure you install new batteries correctly. Most models have a diagram on the outside of the case to guide you.

- Organizations that issue or loan rescue beacons should institute a regular schedule for checking the units. They should verify that the beacon works at maximum range, both in transmit and in receive modes, to make sure an antenna is not broken.

Practising with Avalanche Rescue Beacons

However easy to use your beacon is, it is absolutely essential that you practise searching with it. Many mountain locations now have **Beacon Training Parks** that allow you to rehearse realistic beacon searches. They usually consist of multiple buried signal sources, with a control panel that allows you to turn on beacons to simulate various situations such as multiple or deep burials. There may also be a simulated probe target, so take your probe along. Check with your local avalanche forecast centre for your nearest beacon training park.

Organized clubs and groups should arrange practice sessions for their members at the beginning of each winter season. Hold additional sessions as members acquire units throughout the winter. Because avalanche beacons don't work satisfactorily indoors, use your local park or any open ground where you can hide or bury the units. Some people practise near the trailhead before or after a trip.

Before burying a unit, make sure it's switched on, placed in a plastic bag and well wrapped in a glove or piece of foam to protect it from damage during the digging out. If you intend burying it more than a metre below the surface, placing it inside a packsack will give shovellers a little larger area to search for. Using another unit, check before leaving the burial site that the beacon is transmitting. If, for some reason, the unit quits working you have three alternatives: dig for it (if a large area is trampled down this may take some time), leave it until the spring melt, or persuade the local avalanche rescue dog handler that it's a good exercise for the dog.

The whole purpose of practising is to emphasize that an organized, systematic approach is preferable to haphazard wandering. You can demonstrate, by timing recoveries, that the organized approach is the more efficient, and that practice greatly improves speed. Practices can be set up as competitions either with individual searchers or with teams of two to three persons. Bury two or more rescue beacons with various spacings to simulate an accident with several victims.

You can set your own standards for proficiency. It could be said that a person is proficient when they can lead a group of three searchers in a search area of 100 by 200 m and recover the buried unit in less than six minutes.

Using and Carrying Your Beacon

There are a few important points concerning the use of avalanche rescue beacons that you should remember:

Before a trip Make sure your rescue beacon is working properly and that the batteries are fresh or fully charged. If you are not using rechargeable batteries, use the best batteries available (lithium if your beacon can use them) and change them frequently.

During a trip

- Rescue beacons should be carried under your outer clothing, facing inward, as close to your head as possible. Most models provide a chest strap or harness to hold the unit tight against your body.

- Never carry the avalanche beacon in your pack or in the pocket of a garment such as a jacket that you might take off during the day.

- Keep metal objects such as climbing gear, shovel blades and magnets at least 20 cm away from the avalanche beacon, as they will interfere with the signal, decrease its range and reduce battery life. Electronic devices such as cellphones, radios and any other devices with wireless capability also interfere with the signal. If you don't need them, turn them off and put them in your pack.

- Switch on your rescue beacon at the start of the day and leave it on until you are safely encamped or have finished the trip.

The value of doing this was well illustrated in January 1982 when three provincial park rangers, on their day off, set out on a ski tour in the Healy Creek area of the Canadian Rockies. Out of habit, they switched their beacons to transmit before they left the parking lot. While ascending a small V-shaped valley below treeline, they triggered a small slab avalanche that cleaned off the adjacent side slope right down to the ground, knocking over one of the party in the valley bottom and completely burying him under a metre of snow. Using their avalanche beacons his companions were able to dig him out, shaken but unhurt, within a few minutes. The victim commented later: *We didn't consider that we were in avalanche terrain where the accident happened. It was a complete surprise.* The ending might have been very different had they waited until they reached an area considered hazardous before switching on their rescue beacons.

The use of avalanche rescue beacons during a rescue is covered in the chapter **Companion Rescue**, beginning on page 185.

Shovels

A large shovel and a good shovelling plan are essential for the quick retrieval of a buried victim. It has been estimated that for a victim buried 1.3 m deep, at least 1 cubic metre of snow has to be removed before the airway can be reached. This is a significant amount of snow to remove, especially if you are the only searcher.

There are many light, strong and durable shovels available with folding or collapsible handles for easy stowing.

Points to consider when buying a shovel are:

- Buy a good-quality aluminum alloy, heat-treated shovel. Polycarbonate (Lexan) or newer composite blades, though slightly lighter, tend to flex and bounce off hard, icy snow and have fallen out of favour with people who have used them in actual rescues.

- Get the largest shovel in terms of blade size that you can comfortably handle. A smaller, lighter person can move snow faster and for a longer period of time with a smaller shovel.

- Make sure the handle is long enough for efficient shovelling, and that the grip at the end is large enough to use with gloves on. If you are a powerful shoveller, a D-grip is the most effective. Look for a shovel with a telescoping shaft.

- If you feel the commercial shovels are too expensive, a good compromise is to buy a cheap hardware-store aluminum scoop shovel, knock out the rivet that holds the handle to the scoop and cut down or replace the handle using a wing nut and bolt for fastening. However, this is a compromise, as your shovel will be torsionally less stiff and the blade not as strong as a dedicated avalanche shovel.

Avalanche Probes

Lightweight avalanche probes are an essential part of backcountry rescue. They are mainly used in the latter stages of a beacon search to pinpoint the exact position of the buried person. They can also be used during the initial hasty search to probe around items of equipment and clothing found on the surface.

Avalanche probes are aluminum or carbon fibre sections of tube that are collapsible and assemble quickly using an internal wire cord that keeps the sections together. Like all equipment these days, there are many models on the market.

Choosing probes is a compromise between weight and strength. The stronger and more rigid they are, the more effective they will be in probing through hard, chunky snow.

Probes are longer and slide through the snow easier than ski pole probes, which have fallen out of favour. Probes are sufficiently lightweight nowadays that the additional burden is no longer an issue.

Snow Saw

A snow saw with a blade at least 30 cm long is needed for cutting columns in the "isolated-column" tests described in **Riding Steep Slopes**, beginning on page 163. It is also useful for cutting blocks for igloos or shelter walls.

Again there are many models on the market. You can even get saws that stow in the handle of the shovel and attach to the handle to improve their reach.

AvaLung II™

The Black Diamond AvaLung II is a simple filtration device that allows you to breathe fresh air directly from the snowpack, extending the time your companions will have to dig you out. Exhaled carbon dioxide is directed to the back of the device, away from the fresh-air intake. The Avalung requires that you get a mouthpiece into your mouth and be able to keep it there during the avalanche. Some people ride with the mouthpiece in their mouth during the descents.

It's a great piece of equipment at a reasonable price for committed backcountry skiers and snowboarders who are pushing up their level of risk by frequently descending very steep slopes.

The AvaLung Element is the basic AvaLung ready to attach to any AvaLung-ready pack and easily removable when not needed.

The Avalung II Sling is a modern version of the original AvaLung and is designed to be used for backcountry safety on its own

Avalung II Sling

or with non-AvaLung ski packs. It comes in two different sizes that are reasonably adjustable. Get one large enough to wear snugly over your clothing for the best performance.

There are also a number of specifically designed winter backcountry packs that come with a built-in AvaLung.

Many people feel that while the AvaLung is ideal for within-bounds and tree skiing, riders on large open slopes above treeline are better off using an Avalanche Airbag. Some people own both.

Avalanche Airbag Pack

An Avalanche Airbag Pack, sometimes referred to as an Avalanche Balloon Pack, is an inflatable bag that is stored inside a specially designed backpack that also holds other avalanche safety gear as well as personal items. It is deployed by pulling on a handle located where it is easily reached, near one shoulder. Airbag packs are seeing increasing use by guiding companies and other professionals who spend considerable time in avalanche terrain. The snowmobile community and a few hardcore riders are also using them.

There are now two basic systems on the market that inflate the airbag once the trigger is pulled: the original refillable compressed-air cylinder; and a system using a lithium ion battery-powered fan that will inflate the bag several times on a single charge. Though more expensive initially, the latter system avoids having to recharge cylinders and the packs are more acceptable to airlines. They also allow you to practise with the airbag so you know what to expect if you ever have to use it.

The Backcountry Access Float Avalanche Airbag Pack uses a compressed air cartridge for inflation.

Various makes differ in where the deployed bag is positioned. Some wrap around the head and neck, offering protection for those who do a lot of skiing at or below treeline, while others are positioned at the side to protect the body from the shoulders to the hips. There are advantages and disadvantages to both systems. I leave you to read the literature and reviews and decide for yourself.

The major models presently available feature airbags of either 150 L or 200 L. There is also a difference in compactness and capacity among the packs. If you are buying an airbag pack for heli-skiing you are better off with a lighter, more compact one. On the other hand, self-supported, multi-day ski mountaineers will need a larger-capacity pack.

While undoubtedly this gear is a great advance in avalanche survival technology, its expensive cost will be a significant deterrent for the average rider. With more companies making these, the price will hopefully come down.

It is interesting to note that an airbag system was featured in the first edition of this book, in 1983. It took 25 years to develop a commercially viable product!

The bottom line is that while studies have shown that wearing an airbag reduces the mortality rate significantly, most of those who die wearing an airbag do so from trauma or from failure to deploy it.

The Arc'teryx Voltair Avalanche Airbag Pack uses a battery-powered pump to fill the 150 L airbag.

Cell & Satellite Phones, Messenger Devices and Personal Locator Beacons

There are now many recorded instances of avalanche victims being saved using some of these devices. What will each of these do to help you in an emergency?

Smartphones

We are all familiar with smartphones and their capabilities and they can be life savers providing you have network coverage. In Western Canada backcountry, this is rarely.

Satellite Messenger Devices

Messenger systems such as Spot and DeLorme inReach are hand-held satellite communication devices that can determine your location using a GPS system and send messages via its own commercial satellite network. It will work almost anywhere in the world as long as you can see enough sky to access satellites. Its big advantages are that it works where there is no cellular coverage and that the cost is reasonable.

The survivors of a multiple-fatality snowmobile avalanche incident used a SPOT to alert rescuers, who were able to get a helicopter to them before dark to pick them up.

To use these messenger systems you must subscribe to a low-cost service plan. This will provide for the dispatch of emergency responders to your GPS location on activation. While it functions as an emergency locator beacon, it does not emit a homing signal.

Additional functions will allow your family or friends to track your location using Google Maps and to request help from them in a non-emergency situation.

When you request rescue, these units will send a message via satellite to a response centre staffed 24 hours a day by the service provider, who will pass the information on to local search and rescue units. The device will keep trying to send the message until it can lock on to enough satellites. Messenger Devices are probably the best option for the average winter backcountry enthusiast.

Satellite Phones

Theoretically, satellite phones would seem to be the ideal option for anyone riding in serious avalanche country. However, in practice they are not necessarily the best answer. For starters, they are more expensive than messenger devices to both purchase and use.

Unfortunately the two main networks, GlobalStar and Iridium, are not as reliable as they should be, especially in mountainous terrain where satellite visibility may be restricted. There are many reports of people having trouble getting a signal and, when they do manage to place a call, getting dropped. That said, large touring groups should consider this option.

Personal Locator Beacons

If you are on an expedition to really remote areas and all you care about is getting rescued, then carrying a personal locator beacon is worth considering. But **be warned**: this is not an electronic toy. Activating one will trigger an international rescue effort just as if you were a cruise ship in distress or a missing airliner.

The unit most suitable at present for backcountry (as opposed to marine) use is the ACR ResQlink Personal Locator Beacon. On activation it transmits an SOS signal and your GPS coordinates via satellite at a power level 5–10 times higher than messenger systems, as well as emitting a homing signal.

RECCO Reflector

The RECCO Rescue System enables organized rescue teams to quickly find buried avalanche victims. It can be used on the ground or from a helicopter.

The system relies on a small electronic transponder that weighs about 4 g that is designed into commercially available outerwear, helmets, boots and protective gear. It requires no power, no maintenance and has a virtually unlimited lifespan.

Note that it does not replace wearing an avalanche beacon. It does, however, provide one more chance for skiers and snowboarders to be found quickly by organized rescue.

Climbing Rope

Climbers and scramblers can use their climbing rope for protection when crossing narrow gullies or when kicking snow off from above while descending a steep slope. Because of the large forces involved over a period of several seconds, good belaying techniques are crucial. Static belays to trees or rocks should be used if at all possible.

Helmets

Freeriders, out-of-bounds and extreme skiers and boarders and those who do a lot of tree skiing should consider wearing a helmet. Many avalanche victims die from trauma to the head and chest through contact with trees and rocks.

Inclinometer

If you are a serious backcountry skier or boarder you should invest in an inclinometer. There are several different models available that will help you determine slope angle to within 2 or 3 degrees. Some compasses have built-in inclinometers, and if you have an iPhone there are several good, accurate inclinometer apps (page 136).

Group Shelters (Bothy Bags)

Bothy bags provide immediate protection from the elements in the event of a storm or in case of injury while you wait for help. Usually made of ripstop nylon, they weigh very little (300 g or less for a two-person bag) and pack small. All models have vents and some even have windows so you can see the weather outside. Although the windows add weight, they help prevent claustrophobia.

The main advantage of these bags is the extra warmth provided by two or more people. You can get inside with someone on the verge of hypothermia and give them something to eat and drink. Make sure you get a bag that is easy to deploy and repack — they're great for chilly lunch breaks. The larger ones are ideal survival gear for organized groups.

Don't confuse these with bivy sacs. They are not mini tents — they are designed for people to sit in, not lie down in. The two- and four-person bags are not large enough to completely enclose two people lying down.

Even with this limitation, bothy bags are far superior, in my opinion, to space blankets or the single emergency bags currently available in North America.

Having originated in the UK, where they are considered by many as essential gear, bothy bags come in sizes for 2, 4, 8, 10 or 12 people.

These group shelters are starting to become available in North America, with MEC carrying Rab Superlite Shelters and Amazon.com the Terra Nova line of bothy bags.

Travel in Avalanche Terrain

This chapter covers the basics of travelling in backcountry avalanche terrain. It is intended for **Backcountry Tourers**, **Snowshoers**, and other winter backcountry enthusiasts such as **Ice Climbers** and **Scramblers** who traverse through avalanche terrain to get to their climbs and are generally trying to avoid steep slopes. The needs of **Skiers** and **Boarders** who set out specifically to ski slopes in excess of 30° are addressed in the next chapter, *Riding Steep Slopes*.

The basic law of safe travel is **avoid hazardous areas**. For avalanches to occur, snow must lie on slopes steep enough to allow it to slide, so it follows that if steep slopes are avoided by **careful routefinding**, exposure to danger can be reduced or eliminated.

If you stick to simple terrain and avoid periods of extreme instability you can have a rewarding backcountry experience without any exposure to avalanches.

If you're going to be climbing higher up into the mountains, where the terrain is both steeper and potentially more dangerous, you'll need to refine your winter travel skills in order to reduce the risk. You must:

- Learn to read, interpret and apply **Avalanche Forecasts**.

- Be able to **pick a safe route** through Challenging terrain.

- Acquire sufficient **Snowcraft** to be able to assess changes in snowpack conditions that indicate increasing hazard.

- Carry and know how to use safety equipment such as **Avalanche Beacons**, probes and shovels.

- Be prepared to cope with **emergencies** due to fatigue, benightment, equipment failures, weather and avalanches.

Skills You Need to Acquire

There are a number of skills you need to acquire to travel safely through avalanche terrain. They are:

- Basic navigation skills with map, compass and GPS to determine your aspect and elevation.

- You should be able to determine slope angle with reasonable accuracy. This involves estimating or measuring the angle of the snow you are on and estimating slope angles above you (page 136).

- Snowcraft — understanding the various forms of snow — is covered starting on page 137 but is best learned with the help of experienced friends or instructors.

- The ability to recognize terrain features, particularly those that would be terrain traps in the event of an avalanche.

- You need to be able to determine recent wind direction and understand how slabs are formed (page 69).

- Be able to gauge the water content of the snowpack by squeezing a snowball.

- The ability to recognize signs of settlement in the snowpack.

- Knowing how to manage or interact with the other members of your party.

- A knowledge of the human factors that can lead to flawed decision making.

- Realize that people facing complex problems generally make better decisions using simple rules of thumb.

Accepting Risk

The chance of being caught in an avalanche is often your main concern if you venture into avalanche terrain in winter. The complexities of snowpack, weather and terrain create a great deal of uncertainty, and risk is about accepting this uncertainty. Risk is about enjoying your backcountry experience balanced against the chance of being injured or of dying.

Reducing risk requires recognizing **hazard**, and only by doing that can you use your knowledge and experience to manage risk. Avalanche hazard is forecast using the Avalanche Danger Scale.

There are four factors that need to be considered when managing avalanche risk. The first two, **probability** and **consequence**, can be summed up by two very important questions: What is the chance that an avalanche will occur? and What will happen if it does?

For tourers, the basic answer to these questions is in the risk-based forecast — the "Chance of Avalanche" and "Expected Size" icons and the forecaster's travel advice. Riding steep slopes requires stability assessment and terrain evaluation.

Having determined the probability and consequence of an avalanche, you can now focus on managing the risk. The next question is: How exposed am I to the hazard? Can I reduce my **exposure** by picking a safer line through the terrain or by practising safe skiing techniques. Again there is help, in the "Elevation" and "Aspect" icons in the problems section of the forecast.

The last question is: How **vulnerable** am I if an avalanche does occur and how can I reduce my vulnerability? If you are carrying rescue gear and are with people who have practised companion rescue, you have already taken key steps to reduce your vulnerability. Avalanche airbags, Avalungs and RECCO reflectors are also ways to reduce vulnerability for riders in steep terrain.

This complex route up a crevassed glacier under the east face of Mount Balfour, with its steep slopes and threatening séracs, requires all of the skills described above plus a knowledge of glacier travel.

Before You Go

Follow the Season's History

Each time you go out you add to your knowledge of the season's snowpack. How much fresh snow has fallen since your last trip? Has it consolidated? Does a layer of depth hoar still exist on certain slopes? Have any paths avalanched since your last visit? You should speculate why conditions have changed or why a slope has avalanched.

Don't limit your observations to your ski trip; you can see a lot from your car window just travelling to the area. News items by local papers or radio stations about roads blocked by avalanches, ski area closures or avalanche accidents all help to build up an overall picture as the winter progresses. You've likely seen those pre-season stickers for downhill skiers: "Think Snow." Thinking snow all season will make your trip into the backcountry not only more enjoyable but a lot safer.

Form an Opinion on Snow Stability

If you are skiing in your local area and have followed the buildup of the snowpack and recent changes in weather, you should be able to form an opinion, no matter how rough, about current snow stability. Build up an overall picture as the winter progresses, and revise and refine this picture every time you go skiing. Choose your destination for the day with this picture in mind, and as the day progresses compare your stability prediction with actual snow conditions. Don't let your desire to cross a slope interfere with your evaluation of its stability.

Ed LaChapelle summed it up when he said: *The person who wonders about snow stability only when standing on the edge of an avalanche path about to be crossed has thought of the problem too late.* He also said you *should always have an opinion, no matter how vague or inaccurate, about the current state of snow stability.*

With experience you will be able to revise and refine your opinion to arrive at a more accurate evaluation.

Check the Avalanche Forecast

In many areas you can obtain up-to-date avalanche forecasts prepared by professional forecasters. While these reports are usually for large regions or even for whole mountain areas, in times of high or extreme instability they will sound a warning bell. They will often indicate the conditions that are causing instability such as persistent buried surface hoar or wind-loaded slopes of a certain aspect. Paying attention to all the details in the avalanche forecast is one of the prerequisites for safe skiing.

Assess the Hazard Trend

Pay particular attention to hazard trends. Most avalanche forecasts will indicate whether the hazard is increasing or decreasing. Changes in avalanche hazard are usually the result of changes in weather, so make sure you get the most recent weather forecast. In the field, the presence of any of the Indicators of Danger listed on page 129 will indicate increasing hazard.

Pick a Safe Trail

If there is a warning of High or Extreme avalanche hazard in effect, you should either discard more ambitious plans and pick a completely safe trail or stay at home. Completely safe trails are those which do not cross over or under any slope that is steep enough to generate an avalanche. Even if you consider yourself competent in hazard evaluation, take note of extreme avalanche hazard warnings. Are your predictions likely to be more accurate than those of the professional avalanche forecaster?

Wait for the Right Conditions

Successful (surviving) extreme skiers make meticulous preparations and wait for exactly the right conditions before making their descent. Following their example, you should wait for the right conditions before embarking on a particular tour. Be flexible in your choice of destinations; if conditions are not right, go somewhere else.

Open ridges like this one are safe travel routes. Bowls, like the one to the left of the photograph, are among the most dangerous terrain features. Evaluate snow conditions very carefully before you take off down any steep bowl. Photo Clair Israelson.

Starting Your Trip

A large proportion of mountain accidents, including avalanche accidents, happen as the direct or indirect result of two errors of judgment: late starts and poor routefinding.

Leave Trip Details with Someone

Always leave word of your trip with some responsible person. Key points they, and potential rescuers, need to know are:

- The number of people involved, their names, telephone numbers and contact number in case of an emergency. The contact numbers will also allow the responsible person to contact everyone if the party is alright but delayed for some reason.

- Departure trailhead name, and make, colour and licence number of vehicles, including province or state.

- Details of the trip: route, possible alternatives, date of departure, expected return date and details if the trip ends at a different location.

- For a multi-day trip you should also leave an overdue date and time.

- If you are going into an area with cellular coverage or have a satellite phone, leave the phone numbers and, if necessary, instructions on how to use the satellite phone.

- The responsible person should know who to call in case of emergency. Leave them several phone numbers in order of calling priority.

Re-evaluate the Hazard

- Are conditions as you expected?

- Is the weather forecast correct? Pay attention to the amount of any new snow, rain, high wind or a sudden rise in temperature. All these are potential indicators of increasing hazard.

- Review the avalanche forecast in light of the aspect and elevation zones you will encounter on your trip.

If you get a bad feeling as a result of this re-evaluation, consult with your companions to see if they still want to proceed.

Check-out Your Companions

Some leaders are reluctant to do this, as they feel people might be offended. My climbing partner and I had a rule that we would always check each other, especially when doing high-risk activities such as rappelling under stress. Although we rarely found anything wrong, we felt it added considerably to our safety.

- Is everyone's equipment in good working order: skis, bindings, poles, packs? Does everyone have adequate clothing?
- Does everyone have their emergency equipment: beacons, shovel, probe? No forgotten beacons?
- Is everyone healthy? No flu, pulled muscles or other ailment or injury? If someone has a problem, how will they cope with it? Do they have someone who is willing to go back with them if they can't continue?
- How is everyone's attitude? Is anyone too cold, too tired or somewhat hungover? Do you have a cohesive party? No bickering or personality conflicts? Is everyone still up for the trip?

Discuss the Plan

- Is it still achievable? Do you have enough daylight to complete the trip? Agree on a turnaround time if there is any doubt.
- Brief everyone on possible escape routes if avalanche conditions are more hazardous than you anticipated or snow conditions slow down travel.
- Review how you would deal with an emergency such as an injury. Do you have enough spare clothing to allow a couple of people to wait for help in reasonable comfort? Who has a bothy bag? Does anyone have a stove, pot and provisions to make hot drinks?

Checking Avalanche Beacons

At the start of each day all avalanche beacons should be checked using the following procedure:

- One member/leader turns their unit to transmit and holds it at a constant

orientation, while the rest of the group, their units switched to receive, move off along the trail.

- Each person stops when they lose the signal (changing beacon orientation if necessary to find the optimum position).
- When the group is satisfied that everyone's beacon is working properly, they switch to transmit.
- The leader switches their beacon to receive and joins the group, checking that it too is receiving properly, before switching it back to transmit.

During Your Trip

Every group travelling through avalanche terrain needs to:

- Continuously evaluate potential hazard at every stage of the route.
- Practise safe travel techniques.
- Choose a safe route through everchanging terrain.
- Constantly observe snow and weather conditions.
- Make rational decisions.

Indicators of Danger

Certain indicators of danger should never be ignored:

- Evidence of avalanche activity during the past two days on slopes of similar orientation.
- Settling and fracturing of the snowpack.
- New snow accompanied by high winds.
- Any sudden warming trend, whether due to hot sun on a slope or incoming chinook winds.

If any of these indicators are present the risk has significantly increased. You should pay particular attention to choosing a safe route and be very careful to minimize your exposure to steeper slopes above.

Hazard Evaluation Tools

As I mentioned in the chapter on Trip Planning, there have been many attempts in recent years to develop decision-making tools for the winter recreationist. Research in other disciplines indicates that a simple, easy to use checklist can be an effective way of managing human factors when making decisions. A recent Canadian rule-based decision support tool for avalanche terrain, based on accident data and input from the avalanche safety community, has been found to have good potential for reducing accidents.

Avaluator 2 Slope Evaluation Card

Developed by Avalanche Canada as part of its Avaluator™ 2 Trip Planning Tool (page 111), the Slope Evaluation card helps you recognize dangerous avalanche conditions and make informed decisions.

This resource, a separate, wallet-sized plastic card, contains two lists of factors that are indicators of increased avalanche danger: a list of Avalanche Conditions; and a list of Terrain Characteristics. On each list a score of +1 or +2 is assigned if applicable. The total score for each list is applied to the grid on the reverse of the card to indicate the risk of avalanche danger. You decide whether to proceed depending on your backcountry avalanche experience.

The Slope Evaluation card is primarily intended to be used before you leave the trailhead and during your trip based on ongoing observations. However, you can also use it as an extra step in your trip planning by consulting weather forecasts, avalanche bulletins and knowledge of your destination area.

An accompanying booklet explains the Avaluator 2 in more detail and offers tips on good travel habits and rescue and first aid. It's a major step forward in providing a useful backcountry decision guidance tool for winter outdoor enthusiasts, the culmination of three years of work by the folks at Avalanche Canada.

The most important factor is the **Danger Rating** of **Considerable** or **High**.

Checking this factor alone should be enough to warn you away from venturing onto or near the bottom of slopes steeper than 30°. Remember that most backcountry touring fatalities occur at these danger levels. **This level of risk is unacceptable for inexperienced backcountry tourers whose goal is to travel safely in the backcountry**.

While you may tour safely in Simple or even Challenging terrain at these danger levels, you need good routefinding skills and the discipline to avoid steep slopes.

It is when the **Danger Level** is **Moderate** that you really need to pay attention to the other clues if your route takes you onto steep terrain.

Remember that the Avaluator is a tool that helps you recognize avalanche danger. It does not predict the stability of a given slope, and just because you are in the "green" area of the Avaluator doesn't mean you are completely safe. You still need to be constantly aware of the terrain to avoid straying onto isolated slabs.

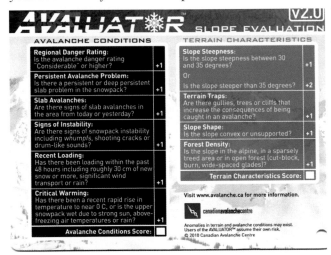

Avaluator™.
Courtesy Avalanche Canada.

Safe Travel

A number of basic precepts for safe travel in mountainous terrain (and therefore, by definition, avalanche terrain) have developed over a century or more of mountaineering. While you may choose to break or ignore some of these rules as a calculated risk in order to achieve a particular goal, you should do so with full knowledge of what you are doing and the extent of the risks you are taking.

Stay Together

It's very important in avalanche terrain that the party travel as a cohesive unit. No one should go so far ahead of the main party that they are only seen at lunch stops. Nor should a person be allowed to fall behind to the extent that they lose sight of the person in front for more than a few minutes. This rule becomes more important as the weather deteriorates; those in front tend to press on faster and faster while the slower members of the group at the back slow down even more. In such cases the leader must use considerable restraint in controlling their tendency to rush ahead. Both psychologically and from the point of view of keeping warm, it's better to slow down the pace than have to stop and wait. When skiing down through trees, encourage the buddy system where skiers pair up and keep in touch with each other all the way down.

Avoid Steep Slopes

When a Moderate hazard warning is in effect, it's generally acceptable to risk skiing trails that cross the runout zones of avalanche paths. Although the chance of being caught by an avalanche is very slight, you should still take the basic precaution of travelling 50 to 100 metres apart on wide slopes and cross narrow slopes one at a time. Avoid slopes steeper than 25°; in other words, any slope the average cross-country skier would think twice about going down on skinny skis. The safest routes are valley bottoms and the tops of ridges.

Rest Stops

Stop well away from the runout zones of potential avalanche slopes. This may sound obvious, but families out ski touring have a habit of stopping for lunch on large, open slopes with a good view, happily oblivious of the avalanche slopes above them.

Food and Drink

Eat and drink regularly during the day. Too many people feel they can exist on a candy bar and a handful of nuts and make up the deficiency when the trip's over. In an avalanche emergency it's important that survivors have the sufficient reserve of energy needed to help search for the victims.

Turning Back

There are two basic safety reasons for turning back from your tour.

- If you are obviously not going to make it out by dark. An impromptu benightment, while inconvenient in summer, is much more serious in winter.

- If there is evidence of serious instability in the snowpack, such as signs of recent avalanching on the slopes around you. Only if you are certain you are not venturing into avalanche terrain should you go on.

Often a decision to turn back can involve a lot of mental courage, especially on the part of the leader of an organized group. No one really likes to turn back unless they are cold and miserable, and on a warm, sunny day few people even think of avalanche hazard. If you do decide to retreat, explain your reasons to the whole party.

Travel during Storm

Sometimes there's no alternative but to travel through avalanche terrain during a heavy snowstorm. Since the greatest danger from avalanches is during or immediately after the storm, make an extra effort to reach safety during the first few hours of snowfall. Observe the buildup of snow and note the direction of the wind. Avoid the vicinity of steeper slopes which may be subject to storm-slab avalanches. Pay particular attention to routefinding—difficult enough in a whiteout—so you don't wander onto suspect slopes unintentionally. Travel will be slowed down and there will be a tendency for the party to bunch up, exposing the whole group to danger at one time.

Consider what happened to a guided party of 24 skiers in the Citadel Pass area of Banff National Park a few years ago. The party, skiing to a helicopter rendezvous during a blizzard, was off the normal route, which crosses an exposed open ridge, and was embarked on a more sheltered route below treeline. Although the party had triggered a small slide earlier on in the traverse which carried one member of the party down the slope for 30 metres, the guide elected to carry on along the same high line; he had arranged to meet the helicopter in the late afternoon. The weather was now worsening; it was snowing heavily and visibility was reduced to a few metres, effectively hiding the steep slopes above. At 2:00 p.m., as the party were skiing across a sparsely timbered hillside, the slope fractured high above them and a large avalanche flowed down

through the trees, taking with it seven skiers and completely burying five of them. Hurried probing uncovered four of the victims almost immediately, but the fifth person, a woman, was not recovered until an estimated 30 to 45 minutes after the accident. By that time she had died of suffocation.

This incident is a prime example of bad route selection during extremely hazardous avalanche conditions. After the first avalanche, which indicated beyond all doubt the instability of the snowpack, the guide should have reassessed his proposed route, taking instead a longer but lower line across gentler slopes even if this meant being late for the rendezvous. Once the original mistake had been made, two other factors contributed to the tragedy: the party had closed up because of bad weather, and they were not carrying rescue beacons, because the normal route they were to have taken didn't warrant them. Had beacons been used, it's probable the victim would have been recovered much faster and might still be alive today.

Photo Bruno Engler.

This relatively shallow slope was the site of the Mount St. Helens accident (see below) in which five people died when their camp was overwhelmed by a slab avalanche. Note signs of further avalanching on adjacent slopes. Photo Ronald V. Emetaz, courtesy U.S. Forest Service.

Campsites

Avoid setting up camp below a slope which could accumulate enough snow to slide. Because slab avalanches can originate on slopes as shallow as 25°, the danger is not always obvious. During the search for two students on Mount St. Helens in 1975, *the majority of the experienced rescue personnel appeared little concerned of the possibility of another avalanche even with the knowledge that at least one had occurred just two and a half days before.* Such a slope rising above the camp established by a beginners Snow & Ice School on Forsythe Glacier was becoming unstable: warm weather in the middle of the month had created a surface crust. Then, between the 23rd and 25th of April, about 50 cm of snow fell, accompanied by a slight drop in temperature. Early on the 26th, the day the 29 climbers were toiling upward to the campsite, the sky cleared and the temperature rose. It would have been a fine day but for the wind, which was gathering strength; in fact, by the time the tents

were up and snow caves built, a strong, gusty crosswind was piling loose snow up against the tents and conditions were so unpleasant that plans for a crevasse rescue practice were postponed. By now the slope above was in prime condition to avalanche and at 26 minutes past 8, some 500 metres above the camp, a soft slab released and came pouring down, trapping most people inside their tents, either burying them or pushing them down the slope as it swept by. Fast action by the survivors probing with anything at hand such as ice axes and tent poles saved many lives.

When speculating why some people lived and others died, some interesting observations were made about the siting of tents. Those placed on cut-and-fill platforms (the angle of the slope was 28°) were propelled down the slope and only partially buried. Other tents dug 2 m into the slope were completely buried; all but one of their occupants died. Snow caves were unaffected, although one entrance was blocked and had to be cleared from the outside. This serves as a reminder to take shovels inside a snow cave with you.

Although snow caves are potentially safe on steep slopes where there is a chance of slides coming down from above, you must be extremely careful in your choice of slope. Don't dig into slab and don't site them in gullies, which are natural chutes for avalanches and stone fall. In certain conditions even the top of a snow gully is hazardous. Consider what happened to four climbers during a winter attempt on the East Ridge of Mount Edith Cavell (Canadian Rockies). All afternoon they had been climbing up a long snow gully parallel to the usual summer route. Around 5 p.m., now close to the top, they decided to bivouac. The deep layers of drifted snow in the gully were supported by a weak layer of depth hoar next to the ground, which, though capable of sustaining the weight of the climbers, collapsed during the deeper excavation of the snow cave. Unnoticed by the climbers, the stability of the snowpack had been further decreased by a substantial temperature rise throughout the day. The resulting avalanche swept the climbers back down the gully and killed three of them.

Ridges are usually safe, but be wary of camping below the lee slope of a ridge. An accident in the New Zealand Alps in the winter of 1966 had several unusual features which are worth thinking about. A rescue party was out searching for a group of four climbers missing on Mount Rolleston in Arthur's Pass National Park. The weather was atrocious; heavy snow, the first of the winter, was being piled on lee slopes by the prevailing northwesterly winds. The rescuers pitched camp on a small spur abutting a face below the summit ridge of the mountain. The face, which lay on the windward side of the ridge, was a perfectly safe route to the summit; the party climbed up and down it all the next day. On the second evening, the storm ended. With the cessation of snow came an unexpected change in the wind: it began to blow hard out of the south, moving snow previously dumped on the southern glacier over the summit ridge onto the previously safe face. A cornice developed and a large area of slab below that. Sometime in the middle of the night, only a few hours after it formed, the slab released. Although most of the avalanche parted on hitting the spur, sliding harmlessly down either side of it, one wave of snow washed over the top, burying tents to a depth of 2 to 3 metres. One man sleeping in the tent closest to the face died.

Recognizing Avalanche Slopes

Most major avalanche slopes can be easily recognized: clean swaths cut through the forest; steep, treeless gullies and steep, open slopes are obvious. While many people, such as highmarking snowmobilers, get caught on the obvious slopes, it's the relatively small, insignificant slopes that catch backcountry skiers and boarders, when no one has noticed subtle changes of terrain features onto which they have unthinkingly strayed. While there is no substitute for local experience in such areas, there are often indistinct clues which can be picked up by careful observation.

Look for signs of previous avalanche activity: trees with lower branches missing or broken, decapitated trees, trees with no limbs or with fresh scars on the uphill side. In open, skiable timber these may be your only indication. Look for fracture lines where a slope has cracked but not avalanched, a change in snow depth and texture, mounds of snow, or dirty snow mixed with rocks and upturned trees. During summer travel notice the location of avalanche debris and of lingering snow patches in gullies and valley bottoms.

Opposite: Small trees which lean downslope are the result of snow creep and regular avalanche activity.

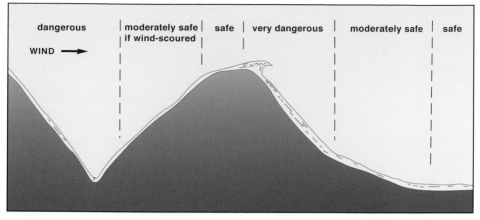

dangerous | moderately safe if wind-scoured | safe | very dangerous | moderately safe | safe

WIND →

V-shaped valley bottoms and lee slopes are the most dangerous routes to travel. Ridgetops and flat ground well away from the foot of steep slopes are the safest.

Choosing a Safe Route

Nowhere is the skill of routefinding more important than in avalanche country. The route must not only be speedy and require the minimum of effort, but also be safe from avalanches. Good routefinding is learned by experience, by following experienced leaders through a variety of terrain in all weather conditions. It depends on planning, careful observation, a knowledge of land forms and snow conditions and the ability to make sensible decisions based on all the available information. Because evaluation of all the factors which may lead to an avalanche is a very complex subject and one which a normal skiing or climbing party is ill equipped to make, always allow a wide margin of safety when making a routefinding decision.

When picking a route through potential avalanche terrain:

- Follow flat valley bottoms, paying attention to the slopes above you and any obvious avalanche paths.
- Minimize exposure to cornices above.
- Choose low-angled (less than 25°) slopes and avoid getting boxed in by increasingly steep terrain.
- Make use of treed ridgelines providing they are not too steep.
- Use ridge crests, but stay well back from corniced edges.
- Avoid travelling above terrain traps.
- If you have to cross a potential start zone, do so as high as possible. Travel where the snow is deepest and avoid weak spots and rocky outcrops.

Determining Slope Angle

Estimating the Angle

Judging slope angle is not easy. Fortunately, most of us tend to overestimate it and so keep off steeper slopes. Here's a quick, simple guide for skiers to use:

25° Intermediate downhill terrain. Competent ski tourers will be able to parallel ski in good conditions.

30° An enjoyable slope for the good skier or boarder and the expert backcountry tourer. Most backcountry tourers will probably be kick turning and traversing. The average talus slope in the mountains is about 30 degrees. If you need to kick turn on your ascent track you are on a slope 30° or steeper.

35° A challenging slope for the good skier or boarder and expert telemark skier. Skiers will be using alpine-style backcountry equipment. Slopes below cliffs and above the talus fan in gullies are 35° or steeper.

40° An expert skier or boarder will feel exhilarated on such a slope. Anyone less than expert will feel decidedly uncomfortable. Few backcountry tourers, even expert telemark skiers, would venture on a slope of such steepness. Dry loose-snow avalanches tend to release on slopes over 40°.

TiltMeter inclinometer app for iPhone.

Measuring the Angle

One problem with measuring slope angle is that you have to be on the slope and so have already made a commitment.

The most accurate way is to use an **inclinometer** (clinometer). Backcountry Access makes a simple, inexpensive Slope Meter, and a number of compasses now on the market have simple inclinometers built into them. There are a number of good inclinometer applications available for the iPhone. Buy an inclinometer that is easy to read when you are out in the backcountry. If you are on a fairly even slope you can point your ski up the slope and put the inclinometer on it; otherwise, sight up the edge of the inclinometer to get the average slope.

Back Country Access Slope Meter.

Slope Angle and the Danger Scale

If the hazard is Considerable or higher, you need to estimate the angle of the steepest part of the slope above you, not just the lower part of the slope you intend to ski or board. If the forecast indicates the possibility of persistent weak layers underlying significant storm slab, then there is a very real possibility of remote triggering of the slope above you. If the hazard is High or Extreme, keep off all slopes steeper than 30°.

If the hazard is Low or Moderate, then you only need to be concerned with the terrain immediately above you and within 20 m either side of your track.

Measuring Slope Angle with Poles

Another method of measuring slope angle is to use two ski poles. Lay one pole up the slope with the tip uphill and the handle nearest to you. Make an impression in the snow at the tip and at the grip. Raise the pole, leaving the tip in position on the snow and, putting the handles of the two poles together, let the second pole pendulum vertically down. If the tip of the second pole touches the snow at the impression of the handle of the first pole, then the slope angle is 30°. For every 10 cm the tip is downhill from the impression of the handle, add 3° to the slope angle.

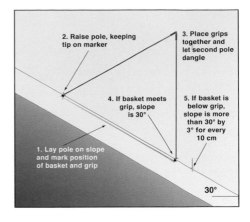

2. Raise pole, keeping tip on marker

3. Place grips together and let second pole dangle

4. If basket meets grip, slope is 30°

5. If basket is below grip, slope is more than 30° by 3° for every 10 cm

1. Lay pole on slope and mark position of basket and grip

30°

Snowcraft

Snowcraft is a little-used term for an almost lost art. Anchorage avalanche educator Doug Fesler calls it "wearing your avalanche eyeballs." Like navigation, it is the art of observing, storing and compiling into a picture a multitude of minute details. Observation is the key to safe travel through avalanche terrain and a major factor in evaluating the stability of a snow slope.

Look for recent avalanche activity, settling of the snowpack or cracks in the surface due to settlement. Feel the snow with your skis to detect any changes to hardness or texture. If you are following in the tracks of other skiers, step out of the trail occasionally. If there is fresh snow, check the depth as you ascend and evaluate how well it is bonded to the old snow surface. Look for signs of drifting. What has been the direction of the wind recently? Keep your eyes open and your senses alert. Gather as much information as you can.

Good ski guides depends largely on "feel." The "feel" of the snow beneath their skis as they turn and a "sense" of terrain. Their built-in wealth of experience attunes them to anticipate potential problems as they ski various types of terrain, just as good drivers sense potentially dangerous situations developing around them on the highway.

Weather

Don't forget to observe the weather. Changes in weather, particularly heavy snowfall, current wind speed and direction or a sudden rise in temperature all have important effects on snow stability.

Observing Snow Conditions

Observation is the key to safe travel in avalanche terrain—observation not only of the mountain scenery but of the multitude of clues indicating snow conditions visible to the perceptive traveller. Some of the things you should look for are as follows.

Evidence of Avalanching

This is the most important clue to instability you are likely to be given. Use other slopes in the area as indicator slopes. If nearby slopes have avalanched, observe how much snow has come down, how far the slides have run, and the depth of the fracture line if they are slab avalanches.

In particular look for recent avalanches on slopes of similar aspect to those you wish to cross. New snow sluffing off cliffs or snowballs rolling down steep slopes are an indication either of settling and strengthening of the snowpack or of isothermal conditions developing.

Note how the slab has fractured around the base of the rocks and at a number of isolated rocks. In this case the slab was recently deposited in moderate winds. Photo Leon Kubbernus.

Wind Direction

You must always be aware of the direction from which the wind has been blowing and of its approximate strength. Snow blowing off ridges or cornices, rime, and drifts around rocks and trees are all good indicators. As a general rule the more pronounced the feature, the stronger the wind. Knowledge of wind direction and strength will enable you to decide if you are on a lee slope and likely to encounter slab. Refer to the section on determining wind direction (page 147) later in this chapter.

Aspect

The aspect of a slope to both sun and wind is most important. If you've ventured onto a lee slope, look for layers of soft or hard slab. On a spring ski tour, watch the shadows; when they point to a slope like a warning finger, the slope is receiving the maximum amount of heat. In depth hoar country, a north slope may consist of little but loose, highly unstable sugar-snow crystals early in the winter.

Rapid Solar Warming

Rapid warming due to strong solar radiation or chinook winds is always a cause for concern. The upper 30 to 40 cm of a previously stable snowpack can become unstable very quickly, even when air temperatures are still below zero.

A number of ice climbers have been swept off shaded climbs in sub-zero temperatures by avalanches caused by rapid warming of sunlit slopes above.

Some recent work on this subject indicates that such warming tends to occur on east- to southeast-facing slopes of 35–40° in March or April. I suspect that latitude will have an effect in that slope angles may be lower for more southerly latitudes. Rapid warming was also observed to occur in low-density new snow, often on the first sunny day after a storm.

The Snow Surface

Observe the texture of the snow surface and note any changes. Is it just a local effect caused by wind or are you on a slope

Windblown slopes such as this one at 16,000 ft. on Mount Steele are usually safe to travel on.

of different aspect? Look for wind or sun crusts, surface hoar, riming or convex furrows, which are signs of rain. Some snow surface features like etching and rippling indicate previous wind direction.

Etching forms beautiful parallel lines on a hard snow surface. The steep edge of the lines faces the direction from which the wind was blowing.

Rippling A light wind causes rippling of the snow surface by sorting particles of different sizes on the ground. Smaller particles are picked up and deposited on the lee side of larger ones, thus promoting the formation of tiny mounds which eventually grow a few centimetres in height. Examination of a rippled snow surface will show that the shallower side of the ripples faces the wind.

One difficulty in determining the direction of wind from ripples is that once the snow has hardened there is little free snow on the surface and so the formation of ripples stops. If the wind continues, erosion begins and changes the appearance of the ripples by cutting into the shallow windward side and depositing snow on the lee side, thus reversing the shape. The only guide you have as to which process is taking place is to test the hardness of the snow surface. Soft, powdery snow is probably forming ripples, while hard, compact ripples are probably being eroded.

Form Widespread areas of wind slab can often be recognized from a distance by the smooth, rounded form the terrain assumes. Look for and learn to recognize such areas. It's interesting to note that in hard wind slab the grains of snow tend to be all one size, thus inhibiting the initiation of rippling.

Cracks Glide of the snowpack over the ground may form cracks in the surface, which should be taken as a warning sign of possible isothermal slides. In spring such cracks may widen over a period of time before avalanching occurs.

In cold snow, cracks running ahead of your skis are a sure sign you are standing on slab, an important warning of instability which must not be ignored.

Pinwheels and snowballs are often seen rolling down steep slopes on warm days and are an indication of surface melting of moist surface layers. Think about what is happening beneath the surface and check for deeper moist layers that might release as a wet snow avalanche.

Snowballs rolling down the slope is evidence that the surface layers of the snow are warming up. The concave, V-shaped channels were caused by rain a few days previously.

The Feel of the Snow under Your Skis

With experience it's possible to assess snow conditions by feeling changes in consistency as your skis slide through the snow.

Change in the Type of Snow

Learn to recognize when you go from one type of snow to another. Sometimes there's no visible indication, but the snow will just feel different. If you're using waxes, you may suddenly find you are slipping or that your skis are balling up so you can't glide as easily. Perhaps trail breaking becomes either easier or harder. Why has the snow changed? There are many answers; think about them and try to decide the reason which fits your present circumstances.

Settling

One feeling everyone will recognize once it has been experienced is the scary, sinking feeling as slabs settle underfoot. Sometimes this is a gentle subsidence, sensed rather than felt, a slight settling which produces no visible signs at the snow surface. This is a sure indication of storm slab. If you're on a steep slope when the settling occurs you'll be relieved to know that the snow has settled without avalanching. But ten paces on, it may avalanche rather than settle. It's your decision: retreat or risk it.

As wind slabs become harder, settlement will be more pronounced and you will actually feel the drop. There will be an audible "whumpf" and often some visible sign of settlement on the snow surface such as dishing or cracking.

Hard Slab

Once experienced, hard wind slab has a recognizable feel to it. It usually feels harder than wind crust and the surface has a sort of smooth, velvety texture. In some instances the point of a ski pole won't be able to penetrate the surface. Sometimes the snow will have a hollow feeling, especially high in the mountains where depth hoar actually creates a space beneath the slab, leaving it unsupported. *On Bridger Peak, Montana, a ski tour leader led his party off a dangerous slope about 15 seconds before it slid. "In spite of the fact that initial testing had given no warning of hazard conditions the party leader became increasingly worried about slab avalanches as the party progressed. He later said that he sensed a kind of "hollow feeling" to the snow. After-the-fact probing indicated a metre and a half slab with 30 cm of depth hoar underneath, which the initial shallow probing had failed to reveal.* Failure of such dangerous slabs is dramatic, with a sudden, jolting drop accompanied by an audible cracking of the surface which may extend for a considerable distance across the slope.

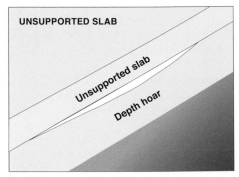

Depth hoar may settle under hard wind slab, leaving a space several centimetres deep. Such slabs have a characteristic hollow feeling to them.

Movement of Skis

The way your skis move through the snow is another indication of snow conditions. If your skis tend to skid sideways, you may be on crust, hard slab or ice. If your skis subside gently into the snow as you break trail but are hard to push forward or lift out, you are probably skiing in soft storm slab. When your skis or crampons ball up in new or settling snow, it's an indication of a rise in temperature. Consider how much the temperature is rising and the effect it might have on the stability of the snowpack.

Observing Your Ski Tracks

You can learn a lot by observing your tracks: how much the snow has consolidated, its moisture content, and whether you are straying into an area of hard or soft slab.

How Far Your Skis Sink

If your skis don't sink in at all, then you're skiing on either hard wind slab, wind or sun crust, or ice. On a side slope, skis will tend to slip sideways, pushing off any loose surface snow. A glance at your tracks will soon reveal if you are on ice, but the difference between wind slab and wind crust is rather more difficult to discern. Both wind crust and sun crust, providing the surface is not obscured by fresh snow, exhibit some form of erosion, deposition or uneven melting. Slab, particularly harder slab, is usually quite smooth and deposited in distinctive, rounded, drift-like shapes with gentle contours. If you find your skis always sinking in to the same depth, you

should suspect wind slab. On the other hand, if the surface consists of alternating breakable and hard crust, you are probably on consolidated wind-blown snow.

Try to relate the depth to which your skis sink to the total depth of the most recent snowfall. For instance, if there has been a 30 cm snowfall and your skis sink in only 5 cm, then the snow is well consolidated; it has either undergone rounding or been formed into slab. If, however, you sink to a depth of 20 cm, then little settlement has occurred and conditions may still be very dangerous.

In practice it appears that the potentially dangerous types of snow are those which produce unusually hard or unusually soft layers in the snowpack. Obviously, if you are sinking in up to your thighs, there is a large enough quantity of unconsolidated snow to give an avalanche of devastating proportions.

Appearance

Good snow at a moderate temperature packs evenly into firm ski tracks. The sides cut down cleanly and hold together without the snow collapsing onto the bottom of the trail. This is a sign that metamorphism is taking place and that the snow has strengthened. If the snow collapses from the sides onto the bottom of the trail and appears sparkling, almost crystalline, then you are probably skiing through recrystallized snow.

Soft storm slab may be indicated if blocks slide out between your skis—the second skier in line will often notice this—or if your skis start slipping sideways or backward on easy grades.

Icy or wet tracks are the result of melt–freeze metamorphism. The snowpack should be examined to see how far down the snow is melting. Free water on the surface is a sign of dangerous thaw conditions in the mountains, meaning that the whole depth of the snowpack is probably close to 0°C. Keep off any slope of 15° or more if these conditions occur.

Suspect soft storm slab when blocks break up between your skis.

When breaking trail in cold, dry climates, particularly early in the season, there will be times when you break right through to the ground. In most cases you'll find a layer of depth hoar at the bottom of the snowpack.

Kick Turns

When climbing a steep slope using kick turns, note the behaviour of the snow at each turn. Does a wedge of snow slide out and if so how thick is it? Is any snow being pulled from above? Where is the sliding layer? Is there more than one sliding layer? Is the snow of the same consistency each time you turn? You may well be in firm, consolidated snow at one end of a traverse and in slab at the other.

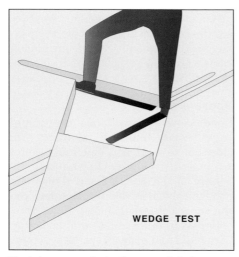

Watch the snow on the inside corner of a kick turn. Does it break loose as a cohesive slab? Do a Hand Shear test.

The Difference between Wind Slab and Wind Crust

Many tourers have difficulty distinguishing between snow that has been shaped by wind such as wind-rippled snow and sastrugi, which are usually safe, and wind-deposited snow such as cushions and slabs, which are often unsafe. Skiers often find it difficult to discern whether they are on wind crust or wind slab, especially if there is a layer of fresh snow on top.

The major difference between slab and crust, and one that indicates whether or not the slope is safe, is that slab has little bonding to the layer underneath, while crust is more firmly attached to the underlayers.

The second basic difference is the aspect of the slope. Slab is found mainly on lee slopes and wind crust on exposed windward slopes. Due to the vagaries of eddying wind currents, however, wind slab has sometimes been found on ridge crests where one would not normally expect to see it.

Wind crust often shows wind rippling or etching; slabs nearly always have a characteristically smooth, rounded appearance. Both forms break up into blocks, but whereas slabs often settle with an ominous "whumpf" sound and cracks shoot out from your skis over a large area, crust will break underfoot only as you pass over it.

Test Slopes

Detour onto any small, steep slope along your route, jump up and down on top, then ski or board back to your uptrack, bearing down to try and cut away a layer of snow. While this is not a conclusive test, any failure is a red flag and another piece of information to file away for later.

Cutting large, steep slopes is a much dicier business and should only be considered by skiers and boarders as part of their evaluation of a slope prior to descending it (page 182).

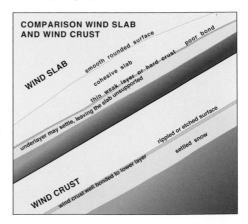

Ski Pole Test

Use

The Ski Pole test is a means of checking snow layers in the top metre or so of the snowpack. It consists of pushing the pole into the surface at a controlled rate and feeling the changes in resistance as various snow layers are encountered. Although used to check for specific indications of hazard such as hard wind slab and depth hoar, it should never be used as the sole judge of snow stability, but rather as an indication that snow conditions have changed and that further testing is desirable.

Limitations

This test has a number of limitations: it's impossible to penetrate more than a few centimetres into heavy wet snow; the length of a ski pole and an arm limits the total depth that can be probed; and finally, the ski pole test will not confirm soft slab, although it will give an indication that slab might exist. If soft slab is suspected, the ski pole test must be backed up by other tests.

Where To Test

Ski Pole tests should be carried out regularly in avalanche terrain; often a second's pause is enough to detect a significant change in the snow. Before venturing onto a large slope, test a small slope of the same aspect first, making sure the elevation is as close as possible to the estimated trigger zone of the larger slope.

How To Test

Always test at right angles to the snow surface. Using the basket end first, push the pole smoothly into the snow with just enough pressure to overcome the resistance. Try not to force or jerk the pole down. Too much pressure and you'll lurch through the snowpack without feeling anything. If the snow is too hard, reverse the pole and use the handle end, making sure before you start that you don't have loose grips. Push in as far as possible, down to the ground if the snowpack is shallow or to arm's length if the snow is soft enough.

Once you've made the hole, withdraw the pole slowly, letting the basket press against the side of the hole. This way the hard and soft layers can be felt. Another technique for examining snow layers is to move the handle in a circle to form a cone-shaped hole in the snow. In this way you can examine the top 30 centimetres.

If you need to know the total depth of the snowpack, use a sectional avalanche probe. Generally, though, the tourer is only concerned with the top metre or two of the snowpack.

When conducting a Ski Pole test, always push the pole in at right angles to the snow.

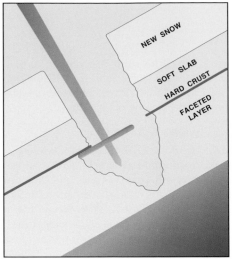

By drawing the basket against the side of the hole, it's easy to feel the hard layers. The thickness of the faceted layer can be estimated by feeling the underside of the settled snow above.

Interpreting Resistance

Little resistance Unsettled new snow, depth hoar or new storm slab.

Stiff Well-settled snow, firm wind crust or soft slab.

Hard Compacted snow, medium slab or wind crust. Handle end will have to be used.

Very hard Hard slab. Point of ski pole will hardly mark the surface.

Ideal situation Steadily increasing resistance with depth and no very hard or very soft layers.

Sudden breakthrough Probably a layer of depth hoar. Check several places in the area to obtain an average depth.

Very hard and very soft layers Any thin (<10 cm) layers that are very hard or very soft in the top metre of the snowpack should be investigated further. Do a Hand Shear test to check whether the layers are well bonded to one another.

Hand Shear Test

Use

Do this test if you suspect a shallow, weak surface layer of snow deposited by wind, precipitation or a combination of both. If you have made a kick turn recently and noticed a wedge of snow has slid, stop and do a Hand Shear test.

Limitations

The Hand Shear test can only be used to identify weak layers in about the top 40 cm of the snowpack and is most effective when done on a slope of at least 30°.

Where To Test

This fairly quick test should be repeated whenever there is a significant change in aspect or if the Ski Pole test indicates a change in snow conditions or a mix of weak and hard layers.

How To Test

Start by scooping out a trench in the snow big enough to allow the block you will cut out to slide. Using your gloved hand, isolate a block about 30 cm square and 40 cm deep on the uphill side of the trench. Some people use their ski pole after digging out the initial trench, punching up the sides of the block first, then across the top.

Put your hand behind the block and try to pull it forward to see if there is a weak layer present.

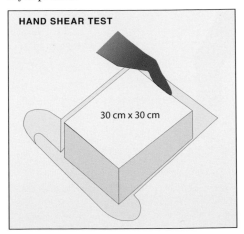

HAND SHEAR TEST

30 cm x 30 cm

Interpreting Results

The only result you are really interested in is if the block slides quickly and easily on a smooth, weak layer.

Pick up the block and check the underside. Check for a clean shear and look at the crystals on the sliding surface. Poke the surface of the snow the block slid on to feel whether there is a hard crust. Is there any sign of loose facets or weak, buried surface hoar?

If the failure was clean and fast, you will need to pay careful attention to your routefinding and avoid potentially dangerous slopes.

If you are planning to ski or board steep slopes, you will need to investigate the snowpack further. See the next chapter, **Riding Steep Slopes**.

Signs of Settlement

In order to avoid periods of instability, you should try to estimate how fast the process of rounding and settling is progressing. The time before the snow becomes stable can vary from a day or two to several weeks, depending on temperature. Small sluffs from steep ground or snow falling off trees are visual indications that rounding is taking place. In early writings on avalanche hazard in the Alps, Arnold Lunn stated that *a good rule is to mistrust all steep slopes after a fresh fall until the pine trees are free from snow*. Unfortunately, vagaries of climate and weather create exceptions to such rules of thumb.

A dangerous slope at Parker Ridge in the Canadian Rockies, the scene of two separate fatal accidents. The wind blows from right to left, loading upper slopes with wind-driven snow and scouring out the snow at the bottom of the slope. Photo Jim Davies.

Observation told us a number of things about snow stability on an unnamed peak on Ellesmere Island. Our shallow tracks and the slightly pitted surface show the snow is well settled. The mature cornices were formed by wind blowing up the ridge from the left. Recent winds blowing directly up the ridge have scoured the surface (bottom right) and helped consolidate the face on the right, which is about 45°.

Determining Wind Direction

Lacking specific meteorological data, wind direction is best evaluated by observing natural features that are the result of either erosion or deposition. As a general rule, eroded features such as sastrugi have their steep sides and sharp edges on the windward side, whereas deposited features such as snowdrifts have smoother, more rounded shapes facing the wind. The most useful features to look for are as follows.

Cornices

Cornices are deposits of wind-drifted snow overhanging the lee side of a ridge or other terrain with suitable configuration. Although they're reliable indicators of past wind direction, they don't necessarily indicate the direction of the wind at the present time.

Double cornices that overhang both sides of a ridge, and cornices that alternate from one side of a ridge to the other, are formed by unusually turbulent and distorted wind patterns which make any kind of prediction of wind direction fruitless.

Blowing Snow

During windy weather you can look up at the mountains and see plumes of snow streaming off the ridgetops. The length of the plume gives you the wind speed—moderate or strong is good enough for your purpose—and the amount of snow indicates how fast deposition is taking place on the lee slopes.

Drifting

Drifts around trees and rocks are a sure indication of wind direction. The smooth, rounded end of a drift faces into the wind; the long tail tapers away on the lee side. In winds of moderate speed, eddies form vertically and scour out wind scoops around the base of obstacles such as trees, rocks and even whole buildings.

Sastrugi

Sastrugi, or Skalvar, is the term used to describe the large-scale erosion of a snow surface into a series of waves and projections. They're usually associated with strong, continuous winds blowing over long periods; in the polar regions they reach a height of a metre or more. More modest formations are found in the North American mountains, but even so, travelling through sastrugi is a wretched, equipment-breaking business. Sometimes the wind removes enough of the surface snow to reach softer layers underneath and then the projection becomes undercut. The steep faces are always on the windward side.

Rime

Rime, a reliable indicator of wind direction, can be observed on any prominent object standing above the snow surface, such as rocks or trees. Rime deposits always grow into the wind; the heavier the deposit and the longer the branches, the higher the wind speed. The presence of rime also indicates that snow on the windward slopes has been strengthened, even cemented in place, by deposits of rime.

Vegetation

In alpine areas near treeline, vegetation is a good indicator of prevailing wind direction. Trees may lean away from the wind or have significantly less growth on the windward side. Small trees leaning downslope are probably doing so from creep of the snowpack or from past avalanche activity.

Hazard Evaluation on Multi-day Trips

Ski mountaineers undertaking multi-day traverses or mountain ascents will be travelling through ever-changing terrain at different elevations and across varying aspects. Apart from the challenges of travel, navigation, and weather and snow conditions, ski mountaineers must be able to assess hazard for themselves without the benefit of Avalanche Forecasts and come up with strategies for reducing the risk at every stage of their journey.

Although the techniques of ski mountaineering are beyond the scope of this book, I hope the following section will provide a guideline for assessing the hazard of avalanches following changes in weather and snow conditions.

It is most important to be constantly aware of the terrain you are travelling through. On a long day with a heavy pack it is easy to get lulled into hazardous terrain as you plod along with your head down.

Let's assume you've arrived at the top of a large, open slope with an undetermined depth of snow that you need to descend. You are aware of past weather conditions and the amount of recent snowfall. How do you go about evaluating this slope? Ask yourself four questions:

1. **Could the slope avalanche?**
2. **Is the snow stable?**
3. **What will happen to me if the slope avalanches?**
4. **Will conditions get worse?**

1. Could the slope avalanche?

Is the slope steep enough to slide? If it isn't, then **are there dangerous slopes above?** If the answer is no to both questions, then you have no worries. But don't forget that wet snow can slide down less steep slopes than dry-slab avalanches. Judge steepness by asking yourself: **Would I ski straight down it or not?** Relate the answer to your skiing ability.

Critical
- *Slopes greater than 30°*
- *Steep rollovers; shallow gullies*
- *Cliff bands*

What's the orientation of the slope to wind? Look for signs of wind direction such as cornices, drifts around trees and rocks, rime etc. Consider the aspect of the slope.

What's the orientation of the slope to sun? If temperatures are above freezing and the snow is showing signs of melting, consider the orientation of the slope. Think about your route later in the day.

Critical
- *South and southwest slopes exposed to strong radiation*
- *First major thaw of spring*

What's the nature of the slope? How long is the slope? How long will you be exposed to danger if you do decide to descend? Are there signs of the slope avalanching previously, such as channels in the snow or debris at the bottom? Examine the collection zone above the slope. Is there a lot of fresh snow up there? Does it have the smooth, rounded appearance of slab?

Critical
- *Open slopes*
- *Thin forest*
- *Confined slide path*
- *Gully or bowl*

2. Is the snow stable?

How deep is the snowpack? In some areas a minimum depth of snow is required before avalanches can develop. The normally accepted figures are 30 cm for smooth ground and 60 cm for rough ground. In the Continental snow zone, however, this general rule doesn't apply. If the base has been weakened by depth hoar, avalanches can occur with as little as 12 to 15 cm of snow; the loose sugar-snow crystals flow around rocks and trees which in other zones would hold the snow in place.

Are there any signs of avalanche activity? Be constantly on the lookout for any signs of instability. Why is snow sluffing off steep cliffs? Why are snowballs rolling down a sunlit slope? Note any slab avalanches, old or new, and consider why they have formed. Are similar slopes still unstable? What about slopes of other aspects? Might they be dangerous too?

What layers are there in the snowpack? Have you investigated the layering of the snowpack by digging a snowpit, doing a shovel test and a Rutschblock test? Do you need to?

Critical

- *Very hard or unusually soft layers*
- *Weak bond between layers*
- *20 cm or more of snow above a weak layer*
- *Loose, cold snow (faceted grains)*
- *Wet snow*

How much fresh snow has fallen? Most avalanches fall during or shortly after storms, so any appreciable snowfall is an indication of potential avalanche hazard. Heavy, damp snow in particular loads a slope very rapidly to the point of failure. The rate of precipitation in terms of mm/h of water content is a better indicator of loading than actual snow depth; a dry, cold snowfall may contain little precipitation. When hazard is already extreme a light snowfall may be all that is required to trigger extensive avalanching. The amount of settlement is important and any settlement of the storm snow at a rate less than 15% per day should be viewed with suspicion.

Critical

- *Snowfall greater than 2 cm/h*
- *New-snow depth greater than 30 cm*
- *Slow settlement of new snow*

- *Very light or very heavy snow*
- *Heavily rimed crystals; graupel*
- *A heavy, stiff layer above a light, weak layer*
- *Rain*

Wind Light winds tend to toughen up the surface of the snowpack by forming wind crust, which gives unpleasant skiing conditions for a day or two. If the wind is warm and dry there is little effect on the snowpack apart from a speeding up of evaporation at the surface. On the other hand, a warm, humid wind that's above freezing will dramatically increase the chance of wet-snow avalanching. Moderate winds pick up loose snow and transport it. Watch for signs of drifting and possible slab formation. Strong winds will scour any large areas of snow, depleting the snowpack on the windward side of a mountain and depositing slab, often hard slab, in smaller pockets and depressions. Don't underestimate how fast strong winds can deposit snow on a lee slope.

Critical

- *Moderate or strong wind*
- *Cracks shooting out from skis; whumpfs*

Air temperature

Very cold, below −15°C. Settlement is very slow. In a shallow snowpack, recrystallization will occur. Check the amount of depth hoar in the snowpack. Bonding of new snow to the old snow surface remains weak when both layers are very cold, particularly if the old snow surface is a cold crust and the new snow is cold, cohesionless grains. During extreme cold over prolonged periods with little snowfall, every layer in the snowpack loses strength, with the result that avalanches can occur without any apparent reason.

Cold, −2°C to −15°C. Metamorphism proceeds more rapidly; watch for sluffs. Avalanches fall during or shortly after a storm. The snowpack then stabilizes and the danger recedes until the next storm.

Warm, −1°C and above. Rapid changes occur in the snowpack. If the air temperature remains close to freezing, the snowpack will stabilize quickly. If it rises above freezing, wet snow avalanche hazard will develop. Check the depth of wet snow—20 cm or more is dangerous—and note whether the snow freezes overnight. Cloudy days when little long-wave radiation is lost to space will often set off a cycle of wet-snow avalanching in early spring when previous clear, sunny days have resulted in little or no activity.

Critical
- *Rapid rise in temperature*
- *Above-freezing temperatures*
- *Sun on slope under consideration*
- *Sun with hazy sky*
- *Temperature inversions*

Humidity It's believed that high relative humidity encourages the formation of slab; it allows snow particles to be carried greater distances without sublimating before they are deposited.

Critical
- *High relative humidity during snowfall or during periods of moderate and strong winds*

3. What would happen to me if the slope avalanches?

Depth of avalanche What depth of snow is likely to slide? How deep are the sliding layers in the snowpack? A few centimetres of snow is not significant if there is a long, almost flat runout but could be fatal if there is an open crevasse below, waiting for the victim.

Critical
- *Deep weak layers in snowpack*
- *Foot penetration greater than 60 cm*

Type of avalanche Loose snow or slab? Wet or dry? Will the whole slope slide at once?

Critical
- *Stiff slab above weak layers*
- *Slope has not avalanched recently*

Terrain How large is the slope you are looking at? What is above? What is at the bottom? How deep will the snow pile up at the bottom? Are there cliff bands below?

Critical
- *Long, open slope above*
- *Restricted deposition zone*
- *Drop-off below*
- *Trees to wrap around*

4. Will conditions get worse?

This depends on the present stability of the snowpack and what is happening to the weather. If you don't have a current weather forecast, you'll have to rely on your own observations. Obviously, any great change must be considered significant. Is it warming up? If so, what will the snow be like later on today, or tomorrow? Has it started to snow? How much and how fast? Is the snowfall accompanied by a strong wind?

Critical
- *Continuing snowfall*
- *Increasing temperature*
- *Strong wind*

Dealing with Hazard

Since most major traverses are done in the spring, avalanche hazard is from wet snow avalanches and fresh snowfall.

- *Travel early in the day; camp early*
- *Camp on a col and descend south-facing slopes the next morning*
- *Take a rest day after substantial fresh snowfall to allow new snow to settle*

Decision Making

Decisions on safe route selection must be based upon facts and not upon assumptions.

It's impossible to write about travelling in avalanche terrain without also considering the impending pressures facing a party in the backcountry. Such concerns include sickness and injury, fatigue, time constraints and weather conditions. Often they're used to justify a certain course of action:

- *We decided to hug the left side of the valley so that we wouldn't lose elevation or time.*

- *Darkness was coming, so we pressed on to the pass.*

- *I had to be back at work by Monday morning.*

- *We had planned the trip for three years and we were not about to throw it all away because of one storm.*

In each of the above cases, the victims felt compelled to make a decision based on factors they perceived as important. When making routefinding decisions, identify the assumptions on which decisions are being made and get into the habit of verifying them. Ask yourself: Do we really need to reach that goal today? Does it really matter if I'm late for work on Monday? What are the possible consequences of my decision to carry on?

You've spent the better part of the day heading toward your objective, a mountain pass, still some 2 km distant. The other two members of your group want to reach the pass before darkness falls. You're tired; breaking trail through knee-deep snow has been difficult. The ridge route you've been following bends abruptly to the east and ends at the bottom of a steep, snow-cushioned slope rimmed by a large cornice. Your objective is on the other side. A light breeze is picking up out of the southeast, but the sky is still clear except for a scattering of pink mare's tails high overhead.

What should you do?

If you haven't done so already, it's time to start asking yourself—and your group—seven important questions:

Why am I here?

This question really asks **What are the objectives to be achieved?** Every decision needs to be measured against a yardstick of purpose. The purpose may be to climb a certain peak. It may be to have a good time and get some exercise. It may be to hone climbing skills. Safety is usually an unspoken objective.

What is the problem?

In the example of the group heading toward the mountain pass, the problem starts to surface when the good ridge route abruptly terminates below the ominous-looking snow slope. Is it safe to proceed farther? The problem rapidly begins to compound itself when you take into consideration other impending factors such as group fatigue, approaching darkness, goal-oriented pressure, deteriorating weather, and alternative routes. The problem now becomes not only the original problem but also all of its consequential ramifications.

What are the alternatives?

Consider your options in terms of your trip objectives. In this case your options are:

- Continue on.
- Stay put.
- Turn around and backtrack.
- Take an alternative route.

What are the probable consequences of these alternatives?

Which alternative gives you the best chance of success as measured by your objectives? If you carry on, what are your chances of getting caught, buried or killed? Are you willing to bet your life on your decision? The real question is **Is it worth it?**

What information is available?

In essence, what's available is everything you've observed in your surroundings and everything you've learned about weather and the snowpack. Only by educating yourself can you expect to understand the physical processes at play and so sort out the information that is relevant.

What are the impending pressures?

This question also asks **Are these pressures really important?** Many times people tend to imagine the importance of a belief which, when viewed in retrospect, becomes meaningless. Try to sort out those impending pressures that have real significance from those that do not. So ask yourself: What can go wrong? Is there an error in my reasoning? Upon what assumptions am I basing my decision? Your boss would rather have you back at work on Tuesday than go to your funeral on Thursday.

What assumptions am I making?

Don't make decisions based on assumptions you haven't verified. When in doubt, check it out. What thinking person doesn't travel through avalanche terrain without doubts? Many assumptions which presume a situation is safe are based on incomplete information:

- *We didn't think the slope was steep enough to slide so we cut across it.*
- *We followed the tracks of another party up the mountain, figuring that if they made it, we could make it.*
- *We thought we would be safe following a route through the trees.*

If, during the tour, things aren't going as you expected, take your time. Get out a map and look around. Don't be rushed into making a hasty decision. If you are leading a party, don't be too proud to ask for another opinion and discuss alternative routes with your companions.

Only after you have asked yourself these seven questions should you make a final decision.

Summer Climbing and Scrambling

Summer climbers are not immune from avalanches. Any fresh fall of snow will avalanche off steep slopes, either because the old snow provides a good sliding surface or because the new snow has lost its internal cohesion. On the plus side, milder summer temperatures and increased solar radiation greatly speed up the settlement of new snow. In very hot weather, or if soaked by rain, the old snow surface will soften and peel off in layers as surface slides which can easily cause a climber to lose their footing.

Wet-snow sluffs in summer can carry the climber over cliffs or into bergschrunds or crevasses. Photo Leon Kubbernus.

Expedition Climbing

In the higher mountain ranges of the world—the Himalaya, the Andes and the high peaks of the Yukon and Alaska—avalanches are a major threat to climbers. They vary in size from small sluffs to some of the largest avalanches known. Members of the Canadian expedition to climb Dhaulagiri IV in winter witnessed an avalanche of monster proportions that fell 3300 metres from near the summit of Annapurna II to the valley floor, then travelled in a boiling cloud of snow dust, finally dissipating below the knoll on which the climbers were standing 15 km distant. Unfortunately this type of avalanche is totally unpredictable, an "act of God" if you like, as are the more insidious ice avalanches caused by the collapse of séracs in the relatively fast-moving Himalayan icefalls. It's a proven fact that the Khumbu Icefall is the most dangerous section of the normal route up Mount Everest. During the first ascent in 1953, the dangers so impressed themselves upon the expedition members that particularly horrific sections were awarded names like "Atom Bomb" area, "Hell-fire Alley" and "Hillary's Horror." Chris Bonington, in *Everest: South West Face*, compares entering these labyrinths of frozen ice to the game of Russian roulette: *All you can do is to try and pick out a route which is as safe as possible, but there will always be sections which are threatened by ice towers which, sooner or later, must collapse. You just hope that no one happens to be beneath them when the inevitable collapse occurs.*

Slab avalanches on lee slopes are much more dangerous because they can occur on relatively shallow slopes which, to the climber, seem the very epitome of security. A slab avalanche killed British climber Nick Estcourt on such a slope on K2 in 1978. Chris Bonington and Joe Tasker, fixing ropes low down on the mountain between Camp 1 and Camp 2, elected to traverse across a snow slope rather than climb the rock ridge above, which looked too difficult and time consuming. The snow slope, steep at first, became so easy angled that no line was fixed across it. Two days of heavy snowfall followed. On the third day the skies cleared but it remained windy. The landscape appeared unchanged, but not quite: the easy-angled slope had been transformed by snow and wind into a death trap. The support party carrying food and gear for Camp 2 found the going very heavy with all the fresh snow, and when they came to the easy-angled slope, which had not been fixed, led out a 5 mm cord which was to act as a steadying handrail in the event of surface sluff breaking away under their feet. Doug Scott made it across without incident. It appears that it was Estcourt, the middle man, who triggered the slope, which fractured 6 ft. down to the old snow about 100 ft. above their traverse line. He stood no chance. Scott had a lucky escape when the line joining him to Estcourt snapped and stopped his whirlwind descent to certain death.

The size and frequency of Himalayan and Alaskan avalanches often make safe placement of camps very difficult. There are a number of reported instances of camps being demolished by windblast from large avalanches even though they were protected from the moving snow.

The problems of avoiding avalanches in these regions are summarized below:

- The short good-weather seasons in the eastern Himalaya require expeditions to tackle the lower slopes of the mountain in the heavy snowfall periods preceding good weather.

- The short time scale that expeditions face when attempting larger peaks requires continuous pushing of the route despite the conditions.

- The necessity to supply climbers farther up the mountain.

- The desire to make progress after periods of inactivity usually caused by fresh snowfall.

- Climbers used to ascending high-angled slopes fail to recognize the danger on slopes of lower angle which they consider easy ground.

An avalanche thunders 3000 m down Mount Steele, well away from our camp on the east ridge. Of interest on this trip was soft slab that formed across the whole mountain from a light snowfall in completely windless conditions.

Waterfall Ice Climbing

Frozen waterfalls form in gully systems or down cliff faces which often have steep talus slopes below the start of the climb and large snow collection areas above. Because difficult ice climbs take several hours to complete, climbers are exposed to possible avalanche hazard for considerable periods of time, during which conditions may change for the worse. You've only got to think of the effect of the sun striking the slopes above the climb, a sudden warming trend in the weather, or the additional weight of further snowfall. Near the town of Field in the Canadian Rockies, two climbers were standing below a climb discussing the best line to take when a small avalanche shot over the top of the ice and carried them several metres downhill over boulders and some small cliff bands. More recently, four climbers were avalanched off the same waterfall and one of them was buried and died. Although it was cold down in the valley, the sun had been on the upper slopes above the waterfall for some hours.

In another incident, during an early ascent of Cascade Waterfall near Banff, the leader was left dangling from an ice screw after being swept off the crux by an avalanche from the bowl above (see photo this page).

John Lauchlan, one of Canada's leading mountaineers, was not so lucky. He was attempting the first solo ascent of Polar Circus, a 620 metre high Grade 6 ice climb in the Canadian Rockies, a route he'd climbed in one and a half days four years earlier. He had completed the first two pitches and was climbing a steep snow bowl to get to

Brian Greenwood moments before he was blasted off Cascade Waterfall by an avalanche from the bowl above. The same bowl released a large daytime slide in January 2009 (danger level High) that reached down to the trees. Six climbers had been on it the day before, when the danger was Considerable.

the foot of the next pitch when the slope fractured just above him and carried him back down the snow slope and over a 20 metre high cliff. Although not buried by the slide he died of injuries suffered in the fall. Later it was perceived from his tracks that John, the most safety conscious of climbers, had recognized the danger and instead of climbing up the middle of the bowl, had been contouring around the top edge in an effort to minimize the risk.

Avalanche Terrain Exposure Scale for Ice Climbers		
Description	Class	Terrain criteria
Simple	1	Routes surrounded by low-angle or primarily forested terrain; possible brief exposure time to infrequent avalanches.
Challenging	2	Routes with brief exposure to starting zones or terrain traps, or long exposure time in the runout zones of infrequent avalanches.
Complex	3	Routes with frequent exposure to multiple, overlapping avalanche paths or large expanses of steep, open terrain; multiple avalanche starting zones; and terrain traps or cliffs below.

Crossing a Suspect Slope

The first thing to do if faced with crossing a suspect slope is to look for another route that will avoid the slope completely.

When it really is impossible to avoid a potential slide area, consider where the likely trigger zone might be. A wide slope can have several distinctly different trigger zones, each of which can initiate an avalanche either locally or over the entire slope. Avalanches often start at the steepest point on a convex slope, or at some discontinuity across a slope such as rocks, a rockband or clumps of trees. Slab avalanches can be triggered from way below the crown line, and in very unstable conditions from relatively flat ground below a slope. Remember also when investigating snow conditions, that a long slope will have different snow conditions at the top than at the bottom.

If you're standing on safe ground level with a potential starting zone, you should either climb to the very top of the slope or drop well down into the runout zone. This may seem like a lot of effort for a tired party, but it is infinitely preferable to conducting an avalanche search and rescue. If you can't ascend or descend on safe slopes because of impenetrable timber or rockbands, the riskier alternative is to use the side of the suspect slope. If it's too steep for sidestepping, take your skis off and walk.

When crossing the runout zone of a wide avalanche gully, space yourselves at least 50 m apart and decide on a point of no return in case a slide starts above you. Post a spotter to warn of incipient slides. After your group has crossed, continue far enough along the trail to be completely clear of any possible avalanche before stopping.

The procedure for crossing a potential avalanche slope is quite different. Try to pick a line where you can traverse downhill, if possible a line that will take you in a series of short traverses from one point of safety to another such as large rocks or a thick clump of trees. It may be that your

This photograph illustrates the wrong way to cross potential avalanche slopes. The wind-etched surface is probably safe, but what are conditions like on the far side of the ridge? Photo Roland V. Emetaz, courtesy US Forest Service.

point of safety is the discontinuity across which the snowpack fails, in which case there is some comfort in knowing that you're at the very top of the slide when it starts and therefore have a good chance of emerging unscathed.

The worst thing you can do is undercut the snow by traversing horizontally across a slope. Try to avoid making turns; the extra force that is applied when weighting the ski in preparation for the turn, and the carving action of the turn itself, could be the trigger that releases the slide.

With the rest of the party watching, **expose only one person at a time to danger**. Never assume that because a slope didn't slide when the first person was crossing, it's safe for the rest of the party to cross en masse; the additional weight of several skiers together could be more than enough to initiate release. Also bear in mind that a slope may still release after several individual skiers have crossed it. On reaching safe ground, the first skiers should wait and watch from a safe spot until the whole party is across. Of course, if the slope is very, wide, exposing one person at a time is not practical. In this case travel at least 100 m apart.

Climbers likewise should cross suspect slopes one person at a time, being careful not to create a trench in the snow and thus undercut a slab. Only rope up if the distance is short and good static belays are available. When crossing a wide slope, you have to decide whether the risk of the slope avalanching is greater than the risk of falling. If the answer is yes, and static belays are not available, cross the slope one person at a time **unroped**.

In the event of an avalanche, using a rope can seriously hinder your chances of getting out alive. A rope will tangle you up, preventing you from making swimming motions, and pull you down even deeper into the moving snow. Moreover, other members of the group, not originally caught in the avalanche, may be pulled into it.

Before crossing a suspect slope, fasten your parka and pull up the hood, put on mitts, remove safety straps if they're being used, take your hands out of wrist loops, undo the belly band of your pack and ensure that avalanche beacons are switched on. Alpine bindings should be set loose enough to kick out of. Pin bindings and cross-country cable bindings can be loosened satisfactorily, but Nordic Norm bindings pose more of a problem because they hold the boot very firmly to the ski and can't be loosened. The best suggestion I have heard of so far is to slacken the laces of the ski boot.

Plan ahead of time what you're going to do if the snow does release. If you have a good downward traverse there's a chance of skiing to the side. But supposing you fall—and the chances are that unless you are a very good skier you will—what then? The first few seconds of mentally rehearsed action on your part may make the difference between survival and death.

Crossing spread out on the shallower portion of this wide 27° slope with a danger level of Moderate.

What It's Like To Ride an Avalanche

The following excerpt is from *The Avalanche Hunters* (pages 16–19), by Monty Atwater, and is possibly the most explicit account ever written of how it feels to be caught in an avalanche.

When a soft slab breaks loose it crumbles internally, losing all its cohesion and flotation. I simply fell through it until my skis hit the hard base of the old snow underneath. Now the snow along the wall of the gully began to curl back towards the main current, taking me with it. I was knee deep in boiling snow, then waist deep, then neck deep. Through ankles and knees I felt my skis drift onto the fall line. But I was still erect, still on top of them. The books tell you, If you're caught in an avalanche, try to ski out of it. With mine trapped under six feet of snow I wasn't skiing out of anything. I wondered what was going to happen when it came time to make that right-angle turn into Corkscrew.

Very fast and very suddenly I made two forward somersaults, like a pair of pants in a dryer. At the end of each revolution the avalanche smashed me hard against the base. It was like a man swinging a sack full of ice against a rock to break it into smaller pieces. Fortunately I took both shocks on the derrière, not on some more vulnerable spot. There was no pain, just a jolt that wrenched a grunt out of me each time. At this moment, the avalanche had taken my skis off for me and in doing so had spared my life, by giving up the leverage with which it could twist me into a pretzel. I didn't know my skis were gone and I don't remember the turn into Corkscrew. I was all the way under by then.

If my memories of this avalanche seem to be rather clear and detailed, it was a memorable occasion. I was a trained observer. In my few years at Alta

as a professional avalanche hunter I'd done a lot of thinking about this moment. I was thinking now and fighting for my life. However, my principal sensation was one of wild excitement.

Under the snow there was utter darkness instead of that radiance of sun and snow which is never so bright as directly after a storm. It was a churning, twisting darkness in which I was wrestled about as if by a million hands. I began to black out, a darkness that comes from within.

Suddenly I was on the surface again, in sunlight. I spat a wad of snow out of my mouth and took a deep breath. I thought, so that's why avalanche victims are always found with their mouths full of snow. You're fighting like a demon, mouth wide open to get more air, and the avalanche stuffs it with snow. I remembered another piece of advice in the books: Cover your mouth and nose. The next time I surfaced I got two breaths.

It happened several times: on top, take a breath, swim for the shore; underneath, cover up, curl into a ball. This seemed to go on for a long time, and I was beginning to black out again. Then I felt the snow cataract begin to slow down and squeeze.

At the mouth of Corkscrew the slope widens out and becomes gentle. The avalanche had swept me onto this slope. The squeezing was the result of the slowdown, with snow still pressing from behind. Whether from instinct or a last flicker of reason, I gave a tremendous heave, and the avalanche spat me onto the surface like the seed out of a grapefruit.

What To Do If Avalanched

When learning snowcraft and studying its application to avalanches, you'll probably become overcautious for a time. Accident reports in the local press will serve as a reminder that the danger is very real. As your knowledge increases, however, you'll tend to become overconfident in your ability to judge slopes in marginal conditions. In other words, the greater your experience, the closer you'll try to approach that narrow dividing line between stability and instability. This may be done unconsciously; because you've crossed many slopes that didn't slide, you begin to assume that all similar slopes are safe. The chances are that one day you'll be caught in an avalanche. What can you do to help yourself if you do get caught?

Hopefully you'll be aware that the slope you're descending is potentially dangerous and will be riding one at a time with at least one other person watching. You will be wearing an avalanche beacon and will have loosened safety straps, donned hat, mitts and parka and chosen the best possible line.

When the Snow Starts To Slide

The strategy for surviving an avalanche very much depends on where you are when the slab releases. The closer you are to the crown or to the sides, the better your chance of avoiding the full ride to the debris at the bottom, with its promise of burial and injury.

When the snow starts to slide:

- **Shout out** so your companions know you are in trouble.
- **Make a quick decision.** Can I ski or board out of it or not? This will depend on your ability as a skier, the depth of snow, the steepness of the slope and the configuration of the avalanche path.
- **Head toward the edge of the slide**, at a downward angle of about 45°, to where the snow is moving more slowly and may be shallower. Try to get right off the moving slab.

- If you get knocked down when the slab starts to move, **try to self-arrest with your hands or poles**. The act of self-arresting will tend to slow the upper body and allow your feet to be pulled down the fall line. It's the same technique as climbers use on a snow slope.
- When your feet are beneath you, **try to stand up and ski or board off the moving slab**. If you are high up on the slab you may even remain on the bed surface as the snow slides from under you.

At Bridger Bowl in Montana, a patrolman who was caught in a dry storm-slab avalanche reported that *when the slide hit, I tried to get my skis pointed straight down the hill, but didn't have much luck, due to the boiling of the snow.* One problem with slab avalanches is that as soon as the snow breaks up and loses its internal cohesion your skis sink deeper into the snow, making it very difficult to force the tips up to the surface. Also, the jarring drop and sudden movement of the slab will throw all but the best skiers off balance.

If You Can't Ski or Board Out of It

- **Throw away your ski poles**; you should already be free of any wrist loops. A ski instructor in Jackson *tried to make swimming motions, but his ski poles kept pulling him down.* He *tried to get his hands to his face to make a breathing pocket, but his poles frustrated his effort.*
- **Kick off your skis.** Getting rid of your equipment is of prime importance; you'll have very little chance of fighting your way to the surface if you are constantly being dragged down and twisted by the leverage of the snow. The same patrolman at Bridger Bowl who tried to ski out of the avalanche then *tried swimming, but this is very difficult to accomplish with skis on, for the instant they are pulled out of parallel with the fall line the feet are pulled uphill with respect to the rest of the body, causing a roll.* He observed *that the snow set up on stopping, even though it was fairly dry.*

- **Boarders** should continue with self-arrest efforts in order to get their board down below them and thus have a chance to pop out onto the surface.

- **Wriggle free of a heavy pack.** If you are wearing a heavy pack, your belly band should already be undone. Keep a small pack on.

- **Grab at trees or rocks.** In the early stages of the slide you may be able to slow your downward plunge and allow some of the snow to slide under you. The farther back up the slide path you are when the snow stops, the better your chance of survival.

- **Shut your mouth** as soon as your head goes under and try to hold your breath for as long as possible. A Banff mountain guide who was caught in a soft-slab said he *took a breath and immediately my windpipe was blocked by snow. Further breathing was impossible. Fortunately after a few seconds the snow melted enough for me to cough out the plug of snow and take another breath as my head came clear. I held my breath while under the snow until my head came clear again.*

The Log Roll

Gerald Seligman recounts the case of a Zermatt guide *who, being thrown down by a dry powder snow avalanche, rolled over and over sideways until he emerged at the side of the avalanche, twelve feet in a more or less horizontal distance from where he had been caught.* More modern writers, particularly those who have skied in the Alps, have also mentioned this technique. It appears that the initial twist of the feet releases the safety bindings and initiates the first roll.

This safety card stresses the importance of doing everything you possibly can to avoid getting carried down through the turbulent area of the avalanche and buried in the deposition zone. Courtesy Theo Meiners, Alaska Rendezvous Heli-Guides.

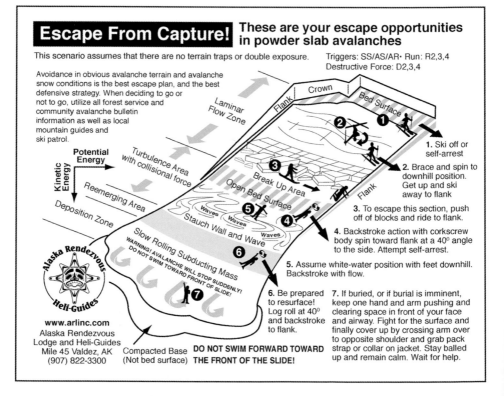

Escape From Capture! **These are your escape opportunities in powder slab avalanches**

This scenario assumes that there are no terrain traps or double exposure.

Triggers: SS/AS/AR· Run: R2,3,4
Destructive Force: D2,3,4

Avoidance in obvious avalanche terrain and avalanche snow conditions is the best escape plan, and the best defensive strategy. When deciding to go or not to go, utilize all forest service and community avalanche bulletin information as well as local mountain guides and ski patrol.

Laminar Flow Zone
Crown
Flank
Bed Surface

Potential Energy
Kinetic Energy
Turbulence Area with collisional force
Reemerging Area
Deposition Zone
Break Up Area
Open Bed Surface
Flank
Stauch Wall and Wave
Waves
Slow Rolling Subducting Mass
WARNING! AVALANCHE WILL STOP SUDDENLY! DO NOT SWIM TOWARD FRONT OF SLIDE!

1. Ski off or self-arrest

2. Brace and spin to downhill position. Get up and ski away to flank

3. To escape this section, push off of blocks and ride to flank.

4. Backstroke action with corkscrew body spin toward flank at a 40° angle to the side. Attempt self-arrest.

5. Assume white-water position with feet downhill. Backstroke with flow.

6. Be prepared to resurface! Log roll at 40° and backstroke to flank.

7. If buried, or if burial is imminent, keep one hand and arm pushing and clearing space in front of your face and airway. Fight for the surface and finally cover up by crossing arm over to opposite shoulder and grab pack strap or collar on jacket. Stay balled up and remain calm. Wait for help.

Alaska Rendezvous Heli-Guides

www.arlinc.com
Alaska Rendezvous Lodge and Heli-Guides
Mile 45 Valdez, AK
(907) 822-3300

Compacted Base (Not bed surface)
DO NOT SWIM FORWARD TOWARD THE FRONT OF THE SLIDE!

Fight for Your Life

- Use a combination of **back stroke** and **log roll** to try to fight your way to the flank or to pop yourself out on the surface. Some skiers have fought their way to the surface by pumping their legs up and down in a treading-water motion and by dog-paddling with their arms. A skier in the Colorado Rockies described the technique: *I worked myself into a sitting position, with my feet downhill, and tried to swim as if treading water. This seemed to work, and I immediately started to rise in the snow.*

- Once on the surface, try to stay on your back with your feet downhill using the backstroke motion. If you get the opportunity, log roll to the nearest flank.

Dealing with Areas of Turbulence

If you go for the full ride, or there is a lot of slab above you when the slide starts, you will almost certainly encounter the area of turbulence. Survivors have described it as like being tumbled around in a clothes dryer. Others have been buffeted around by chunks of hard slab.

- **Go with the flow.** Try to stay on your back with your feet downhill. When the turbulence dies down, start backstroking to try to reach the surface and then log roll toward the flank.

If You Go for the Full Ride

- **Make a last, desperate effort** to pop yourself out if you're below the surface when the slide starts to slow down.

- **Make every effort to avoid the head of the slide**, as the force of the snow piling in from behind will roll you under the front edge.

As the Avalanche Slows Down

- **Get into a sitting position** facing downhill, with your legs out in front and together. You can only do this if you've managed to stay on the surface. As the snow stops you are in a position to stand up and let the snow coming from behind to fill in around you. Clear an air space in front of your face and put one hand above your head if you think you're going to be buried.

- **Work at making a breathing space** in front of your nose and mouth with one hand and arm and reach for the surface with the other hand. Several victims have been found quickly because a hand was seen sticking out of the snow. In an accident involving two skiers in Big Cottonwood Canyon, Utah, *both were located beneath four feet of snow. One victim was uncovered in 20 minutes, having been buried upside down with no airspace; he was dead. The other was uncovered in 25 minutes, hands in front of face and alive.*

- If you feel you are nowhere near the surface, then withdraw the hand that was reaching for the surface, cross it over your chest and grab the opposite shoulder.

When the Snow Comes to Rest

In most slides the snow sets up like concrete on coming to rest, and even if you are only partially buried it may be difficult, even impossible, to dig yourself out. It's very unlikely you can help yourself if completely buried.

- **Don't shout** unless you hear rescuers immediately above you; sound will not penetrate very far through snow.

- **Don't struggle** to free yourself; you will waste energy and precious oxygen.

- **Try to relax**, and if you feel yourself about to pass out, don't fight it. The respiration of an unconscious person is shallower, their pulse rate declines and their body temperature is lowered, all of which reduce the amount of oxygen needed.

In summary, if caught in an avalanche you cannot ski out of, get rid of your equipment, try to stay on the surface, and as the snow comes to a standstill make a breathing space in front of your head. Finally, relax and rely on your companions to dig you out.

Many people are now wearing a helmet when tree skiing. Photo Alf Skrastins.

Riding
Steep Slopes

The needs of **Skiers** and **Boarders** who deliberately seek to make turns, preferably in deep powder, on slopes in excess of 30° are addressed by providing information and tools beyond those needed for backcountry touring. This does not replace the previous chapter—you still have to travel through avalanche terrain and establish a safe uptrack before you can enjoy a downhill run.

While we can take some comfort from the statement made by avalanche guru Ed LaChapelle that *the snow is stable 90% of the time*, there will always be risk when skiing steep slopes in the backcountry. How can you reduce the risk to an acceptable minimum while still enjoying a good day's skiing?

If you are a serious deep-powder hound you will learn to:

- **Distinguish** the good days from the bad.

- **Observe** current snow conditions.

- Evaluate **Snow Stability** from a few simple tests.

- Recognize signs of **Instability**.

- And, perhaps the most important factor in reducing the odds, you will practise **Safe Skiing Techniques**.

Importance of Local Knowledge

I firmly believe that the key to reducing risk is your knowledge, built up over several seasons, of areas where you regularly ski or board. Most of you typically ski or board in a limited number of places, visiting them several times each winter. With a little effort on your part, you can build up a knowledge base of these areas, either in your mind or on paper. Here are some ideas on how to acquire and record this all-important local knowledge.

Local knowledge is especially important for **out-of-bounds skiers and boarders** who start their run at the top of the slope and don't get the chance to evaluate snow conditions on the approach route.

However, Don't Become Complacent

If you ski an area regularly, assess the potential for avalanches each time you go. Are conditions what you expect? Is there anything different from the last time you were there? Don't let your guard down just because you are familiar with the area.

Avalanche Forecasters

These folks love to get out in the backcountry. They are part of the skiing and boarding community and they are constantly in touch with guides, colleagues and friends who have been out making turns in their local areas.

Many forecasters will mention conditions in popular backcountry destinations. Follow your favourite forecaster's remarks over the course of the season, paying particular attention to aspect, terrain features, wind deposition and the times in the season when the slopes you are interested in become potentially unstable.

If you are visiting an area you are not familiar with, don't hesitate to call the forecast centre for their advice.

Locals

Talk with local backcountry fanatics who are out skiing most of the winter. You can find them through the outdoors stores, in the roadside parking areas or out on the slopes. Try Internet blogs, forums, chat groups and social networking sites.

Clubs

Larger communities will often have clubs that run backcountry trips throughout the winter. Again, the local backcountry ski outfitter can usually put you in touch with someone.

Guides

If you are away from your home area and are concerned about snow conditions, hire a certified guide to take your group out for a day. A good guide will teach you a lot about local conditions and can give you advice on which areas you could tackle safely on your own.

Avalanche Terrain Maps

A few forecast centres are starting to make Avalanche Terrain Maps available on their websites that show the boundaries of avalanches superimposed on a map or photograph of the area.

Unfortunately, many of these maps were prepared for other purposes and show historical boundaries of avalanche activity during extreme avalanche cycles. What is really needed are maps prepared specifically for winter backcountry enthusiasts that show pockets of potential activity at Moderate danger level, answering the question *Are there still places I might still get nailed by a small slide even when the danger level is Low or Moderate?* A second layer or overlay should show expected avalanche boundaries at Considerable danger level. You don't go out onto steep slopes when the danger level is High, do you?

In addition the maps could indicate wind directions that typically load lee slopes and show the safest lines for up-tracks and ski-outs.

If your group uses a potentially hazardous area regularly it would be a good project to create your own Avalanche Terrain Map and share it with others over the Net.

Regional Snowpack Characteristics

Anyone who has skied extensively in North America and Europe will realize that snow conditions vary considerably from region to region. Swiss mountaineer and avalanche consultant André Roch classified the western USA, and by that token western Canada, into three major areas of alpine climate: the Eastern Alpine Zone, the Middle Alpine Zone and the Coastal Alpine Zone. Each has a different type of snowfall, a different form of avalanche hazard and requires a different approach to hazard evaluation. The three zones are now more commonly referred to as Continental, Intermountain and Maritime in the US and **Rockies, Interior** and **Coastal** in Canada.

The boundaries of these zones are not always well defined; overlaps and inconsistencies occur and sometimes characteristics of two different zones can be found in one area in the same season. For example, conditions more normally found in the Coastal zone such as rain or snowfall with very high humidity sometimes occur at Whitefish downhill ski area in Montana some 1000 km inland. Alta ski area in Utah exhibits characteristics of both Continental and Intermountain zones, depending on the season.

Try to relate the conditions found in each zone to your own home area.

The Rocky Mountains

Areas such as the Canadian Rockies and Colorado Rockies, tends to receive moderate snowfalls at fairly low rates of precipitation. Few storms deposit more than 30 cm of new snow. One to 2 cm per hour is the more normal maximum, the new snow often falling at temperatures below −20°C and accompanied by strong winds that cause extensive drifting. Cold temperatures and low humidity result in a dry, powdery snow and a tendency for the snowpack to be shallow and unstable. Depth hoar is common. Midwinter rain or melting is rare. **The principal hazard comes from deep persistent slab avalanches** that often involve the whole snowpack right down to the ground.

Early winter has the least predictable snow conditions; the snowpack is often shallow and uncompacted, leading to recrystallization. Without doubt it's the most dangerous time of the year to be travelling in the mountains. In this zone climbers should be especially careful. An accident on Chancellor Peak in early December 1976, that killed Leif Patterson and two companions, was directly attributable to treacherous early-season conditions: drifting snow had formed a hard wind slab over depth hoar in the gully they were climbing. It's surmised that because the snow appeared hard, the climbers believed conditions were similar to those of an early morning in summer.

Professional forecasting is usually based on examination of the snow structure plus evaluation of meteorological conditions, especially wind and new snowfall. You should ask about earlier periods of prolonged cold—an indication of the amount of depth hoar—and look for signs of wind having caused significant drifting. Recent snowfalls of 15 cm or more may be ready to slide on surface hoar or depth hoar layers. Using a ski pole, test all the way down to the ground for weak layers. Because slab formation is often localized, test frequently.

Check for sliding layers using the Hand Shear test and repeat whenever the terrain you are travelling across changes in aspect. If you suspect wind slab, keep off steeper slopes. Suspect all lee slopes, especially minor ones such as the sheltered side of slight hollows, ridges or gullies. Look for signs of wind direction by observing minor drifts, cornices or other wind formations. Ski cutting is not a reliable indication of stability. **Keen observation, good route-finding and extreme caution are the keys to safe travel.**

By mid-season, during February and March, avalanche activity is usually, but not always, more predictable. Obviously the farther north you are, the less predictable the mid-season avalanching will be, because winters are colder and last longer at higher latitudes. Now that the snowpack has built up, the major hazard comes from new-snow avalanches sliding on old-snow surfaces. Observing your tracks on switchbacks and using the Shovel Tilt and Rutschblock tests will give an indication of how deep that sliding layer is and how easily it can slide.

When temperatures start to warm up in spring, wet snow avalanches are the norm. The snowpack must be examined to determine the depth of the wet layer. Spring ski tourers should keep off steep south- and west-facing slopes in the afternoon. Conversely, north- and east-facing slopes, which were the most dangerous early in the season, now offer the safest route if the temperature of the snowpack is several degrees below freezing.

Interior Ranges

The Interior Ranges, for example Rogers Pass in the Selkirk Range of British Columbia, are characterized by heavy snowfalls that can deposit a metre or more of new snow per storm. The snow, which varies from dry to moist, falls at a high rate of 3 to 5 cm per hour and comes with medium-strong winds, medium temperatures and often a high relative humidity. Midwinter rain or melting is rare. Clear skies and high humidity allow for the frequent formation of surface hoar that can lead to multiple persistent weak layers.

This zone is notorious for the fast loading of its slopes by fresh snowfall, often accompanied by wind, which in conjunction with the high humidity common to this area leads to the formation of extensive areas of storm slab.

The principal hazard is from large, storm-slab avalanches within two or three days of their formation that may step down on persistent surface hoar layers.

Warmer temperatures in this zone lead to faster settlement and strengthening of the snowpack than in the Rockies. Depth hoar is rare but when it does occur it can lead to full-depth **climax** avalanches (page 79). Find out the details of any snowfall within the past week. A rate of 3 cm or more an hour is a hazard indicator. Ask about any unusual weather conditions before the last storm, such as very cold spells, recent rain or thaws and clear, cold nights, which encourage the formation of surface hoar; all these indicate a potential sliding layer within the snowpack. Wait two or three days after a major snowstorm before venturing onto or crossing under steep slopes. Ski pole tests will indicate the depth of the new snow but in this area will likely miss layering within the snowpack. Use the Hand Shear test to test right down to the well-settled snow. Repeat the test on each new slope or new exposure and at every 200 m change in altitude. Sliding layers may be deep, so use ski cutting cautiously. Suspect all lee and partial lee slopes but remember that in the Interior Ranges extensive slabs can form over the entire area without regard to wind.

Spring conditions are basically the same. The only difference is that the generally higher temperatures promote a faster settlement and bonding of new snow to the old snowpack. At the same time, changes within the snowpack leading to dangerous conditions are accelerated; rain will warm up the entire snowpack very quickly and then you get an extensive cycle of wet-snow avalanching.

Coast Ranges

The Coast Ranges are typical of most maritime mountain areas such as the Coast Ranges of Alaska, Washington and British Columbia and the mountains of Scotland. These areas have snowfalls of damp to wet snow deposited at moderate temperatures and often at a high rate. Because mid-winter rain and surface melting are common, settlement of the snowpack tends to be rapid, leading to basically stable conditions. Around and above treeline high storm winds form extensive rime deposits on rocks and trees—a good indicator of wind direction. **The principal hazard is from damp storm slab and wet soft-slab avalanches**. Although wind may play a part in avalanche formation, especially on very steep faces which have been plastered with snow from strong, driving winds, the biggest factors in this area are the rate of snowfall, the depth of the newly fallen snow, rapid temperature rises, rain, and dense or icy layers in the old snowpack.

Find out the dates, amounts and durations of snowfalls and rainfalls within the past week. Ask about extended periods of fine weather with clear nights prior to storms, which enhance the quick formation of surface recrystallized grains known colloquially on the west coast of Canada as "West Coast Depth Hoar." Learn what the recent range of temperature has been; specifically, you want to know whether the temperature has been above freezing, whether it stayed above freezing overnight and whether it increased during a snowstorm in the past few days. Look for buried crusts which could form sliding surfaces for the snow above.

Test down to the well-settled old snow, using the handle end of the ski pole if necessary. Use the Hand Shear test to check for sliding layers. Check the snowpack carefully for the presence of free water, especially if you notice water appearing on large rounded ice grains overlying any impermeable layer. Hazard from wet-snow avalanching can develop extremely quickly in this zone, so try to plan your route for the cooler slopes.

Wait two days after a major storm before trusting any steep slopes. The worst avalanche conditions often occur when a crusted or settled old-snow surface is covered with an initial deposit of cold, feathery snow with little wind. If the temperature rises and the wind picks up during the progression of the storm, heavier, denser snow will fall on top of the loose layer, which in turn is lying atop a good sliding layer to which it is poorly bonded.

Rapid thaws are particularly dangerous; firm, stable snow can turn into slush within an hour. Both the increase in altitude and the chilling effect of strong wind make it difficult to detect a change in temperature as you climb higher up the mountain.

In January 1970 four climbers set out to climb the Italian Route on Ben Nevis. Because the climb was in such good condition, they reached the final, relatively easy snow slopes leading to Tower Ridge early in the day and decided to extend their route by taking a more diagonal line that was largely unexplored. High winds had deposited a tremendous amount of snow on the lee side of the ridge.

The survivor recounted: *During this period there was a very remarkable rise in temperature which wasn't apparent to us at the time. The wind was very high—a tremendous wind—and the cooling effect of this wind belied the temperature rise.* (Rescuers later found the snow lower down dripping with water.) As they were crossing a large basin, the snow fractured to a depth of over a metre and carried three of the climbers to their deaths some 300 metres below. The fourth member of the group had, at the critical moment, untied the rope to flick it free of a snag and was left stranded on the climb.

Avalanche Problems

Although the prevalence of the various avalanche problems varies across the climatic zones, the problems themselves can be managed in a similar way in all regions.

There are many different opinions on how best to handle avalanche problems and page-long lists of things to consider have been published or can be found on the Internet. However, for each problem there are some key points that occur again and again.

In Managing Avalanche Problems on the next two pages I have reiterated the way the problems form and listed the most relevant pieces of travel advice.

Managing Avalanche Problems

Loose Dry Avalanches

Loose dry avalanches, sometimes called point avalanches or sluffs, generally occur during or shortly after new snowfall, removing snow from steep upper slopes and either stabilizing lower slopes or loading them with additional snow.

- Be cautious of sluffing in steep terrain until the surface snow has stabilized, and be aware of terrain traps below.
- When descending large, steep slopes, occasionally move across the fall line to avoid being caught by your own sluffs from above.
- Scramblers risk being carried over cliffs by small sluffs, and ice climbers can be at risk from sunlit slopes above.

Loose Wet Avalanches

Loose wet avalanches occur when wet new snow or wet surface snow loses cohesion and starts moving downslope. Melting may be caused by warm temperatures, solar radiation, rainfall or a combination of these factors.

- Avoid start zones and avalanche paths when the snow becomes moist from daytime heating or from rain or does not freeze overnight.
- Avoid travelling on ledges and cliffs where sluffing may have severe consequences.
- Start and finish early before the surface crusts melt.
- Avoid slopes with glide cracks.

Wind Slab

Wind slabs are most unstable when they are forming and shortly after they are first formed. However, in very cold conditions they can remain sensitive for many days.

- Avoid travel in lee areas when wind is transporting snow, and on newly formed wind slabs.

- Allow several days for wind slabs to stabilize before traveling over them.
- Enter your line well below ridge crests to avoid wind-loaded cushions.

Storm Slab

Storm slab is formed by significant new snowfall accompanied by light to moderate wind. Whether the slab becomes an avalanche problem depends on the weather during the storm and on the surface of the old snow.

Fortunately, storm-slab problems are usually predictable; the old rule of never travelling in avalanche terrain for a few days after a storm still holds.

- Make conservative terrain choices during, and for the first 24–36 hours after, periods of intense precipitation until the snow has stabilized.
- Choose slopes that don't lead into terrain traps and from which you can escape off to the flank.
- Pay attention to group management.
- Remember that any significant new snowfall will add load to the snowpack and may activate a previously buried weak layer.
- Does the forecast mention persistent weak layers?

Wet Slab

A wet slab avalanche is the result of a cohesive slab losing its bond with the lubricated layer below. This can result in the entire snowpack sliding directly on the ground, especially where the ground surface is smooth rock or vegetation.

- Avoiding start zones and avalanche paths when the snow becomes wet from daytime heating, rain or lack of an overnight freeze, especially for several consecutive nights.
- Pay attention to slope aspect and time of day. When corn snow becomes mush it's time to move around to a cooler slope.

- Scramblers risk being carried over cliffs by small sluffs, and ice climbers can be at risk from sunlit slopes above.
- Don't underestimate how quickly snow conditions can deteriorate at high elevations on a hot, sunny day.

Persistent Slab

Persistent slab avalanches are avalanches caused by a cohesive slab within the upper to middle layers of the snowpack losing its bond to the underlying layer. Persistent slabs may remain unstable for extended periods of time and be the cause of an avalanche long after they were buried.

- Pay attention to forecasters' comments and blogs and avoid slopes where persistent slabs are forecast to be an issue. The forecast will usually tell you when avalanche activity associated with a particular weak layer has died down.
- Be cautious after any weather conditions such as new snow, wind-transported snow or rain have added load to a slope.
- Allow extra time (36–48 hours) for persistent slabs to stabilize after a period of strong solar radiation or rapidly rising temperature.
- Be aware of the possibility of remote triggering and avoid lingering in runout zones.
- Be wary of slopes that did not previously avalanche.

Deep Persistent Slab

Deep persistent slabs are a different problem in shallow snowpacks than they are in deep snowpacks, and you will deal with the problem differently.

On the Eastern Slopes of the Rockies the deep layer is usually depth hoar just above the ground or on an early-season rain crust.

In the Interior Ranges crusts can be buried several metres deep. Multiple storms build up the snowpack on top of the crust over many weeks, leaving the potential weak layer deep in the snowpack.

- Be very conservative in your choice of terrain, especially if you don't know which slopes have yet to avalanche.
- Avoid shallow snowpack areas where triggering is more likely.
- In very cold, clear weather be wary of steep slopes in shallow snowpacks that are known to have buried crusts, or that have developed a significant layer of depth hoar at the bottom.
- Allow the snowpack time to adjust to stress from changes in weather. Keep off suspect slopes for 36–48 hours after heavy new snowfall (>3 cm/hour) or significant rainfall.
- Avoid exposure to deep persistent slabs if there has been strong solar radiation over the previous days or in the event of rapid warming leading to above zero temperatures.

Cornices

Cornices are overhanging, wind-sculptured snow formations that develop on the lee sides of ridges usually above treeline. They range from small, soft-snow wind features on the downwind side of terrain features to massive overhangs of hard snow.

- Approach corniced ridges cautiously.
- Avoid travelling on or near overhanging cornices and limit time spent exposed to slopes below cornices, especially soon after wind or rain, and during periods of warming temperatures and increased solar radiation.
- Travel early in the day on exposed slopes.

Glide Slab

A glide slab is a phenomenon where the entire snow cover creeps downhill on steep grass or smooth bedrock slabs. They are uncommon in most snow climates and tend to be confined to specific, well-known terrain features.

- They are totally unpredictable—keep off them.

Evaluating Stability in the Backcountry

While simple tools like the Avaluator™ address the needs of backcountry tourers and others who want to minimize risk, it leaves a lot of questions for skiers and boarders who want to descend steep slopes in a variety of terrain without excessive risk.

Even after taking courses and reading books, it's a different world when you are out there looking at steep, snow-covered terrain and trying to decide whether you want to go for it.

In this section I am going to suggest how you might go about making a go/no-go decision—what you have to consider and decisions you need to make.

Avalanche Forecast

Planning a day on backcountry slopes starts with the Avalanche Forecast. There is no better information available for the backcountry skier and boarder. An up-to-date forecast will contain both snowpack and weather information. However, there are a few things to consider.

How Relevant Is the Regional Avalanche Forecast for My Local Area?

Generally it is pretty good, especially for smaller regions and the areas around the forecast centre, which are often the areas around which most backcountry activity take place.

If you are heading into the extremities of any of the very large regions in the interior mountains of western Canada you should check for reports on Avalanche Canada's Mountain Information Network (MIN) at avalanche.ca.

Is the Weather Forecast Current?

If the forecast was issued the afternoon before or the day of your trip, the forecaster will have taken the weather into account.

If the forecast is more than a day or two old you need to consider changes in weather that may have affected the danger level. In particular:

- Has there been any new snow in the past 48 hours or since the avalanche forecast was issued? Has it rained?
- Are there reports of recent high wind?
- Has there been a significant rise or drop in temperature?

Review the Avalanche Forecast

- Accept that the Danger Ratings forecast is for the entire region.
- Are you in an elevation zone or on an aspect specifically mentioned in the forecast?
- Were potentially dangerous conditions such as persistent instabilities mentioned?
- Is the hazard increasing or decreasing?

Do Your Snowcraft Observations Support the Forecast?

As you approach your chosen slopes apply the snowcraft techniques outlined in the previous chapter.

Look for signs of instability:

- Are there any recent slab avalanches?
- Did you notice any signs of cracking or collapsing of the snow on your approach route? Any whumpfs?
- Are there signs of recent wind loading such as obvious cushions of snow or snow of different colour or texture?
- Are there signs of melting? Pinwheels on the surface of cold, dry snow? Can you squeeze water out of a snowball?

Look for signs of stability:

- Are there signs of settlement around trees or rocks?
- Has any snow sluffed off rocks above steep slopes?

Do these observations relate to the forecast danger level? For instance, you would be concerned if you observed large natural avalanches at a danger level of Considerable or whumpfs at a Moderate danger level.

Terrain

Relating Steepness to Danger Level Using the Swiss Slope Angle Scale

The Swiss have created a simplified version of the German Snow Card that relates permissible slope angle to the danger level. Like the Avaluator, the Slope Angle Scale is a graphical representation of conventional wisdom.

While I believe this scale is conservative in times of increasing stability, it is compromised by the wide variation between danger levels. There is a great deal of difference, for example, between a low Moderate and a Moderate that is almost Considerable. This is compounded by inaccuracies in the forecast and the possibility of the danger level changing during the day.

If you decide to accept the increased risk and ski or board slopes at danger levels that fall within the fuzzy area between the green and red zones, you will need the knowledge and ability to evaluate slope stability and manage your party to reduce the risk.

In order to apply the results of the Slope Angle Scale, you must be able to assess slope angle reasonably accurately (see page 136).

Local Knowledge

- How well do you know the area? Have you skied or boarded there over several seasons and in a variety of snow conditions?

- Have the slopes been skied or boarded regularly by others from the start of the season?

- Have you spoken with anyone who has skied or boarded there recently?

- Try to go with companions who know the area.

Examine the Slopes You Plan to Descend

- Are there steeper slopes above you, or steep slopes that could release slides onto your descent line?

- Where are the safe areas to regroup on the descent?

- Where would you end up if the slope avalanched? A long ride through trees or into a gully is a lot riskier than a ride down an open slope with a gentle runout.

- Decide which slope you are going to ski when you get to the area and have had a chance to evaluate stability.

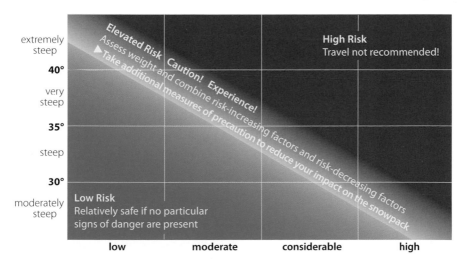

Snowpack

Testing for Stability

If you are concerned about the stability of the snowpack, there are a number of well-researched standard tests you can do on the snowpack in a further attempt to assess stability.

You will need to dig a snowpit in a suitable location to do these tests, which are most pertinent if you suspect buried surface hoar or crusts under recently fallen or wind-drifted snow.

Take a backcountry avalanche course to learn how to do these tests effectively.

Should I Dig a Snowpit?

Some people never dig a snowpit, relying on Danger Level, local knowledge and snowcraft to minimize their risk.

Others believe it is unlikely the average winter backcountry enthusiast can do good-quality tests close to the trigger zone. They also feel that false instability results will spoil many good days of skiing.

I believe that digging a snowpit is **never a waste of time** if it helps you learn more about the snowpack in your area.

Why Dig a Snowpit?

There are two reasons for backcountry skiers and boarders to dig a snowpit: to get a quick look at the **near surface layers** of the snowpack while doing a few stability-related tests, and to make a detailed examination of the snowpack for educational or record-keeping purposes.

If you want to learn how to keep detailed snowpit records you should take a multi-day, hands-on avalanche course.

I emphasize **near surface layers** because it is almost impossible for backcountry recreationists to identify deep-slab instability.

You should dig a snowpit and do stability tests if:

- Your snowcraft observations give you any indication of instability on slopes of any aspect or elevation band.
- If the weather is different from the forecast.

- If the danger level is forecast to be increasing.

Snowpits and Danger Level

Another way to decide if you should dig a snowpit is to consider the Danger Level:

High Why are you out there at this danger level? The only valid reason is if the weather forecast was wildly wrong or you are on a multi-day trip. By all means dig a pit, if only for the educational value or to confirm that you should do some very careful routefinding and keep off slopes steeper than 30°.

Considerable At Considerable danger level you are relying on your local knowledge and experience to find stable slopes to ski or board. You expect some slopes on certain aspects or in certain elevation bands to be unstable.

You can get in some good turns on slopes of less than 35° if you can manage the risk and are willing make conservative terrain choices. You should dig a snowpit and do some stability tests.

Moderate This is a difficult danger level to deal with, as many of the usual indicators of instability are absent. If you are pushing on to higher, steeper and more dangerous slopes, you definitely need to dig a snowpit.

Also dig one if you suspect isolated areas of instability such as rolls in terrain and areas of sudden steepening. It will help you decide whether you need to avoid these areas or can play there after all.

Low You will rarely need to dig a snowpit at this level unless you have some indication that the danger is higher. This is the time to go for steeper descents. Snowpits don't usually help the extreme skier or boarder, as it's unlikely that pits can be dug where they would be useful.

Snowpits

In order to get reliable stability test results you need to take care when choosing your snowpit locations. Look for small, safe slopes that are of the same aspect and character as the terrain you are planning to descend. Consider the consequences if your test slope were to slide. Stay away from trees; avoid drifts or ridges where the wind may have altered the layering of the snowpack; be aware of rockbands, buried bush or other shallow spots; and avoid breaks or transitions in the slope.

According to Bruce Tremper, a professional stability forecaster, *the name of the game is to dig a pit in the most representative spot you can choose without getting killed.* You may have to settle for a smaller test slope and try to extrapolate the results to the larger one, or work your way in toward the middle of the larger slope, digging several quick pits and retreating if there is any indication of instability.

As you dig, pay attention to the consistency of the snow. You can learn a lot about the composition of the snowpack during the digging.

Procedure

- Using a probe or ski pole, check the snow depth and try to identify, by feel, the location of weak layers. If probing indicates that the pit will reach the ground, make sure you're not standing over rocks or tree stumps.

- Note foot penetration by stepping into undisturbed snow and gently putting your body weight on one foot. Also note the depth of your ski tracks where your weight has been on one ski. With experience, foot penetration and ski penetration will give you an indication of how well the snow is settling

- You are now ready to dig the pit. It should be dug with vertical faces and as deep as you have time for. It is usually not necessary for the backcountry skier or boarder to dig more than about

1.5 m deep. In a shallow snowpack you should always dig down to the ground.

- If you plan to do a Rutschblock test the pit will need to be at least 2 m wide (wider than the length of your skis or board).

- Observe the layering of the snow as you dig, especially the hardness, crystal type and free water content of significant layers.

- With the shovel, trim the uphill wall of the pit so that it's vertical.

- The objective is to identify the weakest layer in the snowpack and assess its strength, or to examine the water content of the snowpack if you suspect the snow is close to 0°C.

- Feel the snow with your gloved hand to get an idea what layers are present in the snowpack. Don't bother with brushes or credit cards or with looking at the snow crystals with a magnifying glass. All you are trying to see is the overall

Looking for hard or soft layers in a "Hasty" pit dug down to the ground. Note the thermometer used to record snow temperatures at various depths as measured by the folding ruler.

This large slab in the Bugaboos, British Columbia, fractured and collapsed but did not release. The slope had been skied the previous day. Photo Jim Davies.

picture. Look for the weakest layer and try to estimate how well it is bonded to the adjacent layers.

- Conduct as a minimum a Compression test, or better still an Extended-Column test or a Rutschblock test on the back wall of the snowpit.
- Make an assessment of snow stability based on your observations.
- Fill in the pit if it's likely to be a danger to other people.

What You Are Looking For

- **New-snow instability** Newly fallen and recently wind-deposited.
- **Slab instability in top metre of snow-pack** Buried layers — sun and rain crusts, thin faceted layers (see table on page 63, **Significant Layers in the Snowpack**).
- **Weak layers** Buried surface hoar, depth hoar, graupel, thick faceted layers.
- **Sliding layers** Sun and rain crusts, thin faceted layers.

Dealing with Depth Hoar

If there is a layer of depth hoar at the base of the snowpack, the column you cut for your tests may collapse, either as you are cutting it or after a few taps. While it is obvious there is a very weak layer just above the ground, you really have no indication of the stability of the slope, which will depend on the depth and strength of the layers above the depth hoar. None of these "isolated-column" tests will help you here.

Probably the best solution is to do a couple of Rutschblock tests, one with the back of the block cut, the other with the back uncut. The former will give an indication of the resistance to compression of the depth hoar layer, the latter the strength of the snow layers above.

Snowpit Tests

Limitations of Snowpit Tests

None of the small-column tests use a column large enough to give any indication that the fracture will propagate through the snowpack sufficiently for the slab to release. To address this limitation, two tests on larger blocks have been developed.

The **Extended-Column Test**, developed in the USA, shows the most promise for backcountry use and is described on page 177. Bruce Jamieson has been heard to comment that *it might become the test of choice for backcountry users.*

A **Propagation Saw Test** has been developed by researchers at the University of Calgary. It is not considered suitable for winter backcountry enthusiasts, as it is time-consuming and requires specific knowledge of the snowpack being tested.

Remember that none of these tests should be used as the only factor when making decisions in avalanche terrain.

The depth limitations of backcountry snowpits make it unlikely that you will be able to identify deep persistent weak layers or deep slab instability.

Recent studies indicate that the quality of the shear—pops and drops—is important when evaluating the results of all these tests.

Note: The procedures described in this book have been adapted for use in the backcountry. Avalanche professionals will usually use more detailed and rigorous procedures.

The Nature of the Fracture

In all of the following isolated-column tests, you are looking for the failure (or otherwise) of a layer in a column of snow. Significant results are indicated by:

- The failure is sudden and fast. The whole block pops off and may drop slightly. The terms **pops** and **drops** are commonly used to describe such failures. On steeper slopes it will slide into the pit.

- The shear surface is smooth and uniform. The block slides easily when pulled—if it has not already slid into the pit.

Cutting out Columns for Testing

The procedure for isolating columns for testing is the same for all three of the isolated-column tests described here. Using a **snow saw** makes the job much easier and gives you more uniform columns. You can cut several columns in the back wall of the pit prior to doing the tests. Some people use a knotted cord and probe poles to speed things up.

- Excavate a chimney in the uphill wall just over a shovel's width wide and just over a shovel's width into the hill.

- Mark a square block with sides 30 cm (about a shovel's width) on the snow surface on one side of the chimney. For the Extended-Column test the width of the block should be 90 cm.

- Using a snow saw or the tail of a ski, cut out a triangular wedge of snow at the other side of the column. This allows a block of snow to slide freely during testing.

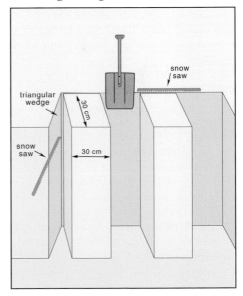

Compression (Tap) Test

This test is used find weak layers in the snowpack and gives an indication of their strength. It only requires a shovel and so can be done by snowboarders and snowmobilers as well as skiers. The following procedure is suggested for use in the backcountry.

Procedure

- Cut the back of the column to below a suspected weak layer. If you have not identified a weak layer, cut right down to the bottom. If there is depth hoar at the bottom, cut the back to just above the top of the depth hoar.
- If the column fails as you are cutting it, the failure is rated as *very easy*.
- Carefully place a shovel blade on top of the column at the same slope as the snow surface and tap 10 times with the fingertips flexing the hand at the wrist. Failures up to this point are *easy*.
- Level the top of the column.
- Tap 10 times, moving your forearm from the elbow. Any failure is *moderate*. Finally, hit the shovel with open hand or fist 10 times and rate any failure as *hard*.
- After a fracture, leave the top of the column in place if the block has not slid right off and will still support tapping. Continue tapping to locate other weak layers.

Interpreting the Results

If a significant snow layer (more than about 10 cm) fails at *very easy* or *easy*, do a Shovel Tilt (Burp) test to see if you get a similar failure. If so, you should reconsider your objective—look for a safer aspect or less-steep slopes. Remember, the failure must be clean and sudden.

If the failure is moderate and below the most recent storm snow layer, you should do an Extended-Column test or a Rutschblock test.

Shovel Tilt (Burp) Test

Used to identify weak layers in soft snow near the surface of the snowpack. A good test for assessing the bond between accumulating storm snow and the snowpack.

Procedure

- Ideally, you should have identified the potential weak layer through the Ski Pole test or the Hand test.
- Insert your shovel horizontally about 20 cm beneath an identified weak layer (or 40 cm down if you have not been able to identify a weak layer).
- Carefully pick up the column on the shovel blade, resting the shovel handle on one knee.
- If you are doing the test on a slope of less than 15°, tilt the shovel so that the layers are inclined to at least 15°.
- Tap the bottom of the shovel 10 times lightly with your fingers, moving your hand from the wrist.
- Hit the bottom of the shovel 10 times with the palm of your hand, moving your lower arm from the elbow.
- Applying more force is unnecessary, as you are testing layers of soft snow near the surface.

Interpreting the Results

If you get a clean, swift failure at any time during the test, you should consider the surface layer unstable. As results from this test vary widely, you may want to move to another location nearby and do another test.

Remember that this is only one test and the result should be combined with other tests and observations before deciding to ski or board. Your final decision will depend on the depth of snow above the fracture and the consequences of a slope avalanching.

Extended-Column Test

The Extended-Column test was developed in 2005/6 by Ron Simenhois and Karl Birkeland as a test to assess both initial failure and fracture propagation in an isolated column. A comparison of the most common isolated-column tests by the Swiss in 2007/8 concluded that the Extended-Column test *was best suited to differentiate between stable and unstable situations.*

Initially developed as a test for avalanche practitioners, I believe it has a place in the backcountry enthusiast's stable of tests. Although it takes longer and requires more skill than the previous tests, it is quicker to do than a Rutschblock test and gives fewer false stability results than the standard Compression test on which it is based.

One of the advantages of this test is that it is easy to interpret — it either propagates cleanly or there is no propagation, even if the block fails. It also works on flat ground. Like all isolated-column tests, this test alone should never be the basis for a decision to ski or board a particular slope.

Procedure

- Isolate a column as for the Compression test, except that the column is 90 cm wide (across the slope) by 30 cm. The back is cut to below any suspected weak layer. If you have not identified a weak layer, cut right down to the bottom.
- As this test is not intended to identify weak surface layers, remove any soft snow and level the portion of the block you are going to use for the test.
- The test is conducted at one end of the block, with the shovel blade pointing upslope.
- Place a shovel blade on top of the column and tap 10 times with the fingertips, flexing the hand at the wrist.
- Tap 10 times, moving your forearm from the elbow. Finally, hit the shovel with open hand or fist 10 times.

- Note the number of taps required to initiate a fracture. Continue tapping and note the number of taps it takes for the fracture to propagate across the entire column in the same layer. Complete all 30 taps if necessary.

Interpreting the Results

In the backcountry you are looking for a clean fracture and swift propagation across the same weak layer. Any other result is inconclusive.

- If the fracture propagates across the whole block at the same time as the initial fracture, or on the next tap, the slope should be regarded as unstable.
- Research into the accuracy of the Extended-Column test indicates that doing a second test at least 10 m away and using the least stable result improves accuracy by a significant amount.

Limitations

- The Extended-Column test is not a good test for assessing the stability of soft surface layers; use the Shovel Tilt test in those cases.
- The developers of the test suggest that the test might *overestimate snowpack instability where a weak layer sits under a thick hard slab.*

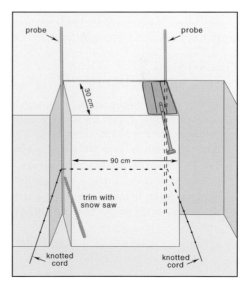

Rutschblock Test

This entertaining and instructional test is used to identify weak layers under a cohesive slab and as an indication of the possibility of human triggering. If you only do one test in a snowpit, this is the one to do. It will give you the most pertinent and reliable information. Because you are using a much larger block (about a ski length square), careful selection of the test site is necessary for reliable results. Probe to avoid logs, brush, rocks etc. before digging the pit. The test has been found to be most effective on slopes greater than 30°.

Photo Mark Shubin, courtesy Bruce Jamieson.

Procedure

- Select a site as close as possible to the slope you wish to descend, and of the same aspect. If you must do this test on slopes of less than 30°, the lower wall should be as smooth as possible and a second person should watch for small displacements (less than 1 cm) that indicate shear failure.

- Dig a pit and completely isolate a block about 2 m wide (a ski length) by 1.5 m deep using a combination of shovel, snow saw, ski tail or knotted rope, whichever is the quickest. Flare the side cuts a little so that the block is free to slide out.

- Load the block in the following sequence and observe when a clean fracture takes place.

Loading Steps

1. The block slides as it is being cut out.

2. Put skis on and carefully approach the block from above. Step down with one ski onto the block, close to the upper wall. Transfer your weight carefully and place the other ski on the block.

3. Flex your knees quickly, without lifting your heels, to transfer your weight to the snow, thus compacting the surface layers.

4. Jump up and land on the same com-pacted spot near the back of the block with both skis.

5. Jump onto the same spot a second time.

6. If the snow is hard, jump on the same spot on the block without skis; otherwise, step down to the middle of the block, push once and jump thee times.

Shredblock Test for Snowboarders

A variation of the Rutschblock has been developed for snowboarders. The following information is courtesy of Andy Gleason from a paper comparing Rutschblock and Shredblock tests that found good correlation between the two.

1. The width of the block can be reduced to 1.7 m

2. The tester should keep their front foot in the binding of the snowboard, leaving their back foot unattached.

3. It may be necessary to build a platform of snow, or use a pack, behind the block so that the tester can step gently onto the block. A ski pole will help balance.

4. While standing with the rear foot on the platform behind the column, the snowboard is lifted up and gently placed on the upper one-third of the isolated column. Do not slide the board onto the column. The rear foot is then placed on the snowboard between the bindings.

5. Subsequent loading steps are the same as for a tester on skis. At some point the tester may need to put their rear foot into the binding, probably for the first jump (step 4).

6. A second person can be put on the snowboard and both can jump together — which requires good coordination!

Interpreting the results

Conservative backcountry skiers will not ski a slope if the Rutschblock test fails with fewer than two jumps (Rutschblock step 5 or earlier).

If the snow fails at any time before you jump on the block, instability is considered to be high on slopes of similar aspect and steepness.

If it fails when you jump on the snow with skis on, local instability should be suspected on similar slopes.

If you have to jump on the block with skis off or jump on the middle of the block to get failure, or if there is no failure, there is a low risk of avalanches.

Limitations

The Rutschblock test will not identify weak layers above the layer penetrated by your skis during the test. For instance, if you sink 20 cm into the surface snow when you step onto the block, a weak layer at 15 cm may not be apparent. Use the Hand Shear test or the Shovel Tilt test to check surface layers.

This popular area close to the highway gets loaded by the prevailing westerly wind. The right-hand slide, on a convex roll (page 100), produced a significant amount of debris (page 196). Photo Jan Uttl.

Safe Skiing and Boarding

Keep your head up and your eyes open.
Source unknown

After stability evaluation, the best way of reducing the odds is to practise safe skiing techniques. The following are pointers gathered from ski guides, avalanche professionals, extreme skiers and boarders, and backcountry ski fanatics.

One thing all these people have in common is that they are willing to turn around and go home if they become uncomfortable about the level of risk. They take their sport seriously. They are willing to wait until conditions are right before making ambitious runs, and they make meticulous plans and preparations.

Take Your Sport Seriously

- Wait until conditions are right.
- Plan your descents.
- Prepare your equipment.
- Practise using safety equipment.

Choose the Right Time

It's difficult to predict snow stability in many areas in the early part of the season. Serious extreme backcountry descents are best done near the end of the season when the whole snowpack has stabilized. Timing is everything!

Don't be an Instagram Rider

There is a lot of pressure these days on young skiers and boarders to seek community approval through social media. A young ski mountaineer in the Tetons describes it as *this invisible pressure to create your own content and become part of this crazy social media sphere.* The desire for an Instagram photo or a GoPro movie should be tempered with common sense.

Key Indicators of Avalanche Danger

Certain indications of danger are relevant to all areas and should never be ignored:

- Evidence of avalanche activity on slopes of similar orientation.
- Settling and fracturing of the snowpack. Whumpfs!
- New snow accompanied by high winds.
- A sudden warming trend.

Managing Your Party

- Plan your descent. Decide where on the slope you will put the first track, who will go first, which side of the first track the second person will ski or board and how far down the slope you will descend before stopping to regroup. Stop at the very edge of the slope or descend right to the bottom.

- If the entire run is not visible, stop (to the side) at any changes in steepness or direction and descend the new section as a separate slope.

- Descend one at a time and watch each person for the entire run. Don't start until the previous person is out of the way. Skiing or boarding one at a time keeps the stress on a slope to a minimum.

- If someone falls, give them time to get up and out of the way. Don't descend to help them unless they are injured, so as to avoid putting additional stress on the slope.

- Don't ski or board above one another. Take care when descending through trees or over rolls and bumps not to descend above your partner. Move well to one side or to a safe position following your run.

- Use the buddy system and stay within sight or sound of your buddy at all times.

Skiing or Boarding the Slope

The first rule of thumb in safe skiing is, if your partner wants to ski first ...let him!
Brad Meiklejohn

There is one overriding rule for safe skiing: **never expose more than one person at a time to avalanche danger**.

- Start the day by skiing or boarding easier-angled slopes and work your way onto the steeper slopes. Descend treed slopes before open ones.

- Typically the first run of the day is always a safe run with several test locations for stability evaluations: a small, steep roll or a short, commonly wind-loaded slope. Continue to sniff around, being constantly aware of changing weather and snow conditions.

- Start at the side of a slope and work towards the centre on successive runs. Take care to avoid areas where the slab may be thinner and weaker.

- Ski or board ridges instead of bowls; stay out of gullies and avoid slopes that channel into gullies. Be alert for terrain traps.

- Be aware of the possibility of snow sluffs on very steep terrain.

- Enter the slope at the top rather than at the sides. Don't cut in from the side below a cornice.

- Take a good look at the slope and consider the possibility of "weak areas" (page 183). Stay where the snowpack appears to be deepest. In depth hoar conditions, stay away from rocks that might be trigger points.

- Descend as smoothly as possible and in control. Sit down rather than crash.

- Ski or board the same slopes as often as you can throughout the season. This not only gives you intimate knowledge of the terrain, but also allows you to follow the buildup of the layered snowpack.

- Put your climbing track on safe, low-angled slopes. Climbing straight up on foot should only be done on the most stable slopes.

- A lesson learned from heli-skiing is to look well above and contemplate triggering an avalanche that starts a long distance away. Be vigilant!

Complex terrain in the Monashees, British Columbia: Christina Ridge. Photo Grant Statham.

Slope Cutting

Slope cutting means skiing or boarding down and across a slope to try to release an avalanche. While it is a useful indicator of stability on small slopes with little chance of injury or burial, cutting large slopes in the backcountry is a serious business. It is far riskier than the controlled cutting of familiar slopes at a resort by experienced ski patrollers.

Cutting large slopes should be used as a safe skiing or boarding technique rather than as a stability test. If your snowpit tests leave you with a gut feeling that the slope might slide, you should probably back off rather than relying on slope cutting to confirm your opinion.

The other problem with slope cutting as a test for stability is that it's rarely conclusive; one pass by a skier is not necessarily an indication that a slope is safe.

However, during your descent there may be places where slope cutting specific terrain features may be appropriate: the top of convex rolls, the sidewall of a gully, or a rib where you cross over to another aspect.

Consider the following:

- What are the consequences if you trigger a slide? Can you reach a safe point before you are carried down the slope?

- Go one person at a time and always have at least one person watching from a safe place. Make sure there is no chance that a slide you trigger will propagate sufficiently to take out your companions.

- You should be a good skier or boarder, able to keep on your feet if the snow begins to move.

- Make a plan that assumes you will get caught. Pick out a feature to aim for and consider that if the snow does slide you may end up below the safe spot.

- Descend at an angle of 45° to the fall line, keep up your speed and aim for an island of safety.

- Never cut below a cornice unless you are sure the slope below is bombproof. A snowboarder became the first snowboard avalanche fatality in Canada by doing this.

Cornice Test

Jump on, shovel or cut through cornices as long as you can do it safely. A good-sized chunk of cornice rolling down a slope without triggering a slide will give you a lot of confidence in a slope's stability.

Riding Moderately Steep Slopes when Danger Level Is High

Many dedicated powder hounds seek out moderate slopes when danger levels are High and there is fresh powder to ski or board—the two usually go together. In many communities such areas are well know and frequently used, further reducing the risk.

While restricting your downhill runs to moderate terrain will significantly reduce risk, there are still dangers you should be aware of:

- The area you choose to ski or board and its approach route should not be threatened by steeper slopes above.

- By definition, moderately steep slopes are less than 30°, but at High danger levels you should choose slopes that average 25° or less with very short rolls that don't exceed 30°. Be very careful not to get sucked into steep terrain.

- If you are tree skiing at a time of high hazard, someone in your group should be familiar with the area in stable conditions. You should also consider wearing a helmet.

- Above treeline, plan your descent line carefully and make sure everyone knows where to go, and perhaps more importantly where not to go.

Weak Areas

On any given slope, the strength of a buried weak layer, or of the snowpack itself, may vary from place to place.

Consider a slope covered with a certain depth of snow. If the slope were perfectly even, you would expect the snowpack to be uniform across the slope. However, if the slope is uneven or if there are buried rocks or brush, then the temperature gradient in those areas will be different and the snowpack will no longer be uniform. In climates where recrystallization (page 51) is taking place, such areas may be weaker and potentially less stable due to the higher rate of recrystallization. These areas are called "weak spots."

In studying a number of slab avalanches which have been triggered by a person adding stress to a weak layer, it has been noticed that the initial rupture of the slab usually begins in a localized area where the weak layer is at its weakest.

Once failure occurs at the weak spot, the fracture propagates rapidly throughout the slab into areas of stronger snow — snow your companions may already have descended safely.

The Implications of Weak Spots

The farther down the weak layer is, the less likely you are to trigger an avalanche; therefore you should try to ski where the snowpack is deepest and keep away from rocks or brush protruding from the snow. On suspect slopes, follow the exact line taken by the person in front.

Remember that the more you concentrate your weight in a small area, the more stress you transmit to the snowpack. A snowboarder will add less stress to a weak layer than a person on skis will. Taking your skis off and walking down a slope is a dubious technique when slab conditions are suspected.

The old concept of moving between "islands of safety" needs revising to stress that the "islands" should be large and stable things such as a substantial clump of trees or a solid rock buttress and not insecure objects such as small trees or rocks sticking up through the snow.

Areas where the snow has slid down to the ground almost certainly represent weak areas in the snowpack, and one of those was the likely trigger location here. Photo Gery Unterasinger.

Stability Assessment Checklist

This is a fairly meaty checklist, but if you are going to ski or board steep slopes you need all the information you can get to reduce your risk. The key questions are: **What is the chance an avalanche will occur? If it does, what will happen?** and **How can I reduce the risk?**

Is the Weather Forecast Correct?

- New snow in the past 48 hours?
- Has it rained?
- Signs of recent wind deposition?
- Significant change in temperature?

Review the Avalanche Forecast

- Are you in an elevation zone or on an aspect specifically mentioned in the forecast?
- Were potentially dangerous conditions such as persistent instabilities mentioned?
- Is the hazard increasing or decreasing?

Do Your Snowcraft Observations Support the Forecast?

- Recent slab avalanches?
- Whumpfs, cracking or collapsing?
- Signs of melting?
- Results of Hand Shear test?

Look for Signs of Stability

- Settlement around trees or rocks.
- Snow sluffed off rocks above steep slopes.

Local Knowledge

- Review what you or your companions know about the area.

Slope Steepness

- Is the slope steepness appropriate for the danger level?

Terrain

- Are there steeper slopes above your descent line?
- Where would you end up if the slope avalanched?

Snow Stability

- Should you dig a snowpit? Why?
- Which stability test should you do?

Snowpit Tests

- **Compression Test** A stability test for finding weak layers and getting an indication of their strength.
- **Shovel Tilt Test** Used to identify weak layers in soft new snow near the surface of the snowpack.
- **Extended-Column Test** Used to determine whether a slab might fracture and the fracture propagate across the slope enough for the slab to release.
- **Rutschblock Test** To identify weak layers under a cohesive slab and indicate the likelihood of human triggering.

Decision Time

- What is your conclusion about stability? Keep it simple. Will it be "stable," "unstable" or are you "not sure"?

If you are "not sure," then there are some more questions to ask:

- What are the consequences of an avalanche? How deep could you be buried? What is the possibility of injury?
- Is the run worth the risk of dying in an avalanche? Are you sure your friends will be able to dig you out alive?

If You Decide To Go

- Make a plan for managing your party and discuss with your companions how you will ski or board the area.

Companion Rescue

Surviving an avalanche in the backcountry depends upon the actions of the unburied survivors. European statistics indicate a fully buried victim has a 91% chance of survival if found within 18 minutes. The chance of survival diminishes rapidly to 50% in the first half hour and few people survive if buried deeper than 2 metres.

After an accident there's always a considerable amount of excitement, anxiety and sometimes numbing fear on the part of the rescuers, especially if friends or loved ones are involved. Having a definite procedure to follow helps restore calm and gives your buried companion the best chance of survival.

Everyone who goes into the backcountry in winter should know the basic procedures of Companion Rescue:

- What to do if someone is caught in an avalanche.

- How to conduct a **Hasty Search**.

- How to search with a **Rescue Beacon** swiftly and effectively.

- The fastest procedure for **digging** out your companion.

- How to care for an avalanche victim.

- Procedures for sending for help and evacuation.

Skiers rush to the aid of a buried companion. The slide was triggered by another skier crossing from right to left above the debris. Photo André Roch.

Three Avalanche Accidents

December 11th was the first day of operations at the Sunshine Village ski area. As usual at the beginning of the season the snowpack was unconsolidated and several of the steeper runs were closed. Three skiers alighting from the Standish chairlift started off in the direction of Bunker's Run, but when informed by the lift operator that the area was closed, appeared to ski off in another direction. As soon as they were out of sight of the lift operator they ducked under the roped fence, ignored a "No Skiing" sign and entered Bunker's Run. As they skied down toward Donkey's Tail they passed several boundary poles and another sign: "Danger – Avalanche Area Closed." Donkey's Tail is a short, steep hillside overlooked by a crowded ski slope, so there were plenty of people to witness what happened, including a group of ski instructors. The first skier got down the slope safely, but the second man fell about halfway down. At the same time, the third man entering the steep slope triggered a small slide 10 m wide by 30 m long that was sufficient to knock the second man off his feet and bury him.

The ski instructors, on the scene in seconds, organized a hasty search and it was during the initial search that one of the rescuers scuffling among the debris had the good fortune to kick the victim's boot. Frantic digging uncovered the rest of his body; his head was 1.5 m below the surface and he was not breathing. Fortunately, a few breaths of mouth-to-mouth resuscitation were sufficient to bring him round. Only seven minutes had elapsed since the accident.

This skier was lucky: the avalanche was witnessed and searching started within a few seconds of his burial. Although he was found within a few minutes he was already unconscious. How much longer would he have lasted?

A highly experienced ski tourer was killed in the Wasatch Mountains of Utah. Out of sight of his companions, he triggered a soft-slab avalanche on a timbered slope, *was carried to the runout, and was buried 4 feet deep. All party members carried rescue beacons and shovels. The victim was located and dug out in 15 minutes, but had died of suffocation.* Brain damage occurs about 4 minutes after the organ is deprived of oxygenated blood, and after 8 to 10 minutes survival is unlikely even if breathing and circulation are restored.

In Jasper National Park a man died because his friends didn't know what to do. Seven ski tourers out enjoying the powder slopes of Parker Ridge were returning to Hilda Creek Hostel in the late afternoon. Five minutes before the hostel they came to a short, steep slope about 30 m high that looked like fun. Unknown to the skiers the configuration of the land allowed the prevailing wind to load the top of the slope while scouring snow from the bottom, leaving a dangerous slab hanging there unsupported (see photo page 145). The same innocuous-looking slope had been the scene of another fatality ten years before. The first man, entering the slope from the side, just below a small cornice, promptly fell face down on the hard slab and triggered a very small avalanche which rolled him down and buried him under 60 cm of snow. Unfortunately, the second man, who up to that time had been watching the leader, had turned his head away at the crucial moment and so didn't see the accident or get any idea of where his friend might be buried. It was at this point that the skiers made a serious mistake: they all left the scene of the accident and returned to their cars for shovels. By the time they'd climbed back up and started digging random holes in the debris, vital minutes had slipped by. It was sheer bad luck that they chose to dig in the wrong places. Had they spent the time immediately after the accident in organized probing with upturned poles they would have located the victim within 5 minutes and almost certainly have recovered him alive. As it was he was found some 2 hours later by Ginger, a Parks rescue dog.

Victims of avalanche accidents may be injured by the twisting force of the snow intensified by the leverage of skis and poles. Photo Bob Sandford.

Backcountry Avalanche Rescue

Overview

There is more to an avalanche rescue than beacon searches and digging techniques. Rescue begins the moment the snow starts to slide and someone is caught in the avalanche. The following overview outlines the key stages in a companion rescue — the exact order will depend on circumstances:

- Watching the person caught during the avalanche until the snow stops.

- Establishing a leader.

- Considering the possibility of further avalanches.

- Calling for help if you have the technology to do so.

- Conducting a Surface (Hasty) Search.

- Searching for a beacon signal and conducting a beacon search.

- Once located, digging the person out.

- Dealing with the victim — injuries and hypothermia.

- Deciding on evacuation: self-evacuation or rescue.

- Sending for help.

- Looking after the rescuers.

- Possibly surviving overnight in a tent or snow cave.

All of the above assume your party is prepared both psychologically and equipment-wise for a rescue. While there are many variables and alternatives in rescues, there are also many well-accepted principles, and these are what I am really trying to get across in this chapter.

Watch the Avalanche

If you're aware of avalanche danger and are using proper slope-crossing procedures and safe skiing techniques you should have only one person to worry about.

Watch carefully as they are being carried down, noting what happens to skis, poles and other abandoned equipment. In particular, fix your eyes on the area where they are last seen and send someone to mark the spot with a ski or some large identifiable object such as a pack. Consider the possibility of further avalanches.

The importance of watching the victim is well illustrated by an accident that happened near Lake Louise ski area in the Canadian Rockies. The first skier had left the top of Richardson's Ridge and was standing in a safe place below the slope watching the second skier come down. The second man, who'd chosen a slightly steeper line, had only made 10 turns when he triggered a slab avalanche which carried him down the slope and finally buried him.

Because the first skier had been watching the whole sequence right up to the time when his friend disappeared, he was able to rush to the most likely area of debris and start probing with his probe pole. The fourth probe was successful. Fortunately he was carrying a shovel. In the few minutes it took to uncover the victims head he was unconscious, his airway plugged with snow. The rescuer said later: *We had no rescue beacons and were both lucky as hell.*

Doing the right thing helps too!

Establishing a Leader

It's important that only one person call the shots, especially if there are multiple burials or people from other groups have come to help out.

- Many large groups already have a leader. If the leader is the one caught in the avalanche, you will need to appoint, agree on and support a new leader.

- For small groups the most experienced person usually takes charge.

The Richardson's Ridge avalanche. X marks the approximate burial location. Photo Kris Newman.

Possibility of Further Avalanches

Consider the possibility of further avalanches. Look for multiple start zones that could release down the same path. If you are at the foot of a bowl, consider the likelihood of other parts of the bowl sliding and whether the debris would end up at your location. If you have any concerns:

- Post a lookout in a safe location if you have enough people.

- Decide and agree on which way to run if another slide comes down. Even if you are the only rescuer, you should plan an escape route.

- If possible, stash gear you are not using in a safe location.

- If you have more people than are needed to search and dig, have them move to a safe location.

- Once you have pinpointed the location of all those buried, take a moment to switch your transceiver back to transmit.

Calling for Help

With the growing popularity of out-of-bounds skiing and boarding near established ski areas there is nowadays the possibility that a rescue team could arrive soon enough to help with a live rescue.

In any event, the sooner the rescue authorities know there has been a accident the better.

If you have the technology—cell phone and reception, satellite or GPS/satellite system—find a moment as soon as possible to call for help. Obviously, when you do this will depend on your situation. If you have enough people, assign someone to call while the others conduct the early stages of the rescue. If you are alone, then uncovering the victim as soon as possible has to be the priority.

Have you been practising transceiver searches? Many areas now have beacon training parks where you and your companions can practise locating one or more signals that simulate buried beacons.

Surface (Hasty) Search

The surface search is the most important part of a backcountry rescue because it offers the greatest possibility of a live recovery.

There are several cases of partially buried victims having died because their companions didn't stop to search before going for help.

An accident report in *The Avalanche Review* stated that *two backcountry skiers were caught in a slide near Aspen, Colorado. The survivor dug herself out, made a fast check of the debris and left the site to notify rescuers. Hours later, a hasty search by the rescue team revealed a ski tip sticking from the snow. The victim, shallowly buried, had died.*

The Hasty Search is a quick scan of the avalanche debris for any sign of the victim. Mark the position of any clothing or equipment found on the surface. You should also mark the last seen area and entry point into the slide if you are able to do so.

Searching with Avalanche Rescue Beacons

An avalanche rescue beacon search is conducted in four phases:

- **Signal Search** to pick up the signal from your buried companion's transceiver.

- **Coarse Search** to home in on the location of the burial.

- **Fine Search** to get a more exact location.

- **Pinpointing** by probing to locate the victim.

These four stages apply to all avalanche beacon searches.

This photograph illustrates two methods of searching avalanche debris to locate a signal. A large avalanche on the Oberalp, Gotthard, Switzerland. Photo André Roch.

Search Methods

If you review avalanche safety literature you will find there are many methods of searching described, some that apply to special situations such as deep or multiple burials, others that describe search methods for various configurations of beacon — analogue or digital, one antenna or two or three antennas and so on. It can be very confusing for the average backcountry enthusiast.

My advice is to purchase a three-antenna transceiver and learn how to use it quickly and effectively according to the manufacturer's instructions.

If you have an older, two-antenna receiver, again use the manufacturer's instructions. If you have an old single-antenna receiver, it's time to replace it.

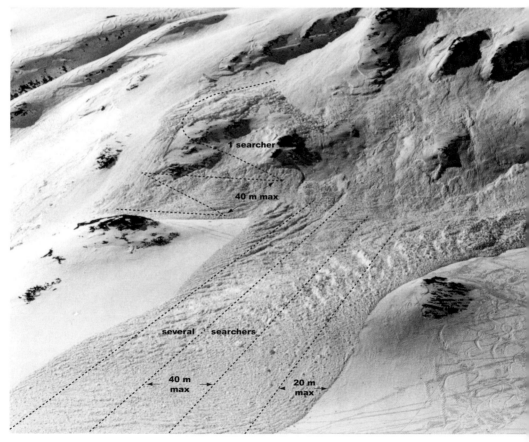

1 searcher

40 m max

several searchers

40 m max

20 m max

Signal Search

The initial search for a signal can often be combined with the **Hasty Search** where the searchers are coming from above and the slide is fairly small.

- Check for danger from further avalanching, especially in multi-branched gully systems and bowls which have only partially slid. If there is danger, post a lookout and instruct everyone to switch to transmit should another avalanche occur. Some receivers automatically revert to transmit mode if they haven't moved for a period of time.

- Keep your skis or boards on for as long as possible, certainly as long as you are going downhill.

- **Everyone** must switch their rescue beacon to receive and make sure they're receiving at full volume if their unit has a volume control, or set to maximum distance for a visual display.

- Spread the party evenly across the slope at intervals of not more than 40 m. It doesn't matter if you search uphill, downhill or across the debris, as long as you ski or board in straight lines parallel to one another. If you're the only searcher, zigzag across the debris.

- Apart from the occasional command the search should be conducted in silence.

- Treat the initial rescue beacon search as part of the hasty search of the debris, and mark any clothing or equipment you find.

- Generally, searchers should wear their packs to ensure that rescue gear is close at hand. Keep ski poles handy in case they're needed as probes or as markers to delineate final search limits.

A modern transceiver uses a combination of visual signals and electronic displays to guide you round the magnetic flux lines (induction lines) emitted by a buried transceiver to bring you close to the burial location. The shape of the induction lines depends on the orientation of the antenna in the buried transceiver.

Coarse Search

The purpose of the Coarse Search is to locate the buried person to within a few metres. Modern transceivers use a combination of visual signals and electronic displays to guide you round the flux lines emitted by the buried transceiver to the victim's approximate position. The exact method will depend on the model.

- When a signal is detected, assign one or two people to track it down while the rest of the group continues to search for other signals. If only one person is known to be caught, assign no more than two people to track down the signal. The remainder of the search party should be getting shovels and probes ready for pinpointing and digging.

- Keep skis on if possible. You will probably have to take your board off.

- If at any time the signal decreases or the indicated distance increases, you are heading away from the victim. Turn 180°.

- You will end up within a few metres of the victim's position. It is now time to do a Fine Search.

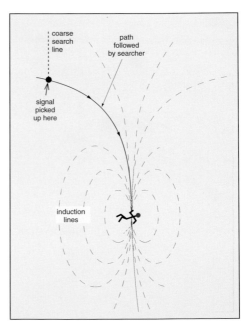

- If there is more than one buried person and you have enough people, assign others to continue searching. Some of the latest beacons will indicate that they have more signals, and the manufacturer will have a recommended procedure for the extended search.

Fine Search

The basic method used in the Fine Search is to orient the unit for maximum signal and sweep the beacon just above the surface of the snow in a criss-cross pattern. Find the location halfway between the points where the signal fades away. Trying to identify the point where the signal is strongest works well with some beacons.

You should be able to locate a buried unit to an accuracy of about one-third of the depth of burial. For instance, if the buried unit is 1 m deep then you should be able to locate the position within 33 cm horizontally.

Again, each manufacturer will have a procedure that you should learn and use.

- **Note** that metal objects will deflect or reflect the signal, so keep skis, poles and shovels away from the burial location until you've finished the fine search. Turn off cellphones, iPods or similar devices.

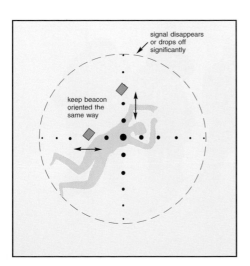

Deep Burials

Deep burials are difficult to narrow down and require a different technique that requires practice and, for best results, a receiver that will operate in analogue mode. If you are concerned about deep burials, check out an article by Manuel Genswein, "Pinpointing in a Circle," at arc.lib.montana.edu/snow-science/objects/issw-2000-357-362.pdf.

Pinpointing
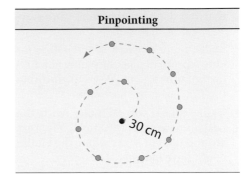

Pinpointing

Time can be saved by locating the exact position of the victim with a probe or ski pole before starting to dig.

- **Note** that at least one beacon on the market has a specific routine for pinpointing that is almost certainly faster than probing.

- Start at the point indicated by the Fine Search.

- Probe perpendicularly to the slope.

- Probe in a spiral pattern with a 30 cm spacing as illustrated above.

- When you hit the victim, leave the probe in place. Note the burial depth.

Search without Beacons

Hopefully this is something you never have to do for someone from your own group. However, there's always a chance that you'll see another party avalanched or be asked for help by survivors. Persuade the survivors to go back to the debris with you and describe exactly what happened.

- Defer to an obviously experienced survivor; otherwise, take charge. Confirm that they don't have beacons. If not sure, start a beacon search.
- Make a quick search of the debris for clues. Leave in place anything you find on the surface; it might serve to indicate the line taken by the victim.
- Using probes, or ski poles with the baskets removed, probe any likely areas around trees or rocks where the victim could have lodged.
- Glance up the runout zone to see if there is anywhere a person could have hung up on the way down.
- After all the likely locations have been probed, set up an organized probe line.

Even if there are only two survivors, it is statistically more effective to probe in an organized manner.

- Keep the slide clean of food scraps, urine etc. in case a rescue dog has to be brought in.

Probing

Probing is the oldest and least efficient method of searching for an avalanche victim. Unfortunately, if either the buried person or the searchers are not equipped with avalanche rescue beacons, it's the only method available to the backcountry traveller. If correct probing techniques are used, there's a 70% chance of finding a victim on the first pass, providing they are not buried too deep. If you don't have avalanche probes, use poles or skis. At least they will allow you to probe to a depth of about a metre. The advantage of probes that extend to 3 metres is obvious.

To be effective, **probing must be organized and orderly**. Establish a leader to coordinate probing; usually the most

Use any item at your disposal when probing. The important rule is to probe in an organized manner.
Photo Bob Sandford.

An organized rescue probe line on Ben Nevis, Scotland. Photo Andy Nicol.

experienced member of the party. The procedure is as follows:

- Probe uphill; it's easier to keep the proper spacing between probers.
- Most victims are found near the toe of the debris. Unless you have a very good reason to suspect otherwise, concentrate on the last few metres of the debris.
- Probe the most likely areas, marking them as you probe them with whatever you have available—skis, packs etc.
- To get the proper spacing, probers should stand hand on hips, elbow to elbow. Keeping this spacing, each prober inserts the probe once between their feet.
- An alternative is to stand fingertip to fingertip and probe first to one side of your body and then to the other side. Use this method when there's a small number of probers.
- After each probe, the line moves forward about two boot lengths or one step and probes again. This procedure is repeated as far as necessary up the slope.

- The leader should call out "probes up, forward, down," at which commands the probers should raise their probes, advance and probe down again. The manoeuvre must be done with military precision and to a rhythm that ensures maximum pace.
- The prober who hits a victim within 1.5 m of the surface will have no doubt about the contact. A tree stump or a rock feels much different.
- Dig out the victim. If you know or suspect there are other skiers buried under the debris, designate one or two people to dig out the first victim while the rest continue to probe.
- If you're unsuccessful on the first pass you must decide whether to probe the same area again or move to an adjacent area. Unless you're absolutely sure that you're probing the right area you should move the probe line each time until you have covered all possibilities.

Strategic Shovelling

In the spring of 2006 Dale Atkins from RECCO and Bruce Edgerly from Backcountry Access (BCA) set out to research and document a more efficient method of digging out a buried person than the random shovelling currently being used. They found very little had been published on the subject, although Canadian mountain guides had unpublished guidelines based on work done by Willi Pfisterer 20 years before. Atkins and Edgerly's work can be found in a paper called "Strategic Shoveling" at https://is.gd/jGWMIz. For links to a handout sheet and several videos, Google the phrase Avalanche Shovelling 101. They have certainly achieved their goal of stimulating interest in the subject among avalanche educators. Strategic shovelling is now considered a critical stage of backcountry avalanche rescue.

At about the same time, Manuel Genswein of Switzerland was developing his Snow Conveyor Shovelling Method, which is geared toward the larger number of rescuers often available in European accidents.

Here is a suggested procedure for uncovering a buried companion, based on the aforementioned works:

- Leave the probe in place, noting the burial depth. Avoid tramping around directly above your buried companion to avoid injuring them or reducing their air pocket.

- Put your gloves back on once you have finished assembling the probe and shovel.

- Mark a rectangle on the snow with your shovel about as wide as your extended arms for a single rescuer or about 2 m wide for multiple diggers. This is to discourage the digging of an increasingly narrower hole that would eventually slow down access to the person's airway. The rectangle should extend downhill from the probe a distance of 1.5 times the burial depth. See diagram on next page.

Single Rescuer

- Excavate the "starter hole," working on your knees if necessary, and throwing snow out to the sides of the hole. Chop

Hard-slab avalanches can deposit a considerable amount of debris that includes large blocks which make for hard digging and difficult probing. Only the most rugged shovels and stiffest probes will be effective in this kind of debris. Photo Bob Uttl.

hard snow into blocks and scoop it out rather than prying. It's faster and uses less energy.

- Stand up when you need to and continue throwing snow to the sides where it won't have to be moved again.

- Maintain the full width of the starter hole as you dig deeper.

- When the snow surface gets to be level with your waist, you may need to dig a terrace on the downhill side so that you can throw the snow clear.

- You will now need to excavate to another level. Start at about half the distance to the probe and work toward the probe. This will give you a bench to sit on.

- If the debris is on a slope and the probe is perpendicular to the slope, make sure you keep the probe exposed all the way down. You may need to begin your starter hole a little above the probe.

- When you first reach your buried companion, dig to uncover their head and clear their airway as soon as possible.

Two Rescuers

- The starter hole should be wide enough for the two rescuers to work side by side, each person throwing snow to their own side. Otherwise the procedure is the same.

Many Rescuers

- Two of the rescuers should begin digging the starter hole, throwing the snow out to the sides as described above.

- You can deploy extra diggers using the principles of Genswein's Conveyor Method. In self-rescue situations you are only likely to be able to use two or possibly three extra people effectively for shovelling. Additional people can be part of the rotation or can be preparing to deal with the evacuated person.

- Rotate shovellers frequently.

- The extra shovellers, offset from each other, clear snow from the downhill

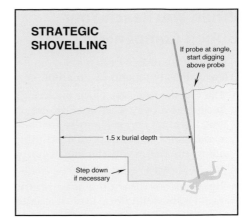

side of the starter hole so as to create and maintain a ramp down toward the burial location.

- The ramp should be flared out at the back to allow the rear diggers room to work. As the starter hole gets deeper it will become easier for the two front diggers to throw the snow up the ramp behind them to where the rear diggers can scoop it out of the way.

- Once the buried person is reached, the extra shovellers can enlarge the hole and maintain the ramp to facilitate extraction while one of the rescue party is attending to the airway.

Take Time To Think

As the victim is being dug out, take a moment to mentally rehearse what you will do when the buried person is uncovered. Preferably, if there's enough help around, let others do the digging and just stand aside for a few minutes and think; it may result in fewer mistakes or serious omissions later on.

Now is the time to put into practice all your first-aid training! Hopefully you have taken a basic first-aid and cardiopulmonary resuscitation (CPR) course.

When You Reach Your Buried Companion

Remember the ABCs of first aid: **Airway, Breathing and Circulation.**

- Dig out the face first. Clear the mouth, nose and airway. Continue digging to free the chest and make room for chest expansion. Be careful not to cut or further injure the victim with the shovel during the final stages of freeing them.

- Spontaneous breathing may return; evaluate breathing for at least 10 seconds or longer. If the victim is not breathing, or breathing is ineffectual, begin direct mouth to mouth artificial respiration. If you can't get a breath into the lungs, the airway may be blocked by the tongue or snow.

- If a neck injury is suspected, the head should be moved as little as possible and the airway opened by placing your hands on either side of the head to maintain the neck in a fixed, neutral position while at the same time pushing the jaw forward with the index fingers. Ideally two people are needed for this method, although one person can do it in a pinch by sealing the nose using their cheek — but it's a difficult and tiring job.

- Don't give up hope at this stage, particularly if the victim is found with an air pocket in front of their face.

- Check for a pulse at the neck by placing a couple of fingers gently on the carotid artery. Assess for at least 10 seconds, or longer if the victim has been buried for any length of time, as the pulse may be faint and hard to detect. If you can't find a pulse, and you've been trained, begin CPR and continue until medical aid arrives or until no longer practical.

- Stop any serious bleeding by applying direct pressure to the injury.

- If there is more than one person buried, **turn off the victim's avalanche beacon** as soon as possible so as not to interfere with searching for additional victims.

Caring for the Avalanche Victim

Asphyxia, or suffocation, is the primary cause of death in avalanches. Avalanche debris is typically very dense and victims may be found with snow in their mouth, or with an ice layer built up around the nose and mouth.

However, recent research spearheaded by Dr. Jeff Boyd of Banff, who is also a certified mountain guide, shows that about one-quarter of all avalanche victims in Canada have died from the trauma of the avalanche. Even small avalanches create very large forces. Until you rule it out, you should assume the victim has traumatic injuries.

Removing Your Buried Companion

It doesn't matter whether the buried person is conscious or unconscious, they must be removed from the snow gently. If a victim is suffering from hypothermia, a cold heart is very vulnerable to shaking or jarring which could cause the heart to lapse into ventricular fibrillation causing death.

- Assume the person has a spinal injury until that is ruled out. Take precautions against causing further spinal damage when moving the victim. The head, neck and back must be immobilized and moved as one unit. Move them as little as possible. If the person is conscious, you may be able to run your hand firmly down the entire spinal column to determine if there is any tenderness along the spine. Ask the victim if they have numbness or tingling in the extremities. Check for sensation and mobility of the extremities. If there is any pain or tingling, or numbness in the extremities, keep the spine immobilized.

- If the patient is unconscious, examine the neck quickly by running the fingers firmly down the upper part of the spine from the base of the skull to the shoulder blades. Feel for any obvious deformity. Sometimes an involuntary reflex movement indicates a neck injury.

Identify Other Injuries

Once the victim is breathing, perform a complete body exam.

- If the victim is unconscious, monitor breathing and pulse.

- Check the pupils for size, equality of both pupils and reaction to light.

- Assume there may be internal injuries and injuries to the arms and legs. Check the rib cage for evidence of chest injuries (pain; laboured, shallow breathing). Look for evidence of internal abdominal injuries (tenderness, rigidity, guarding, distension etc.). Check for fractures of the pelvis or femur. These are all potentially life-threatening conditions and outside help is required as quickly as possible. Make sure the rescue team is advised of these injuries when requesting help.

- Unless you have a definite indication of chest or abdomen injuries, it may be best under the circumstances to leave the patient covered up.

- Look for less serious injuries to arms and legs. Check for and treat any other bleeding.

As soon as you remove the patient from the snow they are going to get very cold. It is extremely important to maintain their body heat by whatever means you have available. See "Keeping the Patient Alive" on the next page.

Sending for Help

Before sending for help, make quite sure that help is required. The leader should gather the group together and discuss with them exactly what kind of help is needed. A problem that plagues rescue organizations is a panic call before the circumstances and consequences of the accident have been determined. Start compiling a log of events and times.

Ideally, the request for help should be in writing; the message may then be passed on by lay people who might otherwise misinterpret terms used by the survivor. It's surprising how quickly and easily a message can become garbled. If possible, send two people out for help. To respond effectively, rescue groups need answers to the following questions:

- Where did the accident take place and at what time? GPS location if possible.

- What travel conditions are like in the area and an estimate of how long it will take rescuers to reach them.

- Exactly what happened.

- How many persons are buried or injured?

- What are their injuries? Will they need special care?

- Some idea of the number of rescuers at the site, their experience and how well they are equipped.

- What help you expect of the rescuers.

- Any other information that might help in planning the rescue such as available helicopter landing sites, snow conditions, elevation of the accident site, weather—especially the amount of cloud, approximate temperature and wind strength.

If You Are Sent for Help

Your prime objective is to get help for injured or buried avalanche victims as quickly and as safely as possible. If you take too many chances and are injured on the way out, not only do you let your friends down but you also compound eventual rescue problems. So take it easy, relatively speaking, and try to arrive at your destination able to describe the accident in a calm and coherent manner.

In national parks or other formally administered areas such as national forests or provincial parks, call the emergency number. In other areas call the closest law enforcement agency, which will get in touch with the appropriate rescue groups.

It's very important that, having given your information, you don't disappear. If you phone in the alarm, give the number you are calling from and stay by the phone until you're contacted; usually the rescue leader will want to talk to you personally. If you're a sole survivor, you may have to return to the scene of the accident with the rescue group.

Keeping the Patient Alive

If the victim is still unconscious, monitor vital signs (pulse, breathing, skin colour, pupils and level of consciousness). Write down these vital signs and convey the information when medical aid arrives. Protect the injured person's airway by rolling them on their side, while maintaining spinal control.

As soon as you remove the victim from the snow, they are going to get very cold. Maintain the victim's body heat right from the time the patient is uncovered. Because an injured person is likely to be partially or totally immobilized, they're much more susceptible to frostbite and hypothermia than the rescuers, who can exercise to keep warm. Cold, coupled with pain, injury and worry, can bring on shock.

Shock and Hypothermia

Fortunately the treatment for shock and hypothermia in a rescue situation is identical. First of all, get the patient into shelter, whether a tent, bothy bag, snow cave or trench in the snow. Remove boots and socks, either replacing wet socks with dry ones or wrapping the feet in a dry wool sweater. The feet and lower legs should be elevated and placed inside a packsack.

Withdraw the arms from the sleeves of the jacket and sweater and arrange inside the clothing against the trunk of the body. Cover the head. Wrap the person further in any material that will help conserve body heat such as a space blanket or polyethylene tube tent. If the patient is very cold and in an advanced state of hypothermia, get one of the rescuers to strip off to their underwear and wrap the two up together using their outer clothing and a space blanket or large group shelter (page 124). A sleeping bag makes this technique much easier to implement. If you have the means to heat water, you can make a hot compress. Soak a shirt or other article of clothing in very hot water, put it in a plastic bag and wrap the whole thing in a sweater. Place the compress on the patient's abdomen just below the sternum, binding it to the patient with spare clothing. If you have the facilities, in a hut for instance, additional compresses can be used against the side of the chest immediately below the arms. Don't massage the victim's arms or legs, as this encourages cold blood to flow from the extremities to the body core.

If the victim is fully conscious, give hot, preferably non-sweetened drinks. Do not give alcohol. Handle gently to avoid any jarring or bouncing that might lead to ventricular fibrillation.

Frostbite

Keeping the patient warm helps prevent frostbite. However, injured extremities, especially if splinted, are extremely prone to frostbite and frequent inspection is necessary to make sure there's adequate circulation. Unless you are several days from help don't attempt thaw out frozen extremities. Do not allow a person to walk or ski once their feet have been thawed out.

Pain

Because pain contributes to the development of shock, a patient who asks for relief should be given it. Do not give drugs if a patient is hypothermic.

Psychological Care

When a person is injured, the accompanying emotional shock can have a great influence on the outcome of the accident. In a backcountry accident there's the additional worry of being far from qualified help and the likelihood of having to survive for a long time in an unfriendly environment.

The accident victim has two immediate psychological problems. First, there's a loss of self-esteem at having been involved in an accident; the realization that they may have done something stupid is further aggravated by the fact that they're now dependent on someone else's skill in order to survive. Second, they have very real fears concerning the extent of their injuries and the quality of care they're going to get. Because an injured person is so wrapped up in their own immediate survival, they become prone to making irrational decisions and voicing seemingly irrelevant concerns.

Rescuers must try to restore a person's dignity. Let the patient discuss the accident, but be careful not to moralize or pass judgment at this stage. If you don't know the victim, find out their first name and use it frequently when speaking to them. Involve them in their own care by giving them something useful to do. Above all try not to give any indication that they are a burden on the rescue party.

It is reassuring to an avalanche victim if the rescue, particularly the first aid, is conducted in a calm, orderly manner. Introduce yourself to the patient and give them some indication of your qualifications: the number of years you've been mountaineering or skiing, your first-aid training and rescue experience. Write down the patient's name and hometown and if they have any medical problems which might affect treatment such as diabetes or drug allergy. Give them an honest appraisal of their injuries, then discuss treatment, explaining as you go along what you are doing and why. Someone should sit by their side at all times.

Evacuation

At some time during the rescue you'll have to make a decision on how the person is to be evacuated. There are three reasonable alternatives:

- The rescue party can evacuate the person themselves before or shortly after nightfall.

- A rescue organization capable of reaching the accident scene before dark can be called in.

- Evacuation cannot be started until the next day and the group has to survive overnight.

Rescue before Nightfall

In the areas of North America where most backcountry activity takes place rescue groups can speedily transport an injured person to hospital by helicopter, snowmobile or rescue toboggan. If it is obvious that such a group can effect a rescue before nightfall it's better to stay put near the scene of the accident and wait for help. Build windbreaks, light a fire, and if a helicopter is expected, stamp out a landing place in the nearest flat, open area.

Look after the Rescuers

By now the rescuers are probably tired, cold and hungry. If it's feasible, send all those who are no longer needed out to the road. Those who stay can keep warm by skiing around or building extra shelters. Watch for signs of hypothermia, frostbite, exhaustion or dehydration. Now is the time to change socks, put on overboots and spare clothing and concentrate on your own survival.

Self-Evacuation

If the victim is merely shaken up or only slightly injured they will probably want to get out without calling in a rescue group. Think carefully before allowing them to do so. Skis are often lost in the accident and walking a long distance in deep snow is exhausting and conducive to frostbite. Don't allow a person who has been unconscious or has developed hypothermia to walk out, even if they say they feel capable.

Building an improvised toboggan from skis and poles, an alternative promoted by survival experts, is only viable if it is to move an injured person a short distance to a place of safety. Long hauls with makeshift equipment in any but the easiest terrain and the best snow conditions require a tremendous amount of manpower, and in deep, fresh snow can quickly exhaust a rescue party, thereby jeopardizing the entire operation. Moreover, moving a badly injured person in this manner can greatly aggravate any injuries and add substantially to the effects of shock. Usually it's far better to spend precious time and energy building a survival shelter and concentrate on keeping the patient alive and warm until professional help arrives.

Surviving Overnight

When an accident happens late in the day or at a remote location, an overnight bivouac is a certainty. If there's enough time, send as many people as you can back to camp or out to civilization.

For those remaining, getting out of the wind and putting some kind of insulating layer between yourselves and the cold air is the first priority. Move to the lee side of rocks or down to treeline. Look for a suitable place to build a snow shelter. Circumstances will dictate how elaborate a shelter you construct; in really foul weather you may only have enough energy left to dig a shallow trench covered with snow blocks. More time, more energy and suitable snow would allow construction of a snow cave or igloo. A small stove, even a candle, will raise the air temperature in a confined space close to the freezing point.

After a Rescue

During or after the incident, everyone involved, including rescuers, may experience an emotional reaction that may impair their judgment or ability to act or carry on. Critical-incident stress is a normal response experienced by normal people to an abnormal event. It may include physical conditions (insomnia, gut aches) or mental conditions such as memory loss, irritability, sadness or reduced attention span.

A debriefing with the help of a trained professional that includes everyone involved can assist with managing the emotional reaction to such a traumatic event. A good rescue organization will usually initiate a debriefing and bring someone in to assist in the process.

Avalanche Rescue Dogs

An avalanche rescue dog's air-scenting ability is a very efficient method of finding buried victims. In Europe between 1962 and 1972, dogs participated in 135 rescues and were responsible for the live recovery of 25 people. The picture in North America is a little different: to date there have only been three or four live rescues of skiers and climbers in the backcountry. Because fewer dogs are spread out over a very much larger territory, the time spent in getting them to the scene of the accident means less chance of finding the victim alive.

In April 1992 a skier just outside the Jackson Hole ski area boundary took a 300 m ride over two cliff bands and was buried over a metre deep. An air pocket kept him alive until found by a rescue dog after being buried for 93 minutes. Ten years earlier, a ski lift operator at Alpine Meadows, California, was found after five days of burial in the wreckage of the summit terminal building.

In reasonable weather, a dog will find all victims who are still alive and those who have just died, regardless of the depth or nature of the snow. If the body has been dead for some time and is frozen, a dog will only be effective to a depth of around 2 m in porous snow, which is further reduced to a metre or less in hard, compact snow.

There are a few things a rescue party should do which will help a dog:

- Keep searching until instructed to do otherwise by the dogmaster. Sometimes the dog can work an area at the same time as a probe line is active. On no account should you stop searching and wait for a dog to arrive.

- Avoid contaminating the debris with food scraps, candy wrappers, urine, cigarette butts etc. If you get the chance, move packs and other surplus equipment off and downwind from the debris.

Photo Kyle Hale, Canadian Avalanche Rescue Dog Association.

The Role of Helicopters in Rescue

- For a helicopter to come in at all requires reasonable visibility. They are highly susceptible to turbulence and high ground winds.
- They can't hover over dense brush or over slopes of more than 10°, but can rest for short periods on one skid. Most rescues are done by slinging the person out, accompanied by a rescuer, at the end of a long cable.

Skiers and climbers should be familiar with a helicopter's limitations and know how to behave safely around one. Photo Bob Sandford.

- Few helicopters can land or take off vertically; they require additional space for a short landing or takeoff run.
- Pilots need a visual reference to pinpoint the snow surface. Skis lying flat at the side of a packed-down area work well. Don't use lightweight items such as jackets or foamies. Don't stand skis up in the snow anywhere near the landing site.

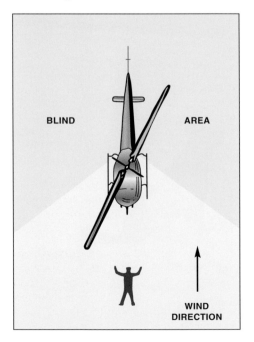

BLIND   AREA

WIND
DIRECTION

- When a helicopter is coming in to land, indicate wind direction by standing with your back to the wind and your arms outstretched in front of you pointing to the landing site.
- Don't leave loose items near a landing site; they're liable to be sucked up into the main or tail rotor, causing damage that will immobilize the machine.
- The most important rule: don't panic!
- Stay where you can be seen by the pilot.
- Never go around the back of a helicopter. Wait for the pilot's signal before approaching. If the landing site has a slight slope, remember that rotor clearance on the uphill side is reduced.
- Beware of the main rotor, tail rotor, exhaust pipes and air intakes. Avoid touching protuberances at the front, which may be either delicate or hot.
- Never carry equipment above shoulder height when approaching or leaving a helicopter.

When approaching a helicopter always remain within the pilot's field of view.

Bibliography

Currently Available

Armstrong, Betsy, and Knox Williams. *The Avalanche Book*, Fulcrum Inc., revised 1992, 232 pp. An informative book on avalanches and their impact on those who live, work or recreate in mountain areas.

Ferguson, Sue, and Ed LaChapelle. *The ABCs of Avalanche Safety*, Mountaineers Books, 3rd ed., 2003, 192 pp. A rewrite and update of Ed LaChapelle's classic pocket guide to avoiding avalanches.

Fredston, Jill, and Doug Fesler. *Snow Sense: A Guide to Evaluating Avalanche Hazard*, Alaska Mountain Safety Center Inc., 5th ed. revised, 2011, 116 pp. Small, easy to read, pocket-sized book for winter backcountry enthusiasts.

Jamieson, Bruce. *Backcountry Avalanche Awareness*, Avalanche Canada, 8th ed., 2000, 78 pp. A well-organized, easy to read booklet, aimed at the backcountry enthusiast, by a leading Canadian avalanche researcher from the University of Calgary.

Jamieson, Bruce, and Jennie Krynski. *Free Riding in Avalanche Terrain: A Snowboarder's Handbook*. Avalanche Canada, 2nd ed. revised, 2012, 74 pp. *Backcountry Avalanche Awareness* rewritten for snowboarders.

Jamieson, Bruce, and Lori Zacaruk. *Sledding in Avalanche Terrain: Reducing the Risk*. Avalanche Canada, 4th ed., 2014, 78 pp. *Backcountry Avalanche Awareness* rewritten for snowmobilers.

LaChapelle, Ed. *Field Guide to Snow Crystals*, International Glaciological Society, reprint, 1992, 101 pp. Snow metamorphism with illustrations of snow crystals.

McClung, David, and Peter Schaerer. *The Avalanche Handbook*, Mountaineers Books, 3rd ed., 2006, 342 pp. A modern version of the US Forest Service's *Avalanche Handbook* that was first published in 1976. Written as a handbook for avalanche professionals, this title is being positioned by the publisher as a book for backcountry recreationists as well. Most people will find it heavy going.

Tremper, Bruce. *Avalanche Essentials: A Step-by-Step System for Safety and Survival*, Mountaineers Books, 2013, 176 pp. A stripped-down version of *Staying Alive in Avalanche Terrain*, focusing on systems and checklists, step-by-step procedures, decision-making aids, visual terrain and weather cues and rescue techniques.

Tremper, Bruce. *Staying Alive in Avalanche Terrain*, Mountaineers Books, 2nd ed., 2008, 284 pp. A detailed and comprehensive book by one of North America's foremost avalanche practitioners. Informative, easy to understand and packed with practical information.

Some Snow and Avalanche Classics

Atwater, Monty. *The Avalanche Hunters*, MacRae Smith Co., 1968, 236 pp. Autobiography describing avalanche studies and the development of control procedures in the USA.

Fraser, Colin. *Avalanches and Snow Safety*, John Murray, 1978, 269 pp. Originally titled *The Avalanche Enigma*. A nontechnical account of snow and avalanches based on the author's experiences in the Swiss Alps.

Lunn, Arnold. *Alpine Ski-ing at All Heights and Seasons*. Methuen, 1921, 1926, 106 pp. One of the first skiing books about snowcraft, snow conditions and avalanches.

Seligman, Gerald. *Snow Structure and Ski Fields*, International Glaciological Society, Cambridge, England, 3rd ed., 1980, 555 pp. First published in 1936. The first comprehensive book in English on snow and avalanches.

Glossary

Accumulation Zone An area where snow accumulates either by direct deposition or by wind transport. In avalanche terminology it usually refers to the starting zone.

Angle of Repose is the critical slope angle at which a granular material is on the verge of sliding.

Aspect The compass direction of a slope looking straight down the fall line.

Avalanche Defined in dictionaries as a mass of snow, rock and ice falling down a mountain. In practice the term avalanche refers to the snow avalanche unless the words rock, ice, mud etc. are specifically used. In the US the term snowslide is commonly used to mean a snow avalanche.

Avalanche Problem A term used in avalanche forecasts when identifying the type of avalanche likely to present a problem to the backcountry traveller.

Avalanche Transceiver An electronic device used to locate buried avalanche victims. Worn by people in avalanche terrain, it transmits a signal that can be received by companions in the event of a burial. The terms transceiver and beacon are interchangeable.

Bed Surface The surface on which a slab avalanche slides. If only the top layers of the snow slide off an underlying snow layer, the avalanche is described as a surface avalanche. If the entire snowpack slides off to the ground, it is called a full-depth avalanche.

Channelled Avalanche An avalanche which is confined by flutings or a gully as opposed to an avalanche on an open slope, which is referred to as Unconfined.

Climax Avalanche Many people consider any large and devastating avalanche to be a climax avalanche but this is not correct. A Climax Avalanche is the culmination of the buildup of several layers on top of a weak one. Large climax avalanches occur in spring when the whole of the season's snowpack may release right down to the ground.

Corn Snow is composed of large, granular snow grains resulting from many cycles of melting and refreezing. Sometimes called Spring Snow, it gives fabulous skiing for a limited time, as it soon begins to melt and becomes so wet as to be slushy.

Creep is an internal deformation of the snowpack reflecting the snow's ability to flow like a liquid, albeit very slowly.

Crown Fracture Line, Crown Line and Crown Surface all refer to the top fracture line of a slab avalanche.

Crust A hard, fairly thin layer formed of well-bonded snow. Bonding may be due to refreezing of melted grains (Sun Crust) or wind packing (Wind Crust).

Crystal A solid whose atoms or molecules have a regularly repeated arrangement. In snow terminology there is sometimes confusion between Grain and Crystal. Rounding causes a snow crystal to lose its crystalline structure and become a blob (grain) of ice. Faceting is the beginning of the recrystallization process, where an orderly arrangement of water molecules begins to build up on a grain of ice. In some processes such a surface hoar, water molecules recrystallize to form new crystals.

Cup Crystal A hollow, cup-shaped depth hoar crystal usually found hanging open end down in relatively large open spaces in the snowpack. A supply of moisture, very still air and a steep temperature gradient are required for their formation. Large depth hoar crystals in the base of the snowpack are also called cup crystals. See also **Depth Hoar**.

Deep Persistent Slab is the result of a layer of facets forming above or below a crust buried relatively deep in the snowpack or a layer of depth hoar at the bottom of the snowpack.

Delayed-action Avalanches are avalanches which release at any time between storms, without warning. Also called Non-storm-induced Avalanches. See also **Direct-action Avalanches**.

Deposition Zone The area where the bulk of the snow carried down in an avalanche comes to rest. See also **Runout Zone** and **Windblast Zone**.

Depth Hoar Recrystallized snow found in the bottom layers of a shallow snowpack after a period of very cold weather. Commonly called Sugar Snow.

Diamond Dust Diamond dust is another form of ice crystal that occurs in very cold, clear conditions. They're often seen early in the day as tiny, glittering crystals floating in the atmosphere a few metres above the ground.

Direct-action Avalanches are avalanches which fall during or shortly after a storm. Also called Storm-induced Avalanches.

Equilibrium Form Used by the snow science community to describe the form of ice grain created by rounding. This form is the result of little or no crystal growth.

Equi-temperature Metamorphism A term formerly used to describe the process of rounding. See **Metamorphism**.

Faceting is the process of building angular grains (facets). It is the beginning stage of recrystallization due to large temperature gradients. Depth Hoar is the culmination of the faceting process.

Firn Snow is snow which has settled and compacted under the influence of both Melt–freeze and Pressure Metamorphism. Common usage considers firn snow to be snow which has survived the spring thaw.

Firnspiegel is a thin, highly reflective surface ice layer formed by subsurface melting due to intense solar radiation during cold, clear weather in spring or summer. The meltwater eventually forms a thin surface layer of clear ice that acts like a greenhouse, allowing melting of the snow just beneath.

Flank Surface The fracture lines at the sides of a slab avalanche. The left flank is the left fracture line as you look downhill in the direction of fall.

Fracture Line The division between the sliding slab and the stable snow above and to each side. See **Crown Fracture Line** and **Flank Surface**.

Full-depth Avalanches are avalanches which clean off the snow right down to the ground.

Funicular Regime The condition, in wet snow, where the liquid content is high enough for the water to exist in a continuous path between grains, resulting in a very weak bond.

Glide is the slow, steady movement of a snow slab over either the ground surface or over a wetted layer within the snowpack such as ice.

Glide Crack The crack formed by the gliding of a slab. Such cracks tend to widen over time and eventually the slab may fall as an avalanche.

Glide Slabs occur when the entire snow cover creeps downhill on steep grass or smooth bedrock slabs. They are uncommon in most snow climates and tend to be confined to specific, well-known terrain features.

Gliding Surface is the term sometimes used instead of Bed Surface when referring to the surface on which a slab avalanche slides. A weak layer above the gliding surface is known as the Slide Layer.

Grain A single particle of ice; the smallest individual component of snow on the ground. A distinction is usually made between **Snow Crystals** and **Ice Grains**. Snow crystals fall from the atmosphere and change into ice grains after they reach the ground. See Metamorphism. In some conditions of temperature and humidity, water vapour around ice grains may recrystallize to form ice crystals. See **Surface Hoar** and **Depth Hoar**.

Granular Snow is snow with relatively large grains or clusters of grains (>3 mm). Examples are large, faceted surface grains, clusters of refrozen melt–freeze grains, or heavily rimed snow crystals.

Graupel Atmospheric snow crystals, heavily coated with rime before deposition.

Hard Slab Term commonly used for slab which forms at higher altitudes with strong winds. Breaks up on release into large blocks which remain intact in the debris. There is no easy way to define hard slabs in the backcountry, though they are considered to have a density greater than 300 kg/m³

Highmarking is an activity where snowmobilers try to get as high up a snow slope as they can before either their machine powers out or the rider chickens out.

Ice Ice grains frozen together, with isolated pores and a density greater than about 830 kg/m³

Ice Grain. See **Grain**.

Ice Lens Formed when free water percolates into a cold region of the snowpack and refreezes. Refers to layers less than 5 mm thick.

Ice Pellet Translucent spheres of frozen water that fall as precipitation that are less than 5 mm in diameter. They are different from graupel.

Indicator Slope Slopes which tend to be the first to release avalanches after a storm are often referred to as Indicator Slopes; they indicate to the observer that snow stability is reaching a critical stage.

Isothermal Slides are wet snow avalanches which occur as a result of the top layers, or even the whole snowpack, attaining the same temperature throughout. In avalanche terminology the temperature referred to is a temperature close to 0°C.

Kinetic Growth Form Term used by the snow science community to describe the process of recrystallization causing faceting and the formation of **Cup Crystals**, and which is the result of rapid crystal growth.

Loose-snow Avalanches are avalanches which start from a point and gather more snow as they descend.

Loose Dry Avalanches, sometimes called point avalanches or sluffs, generally occur during or shortly after new snowfall, removing snow from steep upper slopes and either stabilizing lower slopes or loading them with additional snow.

Loose Wet Avalanches occur when wet new snow or wet surface snow loses cohesion and starts moving downslope. Loose wet avalanches caused by solar radiation are influenced by aspect and slope angle, and the potential danger on a given slope will change as the sun moves across during the day.

Lubricating Layer Normally used to describe a layer within the snowpack which has been wetted by free water percolating through the snow. Sometimes any weak or cohesionless layer, such as a layer of buried surface hoar, is called a lubricating layer.

Melt–freeze. See **Metamorphism**.

Metamorphism means change of form and is the name given to changes in the structure of the snow within the snowpack. The snow science community have made several changes in terminology during the last 30 years.

The terms currently used are: Equilibrium Form (rounding), Kinetic Growth Form (faceting or recrystallization) and Melt–freeze and Pressure Metamorphism.

The old terms Equi-temperature and Temperature Gradient Metamorphism and-Constructive and Destructive Metamorphism are no longer used in North America.

Necks are narrow connections between grains which give strength to the snowpack. They are formed by migration of water molecules from the rounded portion of the grain to the concavity formed where grains come into contact. See **Sintering**.

New Snow The surface layer of snow as it is deposited and for some time after deposition.

Partially Settled Snow New snow which has undergone some rounding. It is usually stronger than new snow and has settled somewhat.

Pendular Regime The condition of snow with low liquid-water content where air exists in continuous paths and grain-to-grain bonds give strength to the snow layer.

Perforated Crust is formed by differential melting by the sun's rays. The portion of the ice grains which receive the greatest amount of radiation melt first, leaving minute hollows in the snow which are enlarged as time progresses.

Persistent Slab is caused by a cohesive slab within the upper to middle layers of the snowpack losing its bond to the underlying layer. Persistent slabs may remain unstable for extended periods and be the cause of an avalanche long after they were buried. As further layers build up the snowpack there may be several weak layers that wake up at different times. Weak layers include surface hoar, sun/rain crusts and near-surface facets.

Pore Spaces are the gaps between grains in the snowpack. In normal-density snow they interconnect so that water or water vapour can flow through. In high-density snow they can be non-communicating and therefore impervious to water vapour.

Powder Snow Avalanches are avalanches in which the snow breaks up into dust and may become airborne. Generally these slides not influenced by obstacles in their path and can flow in a straight line over irregular terrain.

Pressure Metamorphism is metamorphism due to the weight of additional snow layers on the snowpack. The end product of pressure metamorphism, if the snow does not melt, is glacier ice.

Radiation Recrystallization occurs on clear, dry days during the winter and early spring. Slopes with a southerly exposure will absorb enough of the sun's heat for a thin freeze–thaw crust to form a centimetre or so beneath the surface even though the temperature of the snow surface may still be well below freezing due to infrared cooling. The difference in temperature between the cold surface snow and the warmer snow beneath allows recrystallization of the snow on top of the smooth freeze–thaw crust. These thin layers of recrystallized snow form weak, poorly bonded layers when buried beneath further snowfalls.

Recrystallization The process of water vapour sublimating onto an ice surface to form a structured ice crystal. Surface hoar and depth hoar are two examples.

Remote Triggering is the action of triggering an avalanche at some distance from where you are skiing or boarding. It is possible to remotely trigger an avalanche on slopes above you from flat ground at the foot of the slope.

Rime is formed when droplets of super-cooled water impinge on any object in their path. See **Graupel**.

Runout Zone The portion of the avalanche path where snow slows down and comes to rest. The area where the bulk of the snow piles up is called the **Deposition Zone**.

Rutschblock Test A column of snow about 2 m square excavated from the snowpack. The block is loaded by a skier, on skis. The point in the loading cycle at which it fails in shear is an indication of the snow stability at that location.

Settlement The process by which the snowpack becomes denser. In old snow layers settlement takes place at a rate of about 1 cm per day. New snow layers settle much faster. The amount and speed of settlement is an indication of the strengthening of the snow layers.

Sintering The joining together of ice grains by the formation of necks between adjacent grains.

Slab Avalanches are avalanches which start when a large area of cohesive snow begins to slide at the same time.

Slope Angle The angle of incline of a slope measured from the horizontal.

Sluffs are small loose-snow avalanches falling from steep terrain during or shortly after a storm; streams of near faceted crystals released by skiers or boarders on extremely steep slopes; or small, wet point avalanches on open slopes.

Snow Crystal Usually reserved for snow formed by vapour deposition in the atmosphere. Crystals formed in a similar way on the ground are called Ice Crystals. The difference between Snow Crystals and Ice Grains is apparent when viewed through a magnifying glass.

Snow Cushion A smooth, rounded deposit of soft slab formed on a lee slope. The slab under a cornice is a good example. See also **Snow Pillow**.

Snowfall Intensity is the rate at which snow is deposited during a storm expressed in centimetres or inches of snow per hour.

Snowpack The combined layers of snow on the ground at any one time. The snowpack is bounded by the Snow Surface and the Ground Surface.

Snow Pillow A device for measuring the water equivalent of the snowpack based on hydrostatic pressure created by overlying snow.

Soft Slab is slab that loses its cohesion on release and breaks up into relatively small pieces.

Starting Zone The area where unstable snow breaks loose from the snowpack and starts to slide. It's the most dangerous area of the avalanche path for the climber and skier.

Stauchwall The line where the snow released in a slab avalanche rides up over the stable snow below. There is no English translation for this German word.

Storm-induced Avalanches. See **Direct-action Avalanches**.

Storm Slab is formed by significant new snowfall accompanied by light to moderate wind. Whether the slab becomes an avalanche problem depends on the weather during the storm and on the surface of the old snow.

Storm Snow is snow that falls as a result of a continuous or almost continuous snowfall. If a storm is prolonged, settlement and strengthening may take place and slab may form.

Sublimation is the ability of a substance to change from solid to vapour and back again without passing through the liquid stage. Common substances able to sublimate are water and iodine.

Sugar Snow. See **Depth Hoar**.

Surface Avalanches are avalanches which only involve the top layers of the snow and which slide on an underlying snow layer.

Surface Hoar is a bright, sparkling, crystalline growth that forms on the snow surface during cold, clear weather. When buried by further snowfall it becomes a weak sliding layer.

Temperature Gradient The difference in temperature through a given depth of snow. Expressed in degrees Celsius per metre of snow. For example, 10°C/m.

Temperature-gradient Metamorphism The former name given to the process of recrystallization. Now referred to as Faceting or Recrystallization, the process results in the **Kinetic Growth Form** of ice crystals.

Terrain Traps Small terrain features which hold enough snow to bury a person. They're usually places which inexperienced people would not consider to be dangerous.

Track The slope or channel down which snow moves at a more or less uniform speed.

Trigger An Avalanche Trigger is the force which starts the snow sliding. It may be a natural trigger such as the weight of additional snowfall, or an artificial trigger such as the weight of a skier crossing the slope.

Trimline The edge of an avalanche slope that descends through forest.

Unconfined Avalanches are avalanches that occur on open slopes.

Wet Slab is the result of a cohesive slab losing its bond with the lubricated layer beneath. Wet slabs are usually a problem after a prolonged period of warm weather, particularly when overnight temperatures remain above freezing. They tend to occur soon after the snowpack becomes isothermal (0°C throughout).

Whumpf An audible sound caused by a fracture propagating through a weak layer in the snowpack. The occurrence of whumpfs as you travel in avalanche terrain is a sign of instability.

Wild Snow Snow that has fallen in complete calm at very low temperatures. Resembling goose down, it is extremely light (containing 97 to 99% air) and lies very loosely, with the crystals hardly touching each other.

Windblast Zone The area of the runout zone where airborne snow dust is deposited. In very large airborne avalanches an airblast zone may be present around both the track and the runout zone.

Wind Slab forms when strong winds deposit snow in localized areas where wind typically erodes snow from the upwind sides of terrain features and deposits snow on the downwind side. Wind slabs are more common at higher elevations above timberline and often form on the lee side of ridges, bowls and gullies, on the downhill slopes of steep drop-offs and rollovers, and even downwind of stands of trees. The density of wind slab can vary from soft to very hard. Soft wind slab deposited during a storm over extensive areas is usually considered to be **Storm Slab**.

Index